FAYLE'S TRAMWAYS

Driver Eli Kitcatt looks out from the cab of Ruston 48DL 392117 as another day finished. The track leading from the weighbridge to the shed followed the 1907 extension line to Goathorn for a short distance and was completely overgrown at that time of the year. AUTHOR

FAYLE'S TRAMWAYS

Clay mining in Purbeck
Two hundred years, six different gauges

BY

CHRIS LEGG

TWELVEHEADS PRESS

TRURO 2016

CONTENTS

Units of measurement and money used in this book are those which were concurrent with events described. They may be converted as follows:

Money: £1   = 20 shillings (s) = 100 pence (p)
         1 guinea = 21 shillings
         1 shilling = 12 pence (d)
Length: 1 mile = 8 furlongs = 80 chains = 1,760 yards = 1.6093 kilometres
         1 yard = 3 feet = 36 inches = 0.9144 metres
         1 fathom = 6 feet
Weight   1 ton = 20 hundredweight (cwt) = 1.016 tonnes

TWELVEHEADS PRESS

First published in 2014 by Twelveheads Press
Second edition 2016 by Twelveheads Press
Truro, Cornwall.
ISBN 978 0 906294 88 8
British Library Cataloguing-in-Publication Data.
A catalogue record for this book is available from the British Library.

Typeset in Baskerville and Helvetica
Printed by Short Run Press Ltd, Exeter.

Front cover main picture:

Russell, working at Norden.
GEORGE ALLIEZ

Bottom left to right:

Tiny. GEORGE WOODCOCK

Ruston No. 179889. AUTHOR

Special train hauled by *Thames* to Goathorn. STIFF FAMILY

Ruston model DL48, No. 392117. AUTHOR

Back cover:

Ruston passing over bridge 15 on a hot 4 July 1969. AUTHOR

INTRODUCTION

Looking back over 70 years, I wonder what first attracted my attention to clay mining in Purbeck. Could it have been the episode in 1944 at Norden Farm, just north of Corfe Castle, when I stayed with friends while my mother was in hospital? One day a large aircraft transporter arrived, taking up most of the space in the farmyard. The rig was operated by a number of American service men, and I watched them jump over the fence surrounding the clay railway, cross a couple of fields and climb up Knowle hill. As *Tiny* or *Thames* steamed by with trains of clay wagons, the men began to recover a light aircraft that had been stolen and crashed on the side of the hill, bringing the parts of the plane back for loading on to the transporter. Perhaps it was the later influence of seeing Pike's polished steam engines lined up at Furzebrook, exchanging whistles with the crew of the Swanage train as we chugged by the works on our way to school 1950-7. In good weather the siding at Norden always seemed deserted; wrong time of day I suspect! In bad weather, it was the explosion of fog detonators when passing the siding that lingered in the memory.

Those early images had a powerful influence, but it was the later changes in the industry that attracted my attention in 1969 and began my interest in recording the story. I was back in Wareham visiting my parents when some chance meetings with old friends led me to start exploring around Norden. On a hot afternoon in August, I was sitting in the tall grass on West Hill above Corfe Castle, listening to the buzz of bees and watching butterflies as they flitted among the flowers. Having recovered from the steep climb up from Vineyard Farm near the castle, I began to take in the view looking north over Norden. My eyes scanned the countryside, from the nearest point at the foot of the hill where a jumble of buildings seemed to obstruct the clay railway, across the fields where the sidings almost touched the Swanage branch and on towards the haze of Poole Harbour in the distance. A timeless scene, but I was becoming aware of how much things had changed since I stayed at the farm just beyond the rails.

My thoughts were disturbed by the stuttering exhaust drifting up from below, as the Ruston locomotive got away from the mines on its way down to the weighbridge with another load of clay. I could hear the wagons rattling as they passed several pools of water from discarded open pits, bright turquoise in the hot sun. As the

Approaching bridge 15 at Norden, heading towards Wareham is class M7 tank No 30318. For many years these locomotives, introduced by Drummond in 1897, were responsible for day to day workings on the branch. The empty wagons seem destined for clay working; probably some of them would be left at Norden and the rest a bit further on at Pike's siding at Furzebrook.
S. W. BAKER

M7 30050 waits in the south bay to depart from Wareham.
AUTHOR

A train of empty wagons propelled by the Ruston 48DL is approaching the level crossing on the Wareham to Corfe Castle A351 road. The train is on its way back to the mines and just crossing the chalk road used by road vehicles to access the clay mill. The chain links between the wagons are hanging down, as the wagons are pushed up together. Poole Harbour is in the distant background.
AUTHOR

train gathered speed on the run down to the main road, it looked like a model with the farm in the background and I suddenly noticed one of the small diesel locomotives attached at the rear. This was an unusual formation and the small engine was probably returning from some repair at the blacksmith's workshop. There was a distinct slowing down to allow the catch point to be thrown. As the train approached the road I could see the young lad jump down to swing the gate open and unfurl his red flag to stop the traffic at the level crossing. A few cars and a coach gave way and some puffs emerged from the exhaust as Eli Kitcatt accelerated the train across. After a brief stop to close the gate, they went on through the trees and the climb over the Swanage branch. Another stop and points change; then with the boy back on board the

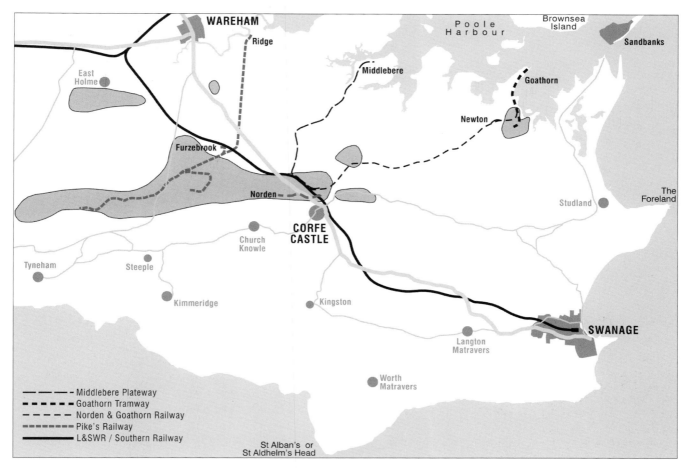

Middlebere Plateway
Goathorn Tramway
Norden & Goathorn Railway
Pike's Railway
L&SWR / Southern Railway

train reversed beside the branch line, through Cattle Creep shed and up to the sidings at the weighbridge. I knew by then that evidence of the beginning of the tramway system and the clay pits it served could be found in the woodland area beyond the farm. I could have seen a similar happening on such a day 160 years before, except the wagons were then pulled by horses and went under the road on their way to a quay at Middlebere.

Eli had worked with horses at Norden for 22 years before taking up steam locomotive driving on *Thames* in the 1940s. He was a direct link to the earlier tradition and eventually his service with the clay company would stretch over 70 years. During that summer we took some time riding, photographing and talking about those years at Norden. While a certain giant step for mankind was making history on the moon, my experience was far removed from rocket science. I was enjoying what remained of the Norden Railway and discovered it was very difficult to keep my balance while riding in a V-shaped skip on the end of a bumping train of empties driven

by Eli. The years that have passed since then have not dimmed the memory of that exhilarating ride. Those small trains moving ball clay would prove to be the last in a long line of industrial railway transport on the south side of Poole Harbour. The very first railroad built in Dorset 1805-6, to serve Benjamin Fayle's clay works had begun the tradition, and after many additions and changes his idea of moving clay by rail would continue on the surface until 1972. The following account will hopefully explain all those developments and trace the changes down the years, until the company's decision in 1954 to use road transport in future saw the gradual run down and demise of the railways.

The story of prospecting and mining for ball clay in the Isle of Purbeck has been greatly enriched by the generations of miners and support workers who lived with their families in the locality. They were employed in the industry either 'getting' clay in surface workings or below ground level. There were also other families and individuals whose interest in clay brought them to visit or to live in the area. These included most

Map of the Isle of Purbeck showing the main clay tramways and their function as feeders from the mines to loading piers for onward shipment. Pike's railway connected Furzebrook to Ridge on the River Frome, itself a feeder to Poole Harbour. Fayle's plateway and tramway crossed the heath to loading piers at Middlebere and Goathorn respectively. Most of the miners/workers lived in Corfe Castle, and some came from Wareham and other surrounding villages.

of the landowners and proprietors of the mines whose mineral rights could not have been exploited without the skills of the local people. The miners were linked by rail through underground passages from the clay face up to the surface. The clay was then transported on other rails to the sidings for weighing, then to various plants and mills for processing before despatch to customers at home and overseas. Other workers were involved in the building of barges and tugs to move the clay from the loading piers to the nearby port of Poole for shipment.

Most of the situations they encountered called for desperately hard work and were sometimes dangerous. Despite that, it was an industry into which sons followed fathers and their forebears before them. The story continues today because ball clay extraction is still going on, but the working methods have changed dramatically over recent years. Some of the record has unfortunately been lost in the passage of time, principally by the moving of company offices and the clearing out of old papers. This account of ball clay mining in Dorset is partly based on word of mouth reporting and other secondary sources. In some places the text includes relevant facts and figures relating to the industry from old company ledgers, historically important because they are new primary sources. The construction of the last drift mine in Purbeck, No. 7 incline, is recorded as a postscript because it has since been moved and re-built as the centrepiece of the Purbeck Mineral & Mining Museum group, part of the Swanage Railway at Norden Station. When No. 7 closed prematurely in 1999, it was time to complete the story of earlier mining activity before the memories of those working days and the men involved were forgotten. Their experience is a testimony to all the families whose lives were shaped by mining and to whom clay offered an alternative living to agriculture.

CHAPTER ONE
The early history and the origins of ball clay

High-quality ball clays are relatively scarce both in Britain and across the world. The area south of Wareham in Dorset is one of only three areas in Britain where economic ball clay deposits occur, the others being the Petrockstowe Basin and the Bovey Basin situated in north and south Devon respectively. The countryside where the clay is mined consists mostly of heathland and although somewhat dull in appearance it has a magical beauty and a brooding aura that draws the attention. Some readers may remember distant holidays in the area, perhaps on the beach at Studland, exploring Corfe Castle or camping under the hills. The Isle of Purbeck as it is known is not a true island, but a peninsula measuring about 12 miles wide from east to west and about 8 miles from north to south. It lies south of Poole Harbour and the River Frome and has a connection with the mainland near Worbarrow Bay. The chalk hills, which run east to west from Ballard Down near Swanage through Corfe Castle to the cliffs at Worbarrow, divide the peninsula into two very distinct parts. A walker along the top of these hills near Corfe Castle will be very aware of the richer agricultural land lying to the south, with evidence in places of the earlier marble and stone industry. In contrast, it is the heathland with poor soils to the north of the hills stretching away to the Frome and Poole Harbour, which presents a very different prospect. This was the area that attracted Josiah Wedgwood when he was searching for suitable clays to use in his potting experiments. The object of his interest lay deep below the surface, but it was the presence of the clay and related minerals deposited below that determined the visual aspect of the scenery that we know so well. Thomas Hardy, coming much later, loved this type of countryside and embraced the broad sweep of land consisting mostly of heather, gorse, stunted trees and sand. It became his 'Egdon Heath' changing its mood and appearance with the day's light, and capturing his poetic imagination. He wrote as if the great heath was unaltered since the prehistoric period, comparing it with the stars set in the heavens, but during his lifetime it was across this land that the tramways were eventually built to link clay mining with the wider world.

The deposition of the clay gets a little

The horse drawn Middlebere plateway is shown following the contours from Norden to the pier. At the Norden end, the original 1807 branch is shown passing under the Wareham to Corfe Castle road, and the diversion to New Meadow (1875) and Matchams (1881) is shown alongside the L&SWR/Southern Railway. Crossing Rempstone Heath near Bushey is the Norden and Goathorn Railway connecting Norden mines to Newton and Goathorn (1907) more usually called Fayle's tramway.

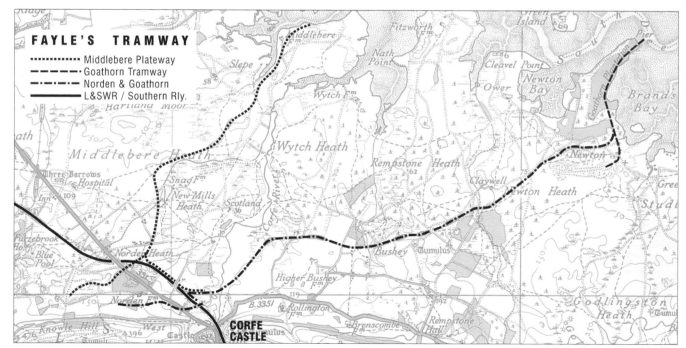

complicated, but some understanding of it will shed light on the mining process and the skill of the clay getter. During the Cretaceous period, which opened about 140 million years ago and is best known for its extensive chalk deposits, there was a relatively warm climate with numerous shallow inland seas, which flowed and receded, rich in marine life with small calcite skeletons. In the area, which later emerged as south Dorset, an east to west (E-W) boundary fault developed along the line of the Purbeck Hills and this had a complicated history of earth movement leading to the complexity of the Norden clay sequences. The E-W fault was subsequently eroded and then covered by the Tertiary ball clay sequences during the geological period which followed the Cretaceous, now more specifically referred to as the Palaeogene, begun some forty to fifty million years ago. It was said that ball clay originated from the decomposition of granite found in Cornwall and Devon and this still applies to the Bovey Basin, which had a large input from kaolinised Dartmoor granite. It is now thought that Dorset clays were derived from weathered mud rocks of various ages, shale, sandstone, chalk and some granite, similar to Devon but with different properties due to the way they were deposited.

The ball clay itself had its origins through the action of steam and acid gases decomposing the mud rocks, the process now call hydrothermal alteration. A period of prolonged rain resulted in a turbulent river following the land contours towards the east. Most of the smaller decomposed rocks and silts, kaolinite (clay substance), mica, and quartz were washed out and carried towards the Great Chalk Sea covering south-east England. Away from the higher ground in the west, the flow of the river eased and eventually slowed down, spreading out to form a large flood plain covering the area of what is now Poole Harbour and the surrounding heathland. In what had become a subtropical climate, the spread of the river formed pools surrounded by luxuriant plant growth, the flow almost stopping and then starting again. The decaying vegetation formed peat and then lignite which is found in seams from a few centimetres to as much as two metres thick between the strata. Some of this lignite, in later years, was used in cottages on the heath as fuel on open fires and was utilised by one of the clay works managers to augment the use of coal in locomotives. As the flow of the river slackened and stopped in the estuary, the very

finest sediments settled to form 'lenses' made up of clay particles. Each lens could cover several acres in extent and be 15 to 50ft in thickness and usually two or three lenses were formed together. The clay was referred to as transported, having been deposited by the water miles away from the parent rock. Then with renewed flow of the water more sand was laid over the clay and slowly, the Bagshot Beds as the deposit became known was built up and completed to a thickness of 70 to 80 metres, covering the area now known as the Wareham Basin.

Until recently this was the best description of clay being deposited in Dorset, but it was puzzling how a seam, such as 'Fayle's Blue' located at Povington could have such uniform properties from top to bottom. It is now thought that the deposition of the particles in estuarine conditions depended on both river and marine conditions. When the clay, carried in suspension in fresh water met brackish water in the estuary rapid flocculation of the particles occurred. Whether clay or sand was deposited depended largely on the river velocity and the sea level at the time. We now know from seismic records in the North Sea that during the Eocene period when the Dorset clays were deposited, there were many rises and falls in sea level of similar frequency to the number of clay sequences now identified in the Purbeck area. Some parts of the deposits were exposed and through erosion and oxidation the clay became mottled and discoloured mainly by oxides of iron. The deeper and thicker clays retained their colour and were actually improved. This explains why host clays can be of high quality in one place but less so nearby and in some cases only a part of the host clay is of good enough quality to be regarded as commercial ball clay.

The sequence of interbedded sands, silts and clay, is now referred to as the Poole Formation in which the ball clay bearing units are named Creekmoor, Oakdale, Broadstone and Parkstone clays in ascending order within the geological sequence. People in the industry usually referred to the different types of ball clay as the Norden, Cotness, Grange and Creech clays, the names being the places in Purbeck where they were mined. After the formation of the beds was completed the gently rolling plain of heathland could have remained undisturbed for thousands of years until man came on the scene prospecting for minerals. However, just to make life more difficult for those miners of the future, a period of renewed earth movements occurred. The land along the Purbeck E-W fault was pushed upwards, folding the strata and elevating the chalk to form the Purbeck Hills, on average 500 feet high. The ball clay sequences along the fault suffered an opposite effect, the stresses producing a downward movement. Because the clays were sufficiently compacted (dewatered), this resulted in complex fractures of the layers, rather than a plastic flow in the fault zone. The complex folding and faulting brought the basal Creekmoor clay closer to the surface, and it is here that a lot of mining work has been concentrated, the most commercial clays being found within a half to one km zone north of the Purbeck Hills. This narrow area extends from Rempstone in the east through Arfleet, Norden and Kilwood as far as West Creech. Because of the fractured ground the mining companies have often found it difficult to predict where good quality clays are located from existing bore hole information. Despite that, core drilling, first using hand drills and much later mechanised rigs, located and mapped the clay over some forty square miles and records still exist from the 1870s. This information was essential in developing the mining operation, but was easily underestimated by the casual observer.

The substance commonly known as ball clay is relatively hard to the touch, consisting of three dominant minerals, kaolinite, mica and quartz with average ratio in Dorset of 4:2:1. Some anatase also occurs. In the natural state it varies in colour from cream to yellow, light grey and blue. Less common in Dorset are darker clays through to chocolate brown and black, the darker colours being due to the presence of carbonaceous matter. This coloured part of the mineral is a colloidal coating of the particles which burns out during the firing process revealing an off white or ivory coloured base substance. Despite the feeling of hardness the raw clay is considered to be soft in geological terms. It has a specific gravity of about 2.25, which means it is about 2.25 times as heavy as water, bulk for bulk. Because of its origins as a fresh-water transported material over a greater distance than other clays, the Dorset product is often claimed to be the best in the world, having finer grain size and greater plasticity than any other ball clay. The technical description of the kaolinite particles of which about 90% are finer than one micron equivalent spherical radius (40% of the particles are less then $^1/_{10}$th micron),

shows they are flattened or plate-like. This is caused by distortion of the mineral lattice, which is referred to as 'disordered' through the inclusion of elements such as iron and titanium. It is probably the particle shape which gives the mineral its high plasticity, which is the quality that gives strength to the ceramic body while being shaped or formed on the potter's wheel.

The high dry strength allows unfired articles to keep their shape and withstand all types of making and conveying during manufacture. For this reason, about 83% of Dorset ball clay gets used in the production of ceramics including domestic tableware, sanitary ware, stoneware, porcelain electrical insulators and glazed wall and floor tiles. The whiter firing clays, which are those having the lowest content of other elements like iron, are favoured for these products. A further 15% of clay which fires less white is used in making refractory articles, where the ball clay also helps with the bonding and shaping of less plastic materials to produce such items as kiln furniture, casting linings, fire cements and crucibles. The remaining 2% of poor quality ball clay is used in the production of pharmaceuticals, fertilisers, rubber and plastics, where it acts as a binder or inert filler. It was also used for a number of years in animal feed stuffs, crayon and coloured pencil manufacture. In addition, ball clay has been used in the production of grinding wheels by binding silicon carbide, corundum, emery and other hard materials.

The use of the name 'ball' which became applied to the clay could have originated from early surface digging of the mineral, when a spade called a Tubil or Tubal was used to cut out approximately square lumps of clay. The weathering process in Dorset and rough treatment during transport resulted in the lumps having their corners rounded off and becoming ball shaped weighing sixty or seventy pounds each. At the other end of its journey to the Potteries in Staffordshire, early transport was by packhorses and as most of the clay was landed at Runcorn it was commonly known as Chester clay. It was considered that 70 balls whether counted or weighed, equalled a ton.

It seems likely that the Romans were the first people to produce true pottery, made on a potter's wheel. In Purbeck the sites of several Roman kilns have been found and investigated. One was located in a field bordering Nutcrack Lane between Stoborough and Ridge, south of Wareham and another to the east of Arne village.

11

Open cast mining at Newton, about 1910. Overburden was being dug out and removed by workers called rubblers who used wheel barrows to move the waste away over a trestle viaduct to a short 3ft gauge railway leading to the waste tip. Two horses in trace harness were ready to move a loaded wagon away and two empties were in a siding waiting to be filled. A fourth wagon, which looked like a tipper had extended axles and may have been a conversion from the plateway type. The steam locomotive *Tiny* was used to haul trains to the pier, but horses remained in use around the mines for wagon assembly and dispatch until 1939. CHURCHILL OF WAREHAM

The site of a Roman villa has been recorded near East Creech village. During 1969, an excavation was being carried out at Norden between the mineral railway and the chalk track running diagonally across the field to Cattle Creep, east of the A351 road. Pottery found in the area suggested there was an established industry in Roman times, but without evidence of kiln structures it was concluded the pottery was fired in bonfires or clamps. In the nearby Matcham's pits during 1882 a fine collection of Romano-British pottery was discovered, along with some 'coins, a bronze weapon and buckle, together with some stone coffins'. During the Mediaeval Period most pottery manufacture was confined to monasteries, the principal items produced being pitchers, bowls, ale jugs and mugs, wine containers and food storage jars. The other important production was tiles for walls and floors, and much of the clay now exported to Spain is still used for this purpose.

Ball clay extraction in Dorset developed rapidly during the period 1580 to 1600, to help satisfy clay-pipe making and the new smoking craze, and because of its end use at that time it became known as pipeclay. Export figures for the year Christmas 1632 to the same date in 1633 show that Poole shipped 30 cargoes coastwise. These were almost monopolised by the 459 tons of tobacco-pipe clay going to London. The demand for pipe clay continued to rise so, for example, the corresponding amount for 1690-1 was 3,114 tons of clay shipped. It was about 1660 that the increasing cargoes to London came to the notice of potters, as well as the pipe makers, and the demand for clay spiralled as potters experimented and realised the pipe clay suited their purpose very well. Some of this clay came from the Arne area, which would become the centre of operations of Thomas Hyde (1731-95) who was paying £30 a year for mining rights. His shipment point, known as Hyde's Quay was established about 1768 and subsequently recorded on most maps of the area.

Rev John Hutchins M.A., who was Rector of the Holy Trinity Church in Wareham, and Swyre for 30 years (1743-73) is famous for his detailed History of the County. In the preface of the first edition, 1773, he referred to the History as 'an extensive and arduous task' and he died soon after aged 75. He introduced the plastic clay of this district by the modest title of 'The Clay Pits'. Long before 1760 it appears to have been known as 'Tobacco-pipe Clay,' and is so called by Hutchins in the first edition. By the time he wrote the following account, the shipment of much of the mineral had become centred on Wareham and the description he wrote before 1760 is given under that town:

> Good tobacco-pipe clay is dug round this town at Arne, Hungerhill, Norden, &c. It formerly sold for

50s a ton, but now at 14s or 15s. Nearly ten thousand tons are annually exported to London, Hull, Liverpool, Glasgow etc., but the most considerable part to Liverpool, for the supply of the Staffordshire potteries, and to Selby, for the use of the Leeds potteries. The principal pits are on Norden and Witch Farms; the former belonging to William Morton Pitt, esq., the latter to John Calcraft, esq., and the clay taken from the same is in great repute with the Staffordshire and Yorkshire potters, from its peculiar excellency, and being the principal ingredient in the composition of the ware commonly called Staffordshire ware, so universally in use in this kingdom, as well as in many other parts of Europe. For want of proper fuel, the manufacture cannot be carried on here; and the clay is consequently exported. In the summer season one hundred and eighty labourers are constantly employed in raising clay from these pits, at the wages of from 6s to 10s a week. The cost of a ton of clay to the potters is from 35s to 37s 6d. The expense of raising the clay and carrying it from the pits to the water-side for shipping, about 13s, inclusive of the ground-rent to the owner of the soil, freight to Liverpool about 11s 6d, commission there 1s, average canal freight 9s 9d, porterage, agents, commission, and other charges 2s 3d. Total cost to the potters in Staffordshire, 37s 6d.

When Hutchins wrote that clay was being 'dug round this town' he was describing the most common way of getting clay, which continued for over 200 years. The ideal situation for open pit working was a level clay lens not far below the surface, which could be uncovered by removing the overburden of earth and other waste. The latter was dug out and removed by workers called rubblers, who used wheelbarrows to cart the soil away or in later days, by transport on a rubble railway. The overburden was taken a short distance to a waste heap, or used to backfill previous digging. It was customary to leave about a foot of earth covering the clay bed, which afforded it some protection from the weather until the miners were ready to cut it. The clay was then finally uncovered and scored across with a rake like tool to give cutting lines. It was then dug out following the marks and transferred to waiting packhorses or wagons. A team of about eight miners worked on the clay shelf or bench, using clay cutting spades to cut out the mineral in lumps about eight inches square. The technique was simple in the sense that each miner lifted his cutting spade, which weighed about 20 to 25lb about 2ft into the air and allowed it to drop vertically, the weight of the tool helping the straight blade to penetrate the clay. Some skill was required, not only to judge the depth of cut and to hit the correct spot, but also to avoid any part of the feet or legs! Each miner had a leather bucket of water beside him into which he dipped the blade of the spade between cuts, which assisted the passage of the blade into the clay.

Josiah Wedgwood had started in his own business during 1759, by which time the bulk of Dorset ball clay was going to the Potteries. At his Ivy House works in Burslem, Wedgwood began researching for a recipe, which would produce a whiter creamware. He acid leached the 'native pot earth' (i.e. local clay), to reduce its iron content and mixed it with Dorset ball clay, flint and lime. When he had perfected the ware, one of the first people to have a complete dinner service was Sir William Meredith who was M.P. for Liverpool from 1762. He recognised the genius of Wedgwood and was active in seeking artistic items for him to model. He was also a supporter of the Trent and Mersey Canal. It was not long before most of the gentry of Staffordshire were using and talking about the new cream-ware and recommending it to their guests and friends. Eventually, the new tableware came to the attention of Queen Charlotte, wife of George III, and she ordered a decorated cream tea service followed by a table-service of the same ware in a plainer style. The elegance of the resulting service was outstanding and became known as the Queen's pattern, or simply 'Queensware' and the resulting Royal patronage was to create a much greater demand for Dorset clay than ever before.

The ball clay used in Queensware came from a pit called Threshers (or Thrashers) situated at Rempstone, east of Corfe Castle. It was the only named clay pit recorded in the late 1700s. A survey map of Rempstone Estate drawn by Donne and James Asser in 1805 has the pit drawn in and marked, *Clay pits in Thrasher's Heath where is dug a very fine clay which makes what is nam'd the Queen's Weare (about 1762-65)*. John Calcraft, who owned the estate, had been active in sending samples to Wedgwood for evaluation over 30 years. For much of that time it was Thomas Hyde who acted as Calcraft's agent in raising the clay. He also acted as agent for the Pitt family of Encombe House who owned clay bearing land at Norden and Arne. In 1770, Hyde was concerned

Benjamin Fayle was born in 1751. Through his business connections in London, which included insurance for ships' cargoes in transit, he came to know Josiah Wedgwood well. This led to a long correspondence between the two families from 1786 to 1825, and probably due to the Wedgwood influence, Fayle became directly involved in the Dorset ball clay industry from 1803. AUTHOR

BENJAMIN FAYLE was just over 50 when he began an active interest in the Dorset clay industry. Born on 10 July 1751 in Ireland, Benjamin's family had Quaker roots, and as a perceived radical group they suffered opposition, sometimes of a violent nature. This may have been the cause of Benjamin moving to England where he started business in London about 1786. Another reason for the move could have been the activities of his first wife, which were said to have caused his bankruptcy. In 1788 he was listed as a merchant in White Lion Court, Cornhill, and in 1793 at Dove Court, Lombard Street.

By 1800 Fayle was well established in the insurance business, mostly of ships' cargoes, which included Wedgwood's ware, and he could boast a substantial turnover and considerable wealth. He was also said to be a manufacturing stationer and a merchant in the clay business. Family memories would suggest he visited Dorset looking for good clay supplies and in 1795 had hoped to obtain these from the Lake Clay Mines at Hamworthy, but the clay was not of the highest quality. Because of that enquiry, it is often recorded that Benjamin Fayle first started clay mining at Norden in 1795, but this was in error and he only became responsible for the workings at Norden in 1803, taking over full control in October 1804. By then he had been married to Charlotte (Adams) for some years and they lived in a 'cottage' in Dulwich with their three children, Charlotte, Richard and Anna Mary. Some records of his activities importing spices from the East Indies survive and also many letters he wrote to Josiah Wedgwood and Byerley. He became a close friend of Tom Byerley, Wedgwood's nephew who ran the London end of the pottery business. A few years later would see Fayle involved in the ball clay industry and a place in history as the builder of the first railway in Dorset.

His best friend was another Irishman, William Babington, five years his junior and they shared a common interest. Born 1756 in Co. Antrim, William studied medicine at Guy's Hospital, London. He was appointed physician there in 1795, resigning after 16 years to follow his private practice. Apart from being esteemed in his profession, he had many other interests, the chief being mineralogy. He became active in the support of Fayle's clay business, which included getting some orders. A meeting he called in 1807 led to the foundation of the Geological Society, of which he was president until 1822. William had married in 1787, aged 31, about the time Fayle was getting established in London. In 1794, William and Martha had their fifth child and he was christened Benjamin (after William's best friend, Fayle) and Guy (after Guy's Hospital where he was born). Some years later the family friendship was sealed when Benjamin Guy Babington married Anna Mary Fayle and they spent seven years in the Indian Civil Service. During this time their health suffered and Benjamin returned to England, a widower with four children. Like his father before him, Benjamin Guy took up the study of medicine at Guy's Hospital and qualified as a physician in 1825, aged 30.

Returning to the clay industry in Purbeck, the Fayle company had always relied on local management to pursue their interests, either as employees/agents or later as shareholders. Benjamin Fayle himself had relied on the Willis family, tenants at Norden Farm to run the day to day clay workings on their land. Over a period of years friendships were forged, so much so the Willis' named one of their daughters after Charlotte Fayle. At some stage, Benjamin Fayle had involved some of his extended family as shareholders, although no written records have been found. These family members were drawn from the Pocock and Adams families. Henry Adams was a master shipbuilder at Bucklers Hard on the Beaulieu River and the Pococks lived nearby and were intermarried with the Adams. We do know that when Benjamin Fayle died he gave several gifts to friends including £100 to his friend William, leaving the residue of his estate divided equally between his two surviving children and his son-in-law. His son, Richard Fayle was more interested in the Church, being Rector of St Mary's Church, Wareham, but he remained a sleeping partner in the business. His daughter, Charlotte was keen to run the business and Benjamin Guy Babington assisted her, becoming a director of B. Fayle & Co. At one period in the 1850s to 1860s the company was known as, or referred to as Fayle and Babington, but later in the 1880s reverted to B. Fayle & Co. Also in the early 1860s the Willis family retired and a new agent was required to run the Dorset end of the business. Richard Pinney agreed to join the company, being the third generation Richard Pinney, his father having married Mary Ann Adams. In London B. G. Babington had retired and his son Stephen Peile Babington joined Charlotte in running the company. B. G. Babington died in 1866, shortly after Richard Pinney started work in Dorset.

that he could not get freight for the clay to Liverpool, the main port for the Potteries, due to the demand for transport of corn to that port. He said it was impossible to get ships at 7s to 8s a ton, when corn paid 15s to 16s per ton. However, he had written to London to see if cheese ships from Chester and Liverpool might pick up clay on their way back. The following year a new deal was agreed to supply Wedgwood with 1,400 tons of clay per annum for 21 years. This must have been a great relief to Wedgwood who needed a constant supply of good clay to keep production busy, and often expressed concern about reliable supplies. He had already written to his partner Bentley saying he had hardly any left and could he possibly buy 20 tons of best Poole clay, adding that his clay came from the Island of Purbeck, but is nevertheless called Poole clay. He offered to send samples to avoid purchasing Teignmouth clay of which there was plenty in store already.

In 1773 Josiah Wedgwood travelled down to Dorset to meet Thomas Hyde, who in a subsequent letter referred to the white clay they had seen at the first work on their way from Corfe Castle. Writing in May, Hyde expressed concern that recent clay specimens sent to Wedgwood, which he thought had good strength and colour had been considered sandy. He went on to say the vein of clay was under land of their acquaintance which was worked by his father 40 years ago (1733), mostly for pipes. The recent clay extractions had been arranged to stop the land falling into other hands with possible success. In this case a pit had not been opened, but the specimens were taken from the top of a boring; he could go no lower because of water. Twenty years later, following some dubious dealings, Hyde was declared bankrupt in 1792-3. For the next ten years, the distribution of Norden clay in the potteries was handled by Barker Chifney, and it was from him that Benjamin Fayle took over running the clay mines.

CHAPTER TWO

Early clay transport and the coming of the railroad
'The New Line'

Many factors were involved in the development of the local transport of clay, some of which originated far beyond Dorset. In 1676, it was reported that wooden rails were used for the transport of coal from the pits to the vessels on the River Tyne, their use having spread from Nottingham and Shropshire over a period of 60 years. The system of squared wooden rails fixed to transverse wooden sleepers was very liable to damage and wear and to prevent this happening, cast-iron plates about 1½in thick were fastened to the top of the track. Richard Reynolds, a partner at Coalbrookdale was the first to introduce such plates in 1767. The iron plates were laid on the wooden under-rails and held by nails. About 1791, the wooden under rails were gradually dispensed with, and the track was then constructed of all cast iron rails fixed to sleepers of timber or stone.

Dorset had a direct connection with those early Tyne plateways through the land owning Pitt family. George Pitt of Stratfieldsaye House, Hampshire, had opened the Tanfield coalfield about 1712 and then developed it by building the most important line of its day, the Tanfield Waggon-way near Gateshead. About 1734, he bought the Encombe estate south of Corfe Castle in Dorset as a present for his son John Pitt, who the following year built the house. It has remained much the same to the present day. John's son William Morton Pitt continued the leasing of their land and the agreements for ball clay extraction at Norden and other parts of the estate. However, William was using up a vast fortune in philanthropic work and other interests, which eventually he could no longer sustain. By 1807 he was compelled to part with Encombe House and parkland in order to satisfy his creditors, the estate being sold to John Scott, Earl of Eldon, who was Lord High Chancellor of Great Britain for 25 years between the years 1801 and 1827. The famous clay mines at Norden remained under Pitt's control until his death in 1836 at his Kingston Maurward home near Dorchester. John Scott's start in life had been made possible because his father William Scott had been a coal factor or trader in Newcastle upon Tyne, so there was a long tradition of mining in both these land-owning families and a familiarity with the movement of heavy goods.

Josiah Wedgwood was also an active promoter and investor in canal and tramway building. With his wide ranging contacts, he and his son Josiah II were in a unique position to bring railroad engineers from one project into touch with clay-mine proprietors and others who were essential to their business. In Purbeck the lanes and tracks were in very bad condition. The early transport of ball clay in Dorset mainly followed the routes which had been used by stone and Purbeck marble, from at least the 12th century. These tracks across the heath led to shipment points on the south side of Poole Harbour of which the most important were Ower and Wytch. Until 1760, packhorses were generally used to transport clay, each one could carry about 2½ cwt or one eighth of a ton, at a rate of a penny a mile. Each horse carried a crate on a pack saddle which took six or seven balls of clay and a small pannier on each side, each holding two or three balls of clay. Some clay was being carted to Middlebere and transferred to clay barges. These were keel-bottomed and each one carried 20 to 30 tons under sail to Poole, but they were soon enlarged. If shipment was delayed for any reason the clay had to be stored in a fairly dry place at the quayside and buildings known as clay cellars were erected for this purpose. These were preferably stone built to be more substantial against the water and completed with a thatched roof. One of the first cellars on record was built at Ower in 1733. In April 1758, John Bishop was preparing to build two cellars each with a length of 100ft and breadth about 17ft. The expense of the mason was stated to be £65 and the carpenter's cost was £45 16s. They were to be thatched with rushes, of which 'there was an abundance at cheap price on the spot'. After 1760, better road surfaces resulted in horse drawn carts displacing packhorses, so four horses could then move a ton of clay. However, on the heath things remained much the same, using the tracks to the various quays where passage houses had been built and local boats provided a ferry service to Poole or Wareham on market days. The passage houses were often multi-purpose with a mix of activities being carried on there. In 1789, John Calcraft leased the building known as Ower Passage & Fishery to Alexander and Thomas Fowler, boatmen, but he retained for his use the west part of the house to be used as a clay house and also the use of the quay there to lodge and ship clay.

The only named clay pit that seems to have been recorded in this period was Thresher's Pit just north of Rollington Farm. Survey maps of the Rempstone Estate drawn by Donne and James Asser in 1805 have the pit drawn in and marked, 'clay pits in Thrasher's Heath where is dug a very fine clay which makes what is nam'd the Queen's Weare (around 1762-65).' In a letter addressed to Wedgwood Byerley & Co. Potters, Etruria, Staffordshire, dated 16 February 1797, more information about Thresher's Pit during the period following the death of Hyde has come to light. The shipping agent Henry Knight revealed that most of the clay was being taken to Sheepstall for loading on to vessels, instead of using wharfs closer to hand such as Wytch or Ower. This would have involved quite a long journey using packhorses or carts to the northwest across Wytch Heath, then over Sharford Bridge to cross the Corfe River and on to the Arne peninsula toward the loading point at Shipstall. There is little doubt that part of the journey was on a well established route, which probably existed from mediaeval times and reached east Purbeck from Wareham via Stoborough and Bushey without having to pass through Corfe Castle. For that reason, it may have been better maintained than the track to Wytch or Ower. In just under two years, from April 1795, more than 2,000 tons were shipped.

A new era was about to begin with the opening of the Surrey Iron Railway (SIR) from Wandsworth to Croydon on 26 July 1803. Even without the Wedgwood influence, the huge publicity surrounding the SIR, almost on his doorstep, must have excited Fayle's business instincts and he could envisage the impact such a line could have on his proposed development of the Norden clay works. No doubt, he would have been aware of William Jessop's recommendation to the SIR Directors to build a plateway instead of a canal. Jessop had written,

> There is another way of obtaining the object in view; if not quite so effectually as by a canal, it will, under all circumstances, be not much inferior to it;

this is by the adoption of an Iron Railway. Railways of wood or iron have many years been in use in the northern parts of England, chiefly among the coal mines; but it is lately that they have been brought to the degree of perfection, which now recommends them as substitutes for canals; and in many cases they are much more eligible and useful.

Fayle decided to embrace the quality build of the SIR and transfer it to the very first Dorset railway, the horse hauled Middlebere Plateway. Although his plateway would be for private use, and it would be worked downhill from the pits to a loading quay, it would be almost a replica of the public line in Surrey.

When Benjamin Fayle took over the Norden clay mines on 1 October 1803, an 'inventory was made of implements taken on Mr Chifney's giving up the clay concern'. It was recorded there were 400 tons of clay in the Wareham cellar near the quay, 200 tons of clay in the Wytch cellar, 136 tons in the Ower cellar and 70 tons at Poole. On 24 June 1804, Fayle paid £365 0s 7d to take over all the implements and boats at the Norden and Newton works. During that period he had paid out £54 19s 2d for new implements, a further £19 8s 6d for some repairs and about £735 for the 806 tons of cellared clay mentioned above. He also took over 45,614 yards of rubbling at Norden, Wytch and Newton for which he paid £820 17s 5d.

Fayle then went on a visit to Newcastle-under-Lyme and in a letter dated 26 July 1804 announced he was appointing John Scarlet of Newcastle to be his agent for the sale of the *Old Blue*, *New Blue* and *Brown Clays*, from 'the Estates of William Morton Pitt and John Calcraft, Esquires.' The start date is also confirmed by the Fayle records, which show that clay was being supplied to Thomas Minton from the year 1804. This shift of responsibility allowed Fayle to concentrate on the building of the plateway from Norden to Middlebere, not only to make the transport of clay more certain in all weathers, but to optimise the efficiency of horse haulage by increasing loads and reducing manpower. It was later recorded in 1810, that since the coming of the iron railway only half the men previously needed were then employed in Purbeck on clay work; however there were still over 100 men working in Poole and Purbeck.

When John Hodgkinson arrived in Dorset to survey the proposed route to Middlebere he found the gentle slope of the land towards the

JOHN HODGKINSON (1773-1861), ENGINEER TO THE MIDDLEBERE PLATEWAY.

In situations where the countryside was steeply graded, canals could not be built and crude railroads were being laid down instead. They were planned as feeders to the water system bringing freight from mines, iron works, quarries and pits. The local population of Purbeck first became aware of the canal and transport revolution sweeping the country when a meeting of Wareham Corporation was called at the Town Hall on 26 January 1793 to consider the Poole and Bristol Canal. It was proposed that this canal would have as its main traffic coal from Bristol and Somerset to Dorset and potters' clay from the Wareham area to the Potteries via Bristol. Later, during 1799, building problems on the related Somerset Coal Canal led to Benjamin Outram (1764-1805) being called in for advice.

Outram had been assistant to Jessop, the leading civil engineer of the day, while planning and estimating for the Cromford Canal and was an able pupil. This was about the same time that Fayle was becoming established in his London business. By 1790, Outram and Jessop were partners with others in the Butterley Company, Derbyshire, who were successful ironmasters and suppliers of rails for railroads or tramways. Gradually the plateways took up more of Outram's attention, he being mainly responsible for the development of the flanged rail, assisted by John Hodgkinson. The two men were probably cousins, Benjamin Outram being the son of Joseph Outram's second marriage to Elizabeth Hodgkinson of Ashover. From 1799 at the age of 26, John was acting as agent for Outram in the construction of the tramroads of the Ashby de la Zouch Canal in Leicestershire where the gauge had been increased from 3ft 6in to 4ft 2in. As canals passed their peak building period or 'mania' in 1792-3 the associated railroads built as feeders to the waterways began to assume more importance in their own right.

Together they had surveyed and built lines similar in construction to the Middlebere Plateway, including a line seven miles long to the Peak Forest Canal opened in 1800 and noted for the 100ft high aqueduct at Marple. They also constructed a double track horse tramroad at Blisworth on the Grand Junction Canal. Outram's advice to the South Wales canal companies to change their edge tramways to plateways must have come to the attention of Wedgwood, who with £7,000 was a principal subscriber to the Monmouthshire Canal. This investment may have been because the canal served, via a private branch tramroad, a colliery in which he had an interest.

During 1801 Hodgkinson surveyed the entire route of the proposed Sirhowy Tramroad and the book of reference and estimates completed and signed by John was ready for submission with the bill by 25 September. It would be 24 miles long with a 1,000ft long viaduct at Risca, by far the largest built to that date. He prefaced his estimate with the statement that it was for making a Railway on Outram's improved plan. Outram was the designer of the project, but when work began on the railway John was engineer in charge at 12 guineas a week. The tramroad was completed in 1804-5 and it was John who took over much of Benjamin's work after his early death in 1805, age 41. Meanwhile, John had converted the Beaufort Works' tramroad from edge to plateway, the first recorded example of such a change. He also recommended railways to the Leominster Canal and also purchased Alteryn House near Newport in December 1803 where he would spend the greater part of his life advising and building numerous railway projects. His next recorded work was in 1808-9, when a bridge was built over the Usk at Caerleon and the route of the Monmouthshire Canal was re-surveyed, leaving a gap between 1805 and 1807. We now know that John spent some of that time working for Benjamin Fayle in Purbeck building the Middlebere Plateway, following Outram's plan but reverting to the 3ft 6in gauge which had been favoured in his earlier years. It was considered ideal for industrial use compared to wider gauges more suited to public railways.

Wedgwood was therefore well aware of Hodgkinson's capability in surveying and building plateways, even if they had not actually met. It must also have been a source of some surprise to him that no-one had done anything about improving the transport of ball clay in Dorset, which had led to delays and uncertainty about stocks of clay in Staffordshire. A new era was about to begin as Benjamin Fayle took over the clay workings and if this was not actually influenced by Wedgwood, no doubt he put forward John Hodgkinson's name as surveyor as soon as he heard Fayle was going to build a plateway in Purbeck.

water's edge ideal for building a plateway. He decided that one fairly deep cutting would be needed west of the Slepe road and the spoil from that work used to build some embankments. With a few sweeping curves the gradient which was about 1 in 100 on average, would be just right for loads going down and the horse-hauled empties coming back. Fayle, with complete confidence put the work into effect in 1805. The Dorset line was initially intended to serve, via two short branches, clay pits just east of the Wareham to Corfe Castle turnpike road and north of Norden Farm. The use of a new form of transport was for Fayle, just an extension of his business in shipping and his interest and investment in canals, until then a prime mover of heavy freight inland. On 1 July, Calcraft was paid £250, and various other payments were noted

Labourers depicted building Fayle's New Line in spring 1806. Plate rails had been drawn up in a wagon by the horse and were being laid on the blocks to extend the railroad. In the distance Corfe Castle dominated the gap in the Purbeck Hills. The stone blocks show the holes that had been drilled to receive a plug of dry oak, into which the fixing nail would be driven.
MICHAEL BLACKMORE, AUTHOR'S COLLECTION

made to J. Willis, (at Norden) and Mr Hodgkinson in connection with the railroad. Willis was the tenant of Norden Farm and agent for the clay mines. On 26 October 1805, Fayle's accounts show the company paid Hodgkinson the sum of £30, and also J. Willis received £200 in Bank of England notes (a payment of £100 had been made on 12 October). At the end of the year, Benjamin Fayle made a new 'inventory of implements at Norden, Thresher's and Newton clay pits, taken on 31 December 1805'. This included 3 boats, 10 tubills, 57 wheelbarrows and 110 wheeling boards, total £319 16s. A large amount of rubbling was recorded at the three sites charged at over £1,000 for labour.

The construction of the new 'road' went well

and considerable progress had been made by a report in August 1806. This was headed, 'Particulars of the length of Railroad 11 August 1806'. The main plateway was then complete, stated to be 4,877 yds or 2¾ miles and 37 yards, from Middlebere Quay to the junction in Norden Common for which Hodgkinson was charging 8s 10d per yard. His contracted distance was 4,530 yards, plus 500 yards turn-outs; or 5030 yards in total, charged at £1,996 11s, plus £100 for the deep cutting, making £2,096 11s. Of this amount, Fayle had already paid £1,935 15s 9d, leaving £160 15s 3d still due on 1 Aug 1806. These payments were made for the tramway construction only, because any extra excavating and making of cuttings to clay pits was undertaken by the Willis family of Norden Farm for £2,000 of which Fayle had paid £500 leaving £1,500 due in 1 August. Willis was employed as land agent to Lord Eldon and would also be responsible for running the clay pits business for over 50 years, while Fayle's business generally kept him London based.

Although the construction of an iron plateway appeared fairly simple, the track was in fact laid to a precise specification. Outram had written a guide, which has survived in several documents:

MINUTES TO BE OBSERVED IN THE CONSTRUCTION OF RAILWAYS.

The line of rail-way being fixed, and the planes and sections by which the same is to be executed settled, the ground for the whole must be formed and effectually drained. The breadth of bed for a single rail-way should be, in general, four yards; and for a double one six yards, exclusive of the fences, side drains and ramparts. The bed of road so formed to the proper inclination, and the embankments and works thereof made firm, the surface must be covered with a bed of stones broken small; or good gravel, six inches in thickness or depth. On this bed must be laid the sleepers or blocks to fasten the rails upon. These should be of stone in all places where it can be obtained in sufficient size; they should be not less than 8, not more than 12 inches in thickness; and of such breadths (circular, square or triangular) as shall make them 150lb or 200lb weight each. Their shape not material, [meaning, not particularly important] so as they have a flat bottom to rest upon, and a small portion of their upper surface level to form a firm bed for the end of the rails. In the centre of each block must be drilled a hole, one inch and a half diameter, and six inches in depth, to receive an octagonal block of dry oak five inches in length, for it should not reach the bottom of the hole; nor should it be larger than so as to be put in easily and without much driving: for if too tight fitted it might, when wet, burst the stone. These plugs are each to receive an iron spike or large nail with a flat point and long head, adapted to fit the counter-sunk notches in the end of the two rails, and thereby to fasten them down in the proper position.

The holes in the blocks were later improved by having a narrow hole drilled right through the stone below the oak plug, allowing proper drainage of rainwater. Two gauges made of iron or wood were used during construction. The gauges had a spike at each end which fitted the holes in the blocks, one being 3 feet long for each rail length and the other for the chosen gauge distance between the tracks. The use of stone blocks without cross-sleepers made it easier for a horse to move freely.

A plateway stone block showing the drilled hole to receive the oak plug. If necessary the top of the block was shaped to give a flat surface for the track. Each rail was cast with a countersunk notch at the end, which formed a hole over the plug when two rails were butted together. Fixing to the blocks was by a single nail driven through the hole and into the plug. AUTHOR

This stone block was found almost in the water of the harbour and still had a nail embedded in the central hole. AUTHOR

Outram continued:

> The rails should be of the stoutest cast iron, one yard in length each, formed with a flanch [flange] on the inner edge about two inches and a half high at the ends, and three and a half in the centre; and shaped in the best manner to give strength to the rails, and keep the wheels in their track. The soles of the rails for general purposes should not be less than four inches broad; and the thickness proportioned to the work they are intended for. On rail-ways for heavy burdens, great use and long duration, the rails should be very stout, weighing 40lb or, in some cases, nearly half an hundred weight each [nearly 56lb]. For rail-ways of less consequence less weight of metal will do; but it will not be prudent to use them of less than 30lb weight each, in any situation exposed to breakage above ground.

The source of the plates used in Purbeck has proved elusive; they could have been cast in Poole but the record suggests there was no previous local demand. There is no record that Butterley supplied the plates, which was a possibility with Outram's involvement with the company. The most likely source would be from Wales, possibly Sirhowy where Hodgkinson had recently been working.

> In fixing the blocks and rails, great attention is required to make them firm. No earth or soft materials are to be used between the blocks and the bed of small stones or gravel, on which they rest. The blocks and rails being fixed and spiked fast, nothing more remains to be done then to fill the horse path, or space between the blocks, with good gravel, or other proper materials, a little more of which must also be put on the outsides of the blocks to keep them in their proper places. This gravel should always be kept below the surface of the rails on which the wheels are to run, to keep the tracks for the wheels free from dirt and obstructions.

In the 1806 statement of work done and items still to be finished, two railroad branches were to be laid from the Norden Common junction by John Hodgkinson, extra to the original contract. Of these, 227 yards of road were needed to reach pit A of which 154 were complete and 176 yards of road were to be made to pit C, of which 44 had been done. The distance above contract was 347 yards on the main railroad plus the two branches 403 yards making a total of 750 yards at 8s 10d per yard outstanding £331 15s. Extra cutting was involved to reach the two pits, 4,925 yards to pit A and 3,791 yards to pit C charged at 6d per yard, total £217 18s. When added to the 'above contract sum' the total was £549 13s extra to pay. Shortly after this the line was in full use and must have caused a sensation among the locals. They saw it as a new kind of road and even the early map makers had a job deciding what name to give to this new type of transport, rail-way or rail-road being common. To this day, professional railway men refer to the track as the road. A local agricultural family living near the Middlebere line moved with the times and called their farm, New Line Farm. It is only in more recent times that the specific term plateway has been used for a railway using L-shaped rails pegged to stone block sleepers, the trucks having flange-less or plain wheels, the common description being 'tramroad'. (This was the opposite system to a modern railway where the rails are plain and the flange is on the wheel, known as an edge railway). On 16 August 1806, Fayle wrote from London to Wedgwood and Byerley announcing the completion of the 'Iron Rail-way from Norden Clay Pits to the Shipping Wharf' and a reduction in the price of blue clay from 20s to 18s. Fayle obviously considered the line was complete without any mention of the later tunnels to be made. The price drop proved too optimistic and was restored to 20s within two years. Fayle was proposing also to install an engine at the wharf for balling clay that had been broken in smaller pieces when taking it out of the pit.

In the meantime, prospecting had revealed new deposits of clay to the west of the existing pits and in 1807 John Hodgkinson was back again, supervising the building of a tunnel under the Wareham to Corfe Castle turnpike road. It seems likely that the construction was by cut and fill because the depth of the tunnel was relatively shallow. The tunnel was about 262 yards from the original junction in the common and the plateway extended at least 350 yards beyond the tunnel to the new pits. This area had been worked lightly by previous proprietors of the pits, but much more intensely by Fayle. A mines map from about 1810-12, shows that the original Pit A was still working, but Pit C was finished. There was now a new Pit B started on the other side of the road. and further to the west, a new excavation was called Pit C, which was so extensive that temporary railways had to be laid to move clay from the digging area to the main

The plateway had been extended under the turnpike road at Norden by 1807. In this drawing showing a scene about 1822, a train of empty wagons passes the tunnel on its way to new clay pits situated on the west side of the road and to the north of Norden Farm. It was reported that the manpower requirements for clay transport fell by 50% with the success of the horse plateway. MICHAEL BLACKMORE, AUTHOR'S COLLECTION

On the keystone at the western end of the tunnel can be seen the letters BF 1807 showing builder and date of completion. The keystone measures 10½ inches across the top, 8 inches at the bottom and is 10 inches high. The letters cut on it are 3 inches high. The entrance to the tunnel is faced with stones about 15 inches deep, but the inner part is lined with brick. AUTHOR

The first Ordnance Survey map for the Norden area published in 1811. The 'Iron Railroad' is shown connecting Middlebere to Norden, where on close examination the two tunnels under the turnpike road can be seen in use. The early mapmakers had a problem with iron roads, hence a variety of terms to describe them.

tramway. It seems unlikely that the Fayle family would have missed the opening of the new extension and the opportunity to view the keystone on the west face of the tunnel. It bears the initials of the builder and date of completion to this day, B.F.1807.

The Middlebere plateway, had been built across land belonging to two estates. At the Norden end of the line, where the mines were situated, the ground belonged to William Morton Pitt of Encombe, and the lease on the mines was

for 21 years from the take-over date of 1804. The main run of the plateway down to the quay at Middlebere passed over land belonging to Henry Bankes of Kingston Lacy. For some reason in 1810 a new arrangement was agreed between Henry Bankes, his son William John Bankes and Benjamin Fayle. This may have been to include new passing places on the line or extensions to beds where clay was left in heaps to weather. The indenture of lease was agreed on or about 25 May 1810, and dated to run from 25 December 1809, the term being 38 years. Under the terms of the lease the Wharf or quay at Middlebere included a piece or parcel of ground around it measuring one acre and thirty eight perches, being in the out parish of the Holy Trinity, Wareham, in the Isle of Purbeck. Fayle had full power to erect any warehouses or sheds on the premises for the storage of any materials brought along the railway. Also included in the lease was 'the piece of land thirty feet in width and 4,323 yards in length situated at Norden, some time since converted into a Tram road or Rail-way'. This strip of land was said to begin from the land of William Morton Pitt and extend along the unenclosed and enclosed lands of Henry Bankes into and ending at the quay or wharf.

From these measurements it seems likely that Fayle was intending to build a double plateway, thus eliminating time wasted at passing loops. The width of land leased conformed to Outram's recommended six yards (18ft) for a double track bed plus 4 or 5ft either side for drainage, fencing etc. Perhaps due to the extra cost of building a double line, this plan never materialised. The yearly rent was to be £50, payable in equal quarterly payments on 25 March, 24 June, 29 September and 25 December. If any payment was 40 days overdue the lessees were considered in default of the terms of the lease.

The first Ordnance Survey map for the Norden area, published in 1811, clearly shows the 'Iron Rail Way' with apparently two branches passing under the Turnpike road, the survey having been carried out in 1805-7. This raises some interesting questions. The 1807 tunnel we

would expect to see but the other one to the south was apparently built at a later date. If both tunnels were in operation at that time it would seem an extravagance to build two tunnels, when one could have sufficed, with the line not branching until it was west of the road. The decision may have been influenced by the cost of moving hundreds of tons of overburden in order to get the direction of the lines required. Moving down the line from Norden clay pits towards the harbour, a short branch to the east of the turnpike road was shown leading to some open pits. Further on again, a passing place was in use just to the west of the large cutting in Middlebere Heath, and another near Middlebere Farm, before approaching the quay where one or two more passing places were provided. By 1822 the southern tunnel appeared to be disused because it is omitted on a map drawn that year and only the line through the 1807 bore is shown, leading to extensive clay pits. Although apparently discarded by the mid-1820s the second tunnel would be re-instated at a later date.

Soon after the opening of the plateway, William Stevenson came past Corfe Castle in 1811, collecting material and observing the County of Dorset for his 'General View of the Agriculture of the County of Dorset', published in 1812. He was so impressed with the new road that he enquired from Willis and wrote a description of it:

A road of this kind, 3½ miles in length was made in 1806. It extends from the pits of Potter's clay at Norden near Corfe Castle, to a place opposite Poole, where the clay is shipped for Liverpool. The iron rails of which this road is composed are 3 feet long and five-eighths of a inch thick at the bottom, where the plate on which the carriage wheels run is 3½ inches wide, with vertical edging 3 inches high on the side next to the horse path and they weigh about 40lb each. The ends of the rails are supported on stones of 60 to 70lb weight, in each of which is made a hole to receive an oak plug, to which the rails are fastened by means of a large headed nail driven between the contiguous ends, through a small cavity which is left for the purpose. The declivity of the road is in some places 4 inches, and in others 5 inches every 20 yards, (that is about 1 in 180 and 1 in 144) and the expense attending this work is stated by Mr Willis (agent of Norden Works), at about £2,000 a mile for new work. The clay is conveyed on small carriages with four iron wheels carrying two tons each. Three horses draw 10 tons to the seaside, three times a day, at the expense of about six-pence a ton-weight.

William Stevenson's report said, 'Three horses draw 10 tons to the seaside, three times a day, at the expense of about six-pence a ton-weight.' A similar train well loaded at the Norden beds is about to depart for Middlebere. The clay beds were at a higher level than the track, with a 'platform' running alongside to facilitate loading the clay. In the background some men are busy loading a second line of wagons. The wagons have cast iron wheels with dished spokes and deep wheel boxes with caps to retain a reservoir of oil. About 1894.
STOBOROUGH SCHOOL

Part of a set of points recovered from the Middlebere Plateway, held up by Gordon Bartlet on the left and Rodney Lissenden on 27 July 1956.
MARTIN GALLEY

the rail at each end to resist any inward pressure when trains passed. The vertical edge or flange was often curved along the top in the form of a fish-bellied girder to give extra strength to the relatively brittle cast iron rails. In some cases, for the same reason, a longitudinal rib, convex in section was cast under the running surface of the rail. A fairly crude type of point was used with a small pivoting tongue, for access to sidings and at the passing places. The bar of iron moving on the pivot was generally pushed over by the boot of the carter and at low speeds this proved quite adequate.

The quantity of clay carried is slightly ambiguous and three horses could mean that each horse pulled a load of 10 tons three times a day to the sea-side, the alternative being three horses working in line on each train of 5 wagons. However, from the tonnage figures for clay reported sent from Poole or Purbeck at the time, it confirms the three horses worked together. This would mean 30 tons being moved every day; say nearly 300 working days a year at that time, a total of 9,000 tons. This fits well with Fayle's calculated average for 1811 of 8,000 to 10,000 tons, being about half the amount from Purbeck as a whole which was stated to be 16,000 to 20,000 tons. The horses would then have worked a distance of 18 to 20 miles a day, which was about average. It is likely that on the gradients involved no braking of the wagons was needed, although this could have been achieved using metal slippers, which the driver placed between the wheels and rail, or sprags thrust between the spokes of the wheels. Once started, gravity would assist the horses pulling the load, but a less than

To clarify one or two points, the 3½ miles he mentions must have been measured from the furthest pits, the main plateway as built being only 2¾ miles long. The 'side next to the horse-path' would have been the inner area between the two vertical flanges of the iron track. Following Outram's minutes, this was an early method of construction with the rails spiked directly to a wood plug in the sleeper block. The rails had a rectangular tapered notch at each end of the running surface or sole, so when two rails were closely butted together the adjacent notches formed a hole through which the iron nail was driven. In a very short time the design was modified and the sole of each rail was thickened at each end for 3 to 4 inches. This improved their footing on the stone sleeper blocks. In addition, semicircular lugs were cast on the inner side of

Diagram and calculations of weight of a plate rail found by R. Taylor of Hamworthy, whose early research notes on the plateway are held at Birmingham City Library.

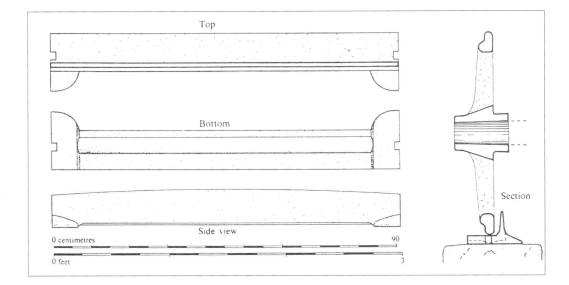

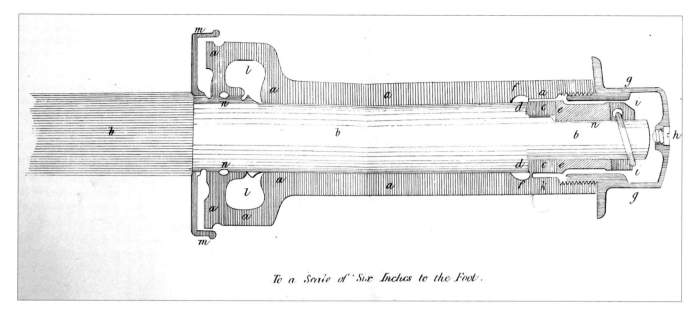

To a Scale of Six Inches to the Foot.

perfect track and uneven wear would provide enough friction to prevent the train running away. Some of this was due to the weather, for example metallic surfaces wear much more when they are dry (south facing) than wet (north facing). The north wheels being less worn would tend to outrun the south wheels and rub more against the north rail thus retarding the speed of movement or any tendency to run away. A plate rail also harboured dust, dirt and stones deposited by wind or horses hooves, thus increasing the friction of the wheels. On cast iron railways wagon capacities were generally low and varied approximately with the gauge. Nearly all the wagons built between 1603 and 1830 were constructed with wider tops than the wheelbase. On a plateway like the Middlebere line each wagon would have weighed about 15 to 20 hundredweight. Connection between wagons was by a chain each side, fixed at buffer level, the horses' trace harness being connected to a bar attached to the leading wagon in a similar way. The height of the harness was cut down because of limited clearance through the tunnels and the horses could be easily changed around in the line to gain experience.

About the same time as Stevenson's report, John Collinge of Bridge Road, Lambeth supplied new patent axletrees in 1811-2 for use on the wagons, resulting in much better lubrication. This event was reported by John Farey in his *General View of the Agriculture of Derbyshire, (1817, vol. 3, p. 297.)* where he said;

It is nevertheless true, that a large share of the friction and labour of drawing TRAMS,

originates with the imperfect form and workmanship of the Axle-trees, as has been proved since Collinge's 1811 patent Axletrees (made in Westminster Road, Lambeth), have been applied to the trams on the Railways to the famous Pipe-Clay Pits near Corfe Castle, in Purbeck in Dorsetshire, and others in the south of England; by which also there is a great saving made, in the cost of incessantly greasing the wheels; and in the great durability of these new Axle-trees, and their Wheels.

This was a very surprising development as this type of axle was normally used for faster moving vehicles such as mail and stagecoaches. Plateway wagons normally adopted the very simple arrangement of cast iron wheels revolving on a fixed axle. The wheels were held roughly in gauge, and prevented from falling off the axle, by a linch pin or cotter through a hole near the end of the axle. There was no obvious reason for the Middlebere wagons to require anything different and no doubt they were originally built to the usual pattern and would have remained so.

John Collinge had been granted the patent, No. 3410 on 9 March 1811, for his invention of, 'Certain improvements in and upon carriages and other wheel boxes and axletrees'.

In his statement under the patent he said,

...in preference and from experience I use axletrees made of wrought iron case-hardened, and the carriage wheel boxes of cast iron case-hardened.

John Collinge's 1811 patent axle-trees were fitted to Middlebere wagons, as noted in Stevenson's report of 1817.
CENTRAL LIBRARY SHEFFIELD

27

The second choice he listed to make the wheel boxes was of brass. The lince pin, as he called it, at the outer end of the axle was improved to prevent fracture or loss and its function was modified to keep a fixed collet (or collar) in place on a flattened part of the axle. This collar acted as a bearing against an inner bridge or ring on the axle of smaller diameter than the main axlebox. It was claimed that the collar was able, through plates or washers, to absorb shock from the movement of the wheel box (or centre of the wheel), as it revolved around the axle and to give smoother running. An outer cap was screwed into the box to cover the end of the axle, which prevented the linch pin coming out, and also retained oil for constant lubrication of the wheel box on the axle. An agreement was reached for Collinge's new patent axle to be applied to the wagons on Fayle's railroad. No doubt, the manufacturer received many more enquiries following the endorsement by Fayle, and the clay

works had wagons which were smoother in operation and more sparing with lubricant. Axles were usually fitted at 36 to 38in centres, so each rail was never loaded with more than one fourth of the wagon weight at once, but this did not prevent frequent breakages to the road. Outram stated the standard gauge of a plateway to be 4ft 2in between the upright rail flanges but Hodgkinson later adopted 3ft 6in and the Dorset line was probably the first one built to this specification. Measurements made by Michael Wilmott in 1996, from blocks in situ near Middlebere confirmed a gauge of approximately 3ft 6in.

By 1800 it was customary to bore for clay samples, usually at intervals of 30 yards. The information gained from the boreholes helped to map each clay lens and if commercially viable a plan was adopted for getting the clay by sinking shafts or open pit working. Traditionally, drilling was done by hand so earth samples could be taken at each foot of depth, thus giving more accurate results. The 'getting' of clay and changes in mining practice developed in tandem with the new transport. In the early days various tunnels had been driven in the search for clay, such as the Norden Tunnel pit of 1807. The clay cutters began to use this method when the clay lens was at a deeper level and not parallel to the surface, and therefore not convenient for a shallow open pit. After digging down to uncover some of the clay the miners stuck to the seam grimly until short tunnels had to be driven to follow the lens. Eventually lack of oxygen guttered the candles or made breathing and working difficult. The depth and extent of the pit was limited by the lack of any ventilation to disperse bad air.

There were two other limiting factors in those early tunnels. One was the threat of water flooding the work place together with sand. It was hardly surprising, given the location and the porous sediments of the Bagshot Beds surrounding the clay, that nearly every mine suffered water problems at some time. These could be quite minor and easily dealt with by using pink slub clay, puddled behind a timber barrier with bundles of dried heather pushed well in behind to form a natural filter. From long experience, the miners knew that heather was best for holding back the sand and letting the water filter through. For generations they had come to work prepared for any water problem by cutting a few bundles of heather as they walked across the heath. A large ingress of water would

The hand drilling rig remained virtually unchanged for generations. In this picture from the 1930s, Frank Kitcatt (Eli's father) supervises another borehole, assisted by Bill 'Sticky' Marshallsay. AUTHOR

In the old mill at Norden bundles of heather were stacked on two of the Lister wagons. The miners used the heather in the building of dams when water broke into the workings underground. 26 June 1968.
GEORGE MOON

require the building of a timber dam to block off the whole lane, mining continuing round the obstruction. Another solution was to use a metal cylindrical structure, such as an old ship's boiler to form the upper part of a shaft to keep water out, the lower part of the shaft being the usual timber construction. One of the mines at Norden, which was about 70 feet in depth, was constructed in this way and always known as Tankhole. As the clay was taken out underground, excavated areas were left with the roof supported by timber cages. A cage was made up using old timber props, stacked in a criss-cross fashion from floor to roof, which helped to support the working area while the next block of clay was mined. As mining moved on, some timbers were withdrawn allowing the 'plastic' clay and the ground above to be let down in a controlled manner. This prevented cracking of the clay above and sand and water breaking into the mine.

The other significant factor limiting early clay mines was the manual transport of clay along the tunnels using wooden boxes like sledges or wheelbarrows before the advent of underground rail haulage. The mines remained fairly basic using just single shafts, square in cross section, made of interlocking timbers. The head frames were also built of timber and the simplest type had a single wheel and bucket, and the clay

originally hauled to the surface in boxes. It was said that a few of the earliest mines on Fayle's property were hand wound using two men on a gin with ordinary hemp ropes, pre 1840. With the advent of coal mining techniques deep vertical shafts were soon being sunk to reach clay at lower levels. The first reference to underground mining at Fayle's was a report in a letter from 1816. Fayle said he had got two miners from South Wales to mine Thresher's clay. They must have had a difficult time because six years later he wrote,

> The miners for Thresher's clay have had heavy expenses of timber and unfortunately they are checked by water which has happened since I left Norden. Of this clay there can only be saved three feet clear of ordinary clay; the depth of this clay through a variety of strata is great and the timbers necessary for support are expensive and liable to be lost.

The shafts at Norden were not so deep as those mines in coal measures, rarely exceeding 100ft. Working lanes (or roadways in coal mining parlance) were driven off from the bottom of the shaft, and in some cases at several levels, to the extremity of the clay lens. The bottom of the shaft was designed to be the lowest part of the mine so the lanes would have a slight upward gradient toward the clay miners or getters at the working face, which helped when pushing full wagons out to the shaft. The miners were also responsible for the support to the tunnel, the simplest pattern or 'set' being a vertical timber prop each side with a horizontal one laid across the top close to the roof, and building their workplace was part of the job. Over a period of years the clay getters worked back from the boundary of the deposit to the shaft, a process known as retreat mining. The clay was hand cut from the face using a short handled pick or mattock, the head of which had two cutting edges made razor sharp by the local blacksmith. The miners were trained to recognise the different grades of clay, either by sight or by putting a piece in the mouth and feeling the consistency between the teeth. Lighting at the face was by candles made of tallow (rendered down from animal fat by local butchers). No. 16s were used in mining, thinner and longer than the usual household type. It was generally agreed that getting clay using hand tools demanded extreme physical input from the miner, but being a 'runner' pushing the wagons was worse!

Although Wedgwood said he preferred his clay to be unweathered it became accepted practice over the years for Dorset clay to be weathered at beds, which then became the focal point of the railway system. At that period the Norden beds were situated near the office and weighbridge on the common. The weathering process was supposed to increase the clay's plasticity before despatch to the customer. The clay was dumped in discrete heaps and apart from some watering and turning was left for a period from 6 months to three years before being dug and loaded for the customer.

For eighteen years, Benjamin Fayle had enjoyed full use of the railroad for the 2½ miles to Middlebere at a favourable rent of £50 per annum, which had been a vital factor in developing the clay business. There had been a few farm crossings with some repairs to be done, but soon dealt with under the terms of the lease. Although there was a covenant in the lease allowing the landlord Henry Bankes and his business partners to use the line, the option had never been taken up. It also allowed for any tenants of land belonging to Bankes to exercise an option over the railroad, but likewise this had not arisen. In the early 1820s, Fayle became aware of interest being shown in the railroad as a means of getting goods to Poole Harbour, but as far as he knew these persons were not existing tenants of the Bankes' estate, so would have no rights over the Railroad.

In January 1824, Fayle wrote a letter to Wedgwood in which he described a renewal of his lease with Mr Pitt, and re-stated his exertions to serve the potters well over the previous 20 years.

> If I had not expended £10,000 on making a rail road and introducing other accommodations, the quality of clay required could not be supplied and the price must have increased.

It came as a shock therefore to receive a letter from Henry Bankes in November 1824, announcing the fact that someone who was a tenant had applied to use the railroad to Middlebere and this had been granted. The shock derived from the fact that the tenant was none other than William Pike, their main competitor in the clay trade. After quoting from the lease, dated 20 May 1810, with regard to usage by associates or tenants, the letter stated that,

> ...no person using the said railway could carry or convey any clay or minerals in any greater quantity or weight usually conveyed thereon in any one carriage by the said B Fayle.

The letter continued

> Now wherefore pursuant to the said Covenant and the power thereby reserved to us, we give you notice that William Pike a tenant of ours of lands and tenements in the said Isle of Purbeck will from henceforth use and exercise the right and liberty of ingress, egress and regress in, to, from and upon, the said Road or Railway and will unite and join any other Road or Railway thereto which he may choose to make for the purposes – Witness our hands this eighteenth day of November 1824, HB WJB (Henry Bankes and William John Bankes).

Pike's argument was that the Landlord would benefit from getting more rent. When he took advice on the wording of the 1810 lease he concluded that he was not due to pay any compensation to Fayle. However, Pike writing from his Bucknowle home near Wareham on 5 August 1825, consulted Matthias Dunn, who was an expert on such matters in the coal industry. He advised Pike that it was normal for, 'a fair compensation to be paid for the use of Fayle's capital and also for the annual wear, tear and maintenance of the Way.' Pike estimated a reasonable wayleave charge would be 2s a ton with no repairs, which was little more than a halfpenny per ton per mile. Benjamin Fayle reacted in angry style objecting to the proposal that Pike might build a new plateway from his clay pits to unite with the Middlebere line, expecting virtually free access. Fayle objected to the extra loading, believing that more trains would hinder the existing clay business. Although Pike claimed, that under the terms of the lease he also had the right of access to the clay cellars and pier at Middlebere, he decided to make a new Wharf 'a few score yards further down the river.' He then complained that Fayle had not given him similar consideration, 'for he has taken up two railroad Turns out and says I cannot go over his 30 feet so as to join.'

The outcome of the disagreement does not appear to be recorded. William Pike for reasons unknown, decided not to pursue the plateway connection and the whole action may have been to irritate the opposition. Pike was known to be difficult in his dealings. Also, by that date an edge railway should have been first choice for a new build. Whatever the reason, the Pike operation continued in its traditional form for another 13 years until the next generation started building their Furzebrook Railway. Back in 1805, Fayle had set his business on course, by building the first railroad in Dorset. The Middlebere plateway had proved so successful it would celebrate its centenary, still using horses to provide motive power. Perhaps the disagreement with Pike had set Fayle's business mind working, because about 1828, despite being in his late 70s, his attention was taken up by the improvement of transport from his pits at Newton, five miles to the east of Norden. A strong verbal tradition among older employees suggested a new plateway similar to Middlebere was operating by 1830, the distance to the pier being about 1¼ miles. It was this second plateway built at Newton and opened barely a year before his death, which was destined to maintain the clay business after 1907. Clay had been loaded into ships at Goathorn for generations, probably 100 years before the Newton line was built. This long tradition of shipping ball clay at Goathorn was described in a letter to John Calcraft the estate owner. In April 1766 John Bishop of Hayes Farm, who was the agent for the Rempstone Estate wrote to Calcraft at his London address in Sackville Street about contracts and prices which he needed to agree.

...before building a seler (cellar) on Goathorne

Poynt for the clay we dig from Kingswood and Ower Farms, as it is much the best place for shipping it and where it was always formerly done which is on Newton Estate.

This plateway, said to be 3ft 6in gauge, apparently followed the Middlebere practice being horse-worked, and was later converted to edge rail and became part of the Corfe to Goathorn Railway, now commonly known as Fayle's Tramway. Fayle's personal involvement was brought to an end with his death at the beginning of 1831. In his will the clay business was divided equally between his son Revd Richard Fayle (Rector of St Mary's Church, Wareham from 1828, in the gift of John Calcraft), his son-in-law B. G. Babington (whose wife, Fayle's daughter Anna, had died) and his daughter Charlotte aged 36, who remained unmarried and took up the reins of the business. Charlotte had purchased her Freedom of the City of London in 1831 (as a patern maker) and the business remained based in London at 16 Aldermanbury.

Unfortunately, the year that Fayle died in London was marked locally by an accident at the Norden mines, when a boy was killed on the plateway. Clay mining, like any business involving heavy manual work, suffered a fairly regular accident rate, which often affected young and inexperienced workers, and it was a sad day when the railroad had to record a fatality in July 1831. Robert Bennet was about 14 years of age and in the employ of Farmer Ricks. Robert was killed when he fell from a wagon, which was drawing a ton of clay. The driver of a following wagon about 100yds behind ran to the spot and found the deceased lying on the road, his head on the wheel-plate and the off-wheel before jammed against it. Blood was flowing profusely from the head. It was a general rule on tramways that the driver should walk and not ride on the wagons or horse. The men usually followed these instructions, but it must have been difficult getting trains through the road tunnels with limited access.

A few years later, in 1838, following the death of William Morton Pitt, Norden Farm and the Clay Pits became Lot 31 in the sale of his estate. The sale took place on Saturday 18 August 1838 at the King's Arms Inn, Dorchester. The farm consisted of 524 acres,

...with the well known and celebrated Norden Clay Pits. The clay pits are let, on lease, for a term

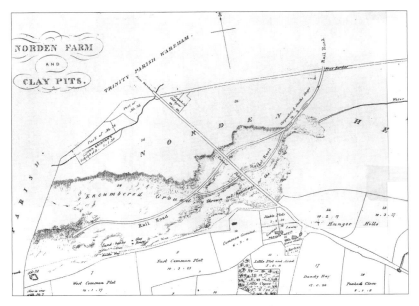

The 1838 estate map of Norden, drawn for the sale of the mines. It shows the plateway in use through both tunnels under the turnpike road and connected either side of the road. The northern one is dated 1807 on the west portal and the southern one was dated 1848 on the arch facing Middlebere.

The terminus of the Middlebere plateway showing a short branch leading on to the pier, and the extension referred to in the 1838 lease running past a second pier to the boundary of the property. The boat slip was used for hauling lighters up for repair

of twenty-one years from the 24th day of June 1825, at a clear yearly rent of £800. The works, which are now, and have been for many years past in full activity are provided by the tenants with a railroad to the waterside of the estuary of Poole Harbour, where the clay is shipped.

The Right Hon John Earl of Eldon, wanting to extend the Encombe Estate, paid £27,000 for lot 31. A map of the pits produced at that time showed the lines joined up, making junctions east and west of the two road tunnels and this formation could have enabled empty wagons to be brought in through one tunnel and full trains for Middlebere to leave through the other. It is worth noting the difference between the two junctions as drawn on the map. The one to the east appears to be a normal junction with conventional points, but to the west the southern

branch meets the other at a sort of T-junction. It is possible that loaded wagons were brought individually from the mines, as described in the 1831 accident above, the junction being an exchange point for empties, so the usual connection with points was not needed. After some years this arrangement was abandoned, probably due to accumulated waste spoil covering the southern part of the loop and the two branches became quite separate again. In a short time the southern branch fell out of use and the tunnel became redundant. It was later restored and used again after 1848.

By 1839, Henry Bankes who had granted the 1809 lease for the plateway land had died, as well as Benjamin Fayle, so a new agreement was made, the annual rent being set at £150. The new lease allowed for an extension to that part of the plateway and quay on Bankes' land. One of the reasons for this may have been the Pike's decision to build their new line from Furzebrook to the River Frome at Ridge, which was half completed by 1839. With this new competition, Fayle's may have felt the need to increase their capacity at Middlebere quay.

The lease was dated 25 December 1839, and made between William John Bankes of Kingston Lacy, the lessor, and the three beneficiaries of Fayle's will: Rev Richard Fayle, Benjamin Guy Babington and Charlotte Fayle.

Bankes had apparently established a quay or slipway for his own use, a short distance to the east of the Middlebere clay wharf. If Fayle's could extend their plateway up to the boundary of Bankes' quay, this would give them room for a second pier to load clay if needed. The main details of the Middlebere quay and tramroad were as stated in the 1809 lease, with an addition to cover the extension, which stated:

> The said lessees shall and will within twelve calendar months from the date hereof make or cause to be made and laid down in good substantial and workmanlike manner a branch Tram road or Railway of the width of twenty feet, rails thereon corresponding in all respects with those on the existing Tram road, which said Branch Road or Railway shall unite with the existing Tram road, and shall extend from thence in an easterly direction up to and as far as the boundary between the Middlebere Quay ground, and the wharf belonging to W. J. Bankes. The lessees to maintain and repair the extension to the same condition as the main Tram road.

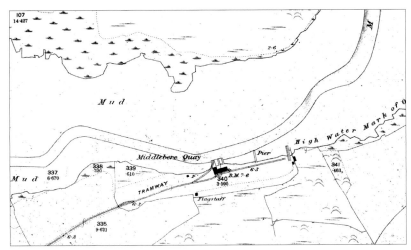

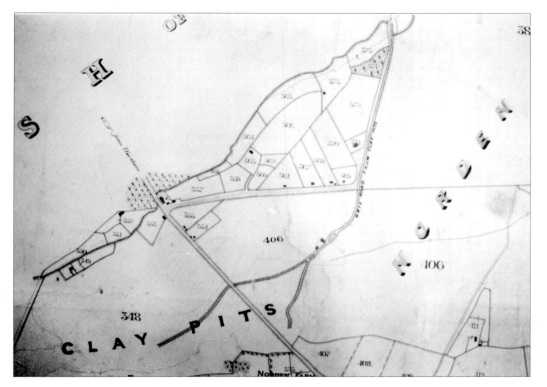

Tithe map of Corfe Castle, 1844. Six years after the sale of the clay pits in 1838 the original 1807 tunnel was still in use, but the second tunnel, which apparently was in use from 1811 to 1838, appeared to be disused. Soon after the turnpike road would be slewed to a new position. Two loops or passing places were shown in the plateway near the weigh house, the longer one being about 53 yards and the other 36 yards. From there it was about 262 yards to the tunnel, and the branch through the tunnel extended another 340 yards to pits that were still being worked in the 1870s.

The extension was to be a single line as defined by Outram, a twelve feet wide bed and about 4ft either side for allied construction such as drainage. A restrictive clause was inserted to allow only the conveyance of any clay minerals or materials or merchandise raised at the works or belonging to them. The Branch road or Railway was to be worked with horses and suitable carriages, the limit of quantity or weight on any one carriage to be 30cwt (40cwt was allowed on the main plateway). They were however given permission to make any number of turnouts in addition to those at present on the railway. It was allowed on both sides for them or their agents to enter the land for the purpose of laying down any Tram road or Rail way across the existing line, the time taken to be as short as convenient, and any damage made good as soon as possible. Bankes reserved the right to purchase the

materials of the warehouses or sheds, and all or any part of the iron, stone, wood and other materials constituting or forming the Road or Railway at the end of the term of the lease. A valuation to be set by three referees.

By 1844, the Corfe Castle tithe map showed only the 1807 tunnel being in use, leading to the common west of the turnpike road, which extended to 83 acres. Following a further renewal of the mine lease in June 1846, attention was given to getting the clay, which had been left under the turnpike road around the second tunnel. To achieve this the road itself was slewed

The second tunnel was built under the turnpike road about 80 yards south of the 1807 bore. It took some time, on 16 February 1980, to cut brambles and undergrowth away to uncover the end facing west and venture inside. The date of building is not recorded, but it is generally referred to as the 1848 tunnel because of a date stone attached to the east (Middlebere) side when repairs and part re-building were carried out 1846-8. From then on, the plateway branch emerging from the west end of the tunnel, turned sharply south leading into a large open pit of about an acre in extent. AUTHOR

View through the 1848 tunnel looking towards Middlebere. The depth of the water was too deep to walk through in safety. AUTHOR

On the end of the tunnel facing Middlebere was the stone which recorded its second building and repairs, 'Dated in 1848'. AUTHOR

to a new path east of the previous route, producing a noticeable double bend in the highway, instead of being straight as shown on all older maps. The tunnel was extended under the new piece of road, and repaired and dated 1848, the old section being dismantled to allow mining. Another reason for the 1848 work being carried out was the renewal of the lease for the Middlebere Plateway, the 1809 agreement having expired after 38 years on the last day of 1847.

Within four years of the tunnel work at Norden, Fayle's were looking to re-build and enlarge the pier at Goathorn and to convert the Newton Plateway to edge rail. They knew that Pike's were hoping to build on the success of their 1840 edge railway to Ridge, having applied in 1848 for access to a deep-water pier. Fayle's also decided it was time to compare both types of railway system in their business. On a map of Poole Harbour 1848 Fayle's depot was called, 'Middlebeere Quay and Clay Shed' and the channel was only three feet deep, but another five years would pass before the upgrade was finished. The 1853-4 winter was very hard and the miners had been unable to work as much as normal. Lower production on piece rates severely affected their weekly income. In a philanthropic move B. Fayle & Co. supplied the miners with 240 loaves a week as long as the bad weather lasted. By May 1854, the Newton line conversion was complete, using bridge rail, and a grand opening day was planned. Charlotte Fayle came down from London with her brother-in-law Benjamin Babington and brother Richard came up from Torquay where he was living. Assembled on the new pier, they shared a celebration dinner of roast beef with Rev J. H.

Evans of Corfe Castle, mines manager Joseph Willis and 170 clay workers, some of the latter from Norden works. It was later reported that the new line worked by horses was built to 3ft gauge, but this should be compared with other reports, which said the initial gauge was 3ft 6in. It was re-gauged to 3ft 9in for steam operation in 1868.

Five years later the men were feeling less happy. Changes in pay structure had been announced at Fayle's clay pits. The way in which miners were paid piecework had a long record of change down the years and was nothing new. However it was not always received very well and in this case a strike was called because the men felt hard done by. No doubt, a recent accident at neighbouring mines when two men were trapped underground by a collapsing shaft was still fresh in their memory. They knew only too well the dangers involved in mining. On 12 May 1859 the report was headlined,

A STRIKE. All the men on the clay works of Fayle and Co., have been on the strike for wages since Monday 1st. For many years the workmen there have been employed as day labourers, but the company having determined upon having the work done by measurement, submitted to the men their list of prices, to which the men object as being much too low. It is generally difficult to know the right and the wrong in such cases. Neither party seems inclined to give way at present; but we hope the matter will soon be adjusted to the mutual satisfaction of both.

On 19 May, the *Dorset County Chronicle* was glad to report,

...the temporary misunderstanding which, during

the last week, existed between the company of Fayle and Babington, and their workmen at the Norden and Goathorn clay works, has come to an end. The men cheerfully resumed their employment on Wednesday morning. We believe the grievance was more nominal than real. The company is of the wrong stamp to impose a real hardship upon the workmen and the latter too wise and tractable to hold out after being reminded of their employer's well known character for fair dealing exhibited towards them for so many years.

About the same time as the pay changes the men had to contend with other changes in working practice. Some miners reported the hand windlass being used prior to 1840 for winding clay and also for winding water out of the shaft. Horse winding devices called gins may also have been used. When steam winding of pits came in, between 1860 and 1870, a much earlier start to the day had to be made usually by 4am to build up steam from the previous day to working pressure, but no wages were paid for 'Steam time'. When sufficient power had developed the winch-man would wind the shaft to pump out accumulated water and the movement of the empty cage up and down the shaft helped to disperse bad air. A crude test for the air was to let a candle down in the cage and see if it stayed alight on return. It later became a tradition that men with steam experience from mine haulage were generally promoted to locomotive driving.

Two years later in 1861 the Third Edition of Hutchins' *History of Dorset* appeared. The new editors recorded the extended demand for Dorset clay since the account written in the First Edition. Shipments from Poole had increased from the 10,000 tons mentioned by Hutchins in 1760, to 14,796 tons in 1802, 22,000 tons in 1808 and 62,932 tons in the year 1859, of which about 50,000 tons were from Purbeck. The average annual exportation for 1861, including that sent by rail, was estimated to be 75,000 tons. The various British ports and places to which the clay was consigned were given as, 'Bowness, Bristol, Cardiff, Chester, Dysart, Falmouth, Gainsboro', Glasgow, Gloucester, Goole, Grimsby, Hartlepool, Hull, Kirkaldy, Leeds, Liverpool, Llanelly, London, Middlesboro', Milford, Newcastle, Plymouth, Runcorn, Saundersfoot, Shields, Spalding, Stockton, Sunderland, Swansea, Teignmouth and Whitehaven'. The foreign ports listed were 'Bremen, Brussels, Carthagena, Dordt, Elsinore, Growgen, Hamburg, Kyn, Rotterdam, Seville, Saint Cyprian and Saint Michael'. The report continued:

> The establishments which supply this immense demand, are conducted with all the improved appliances of modern engineering. There are three firms in Purbeck working the clay technically known as the blue clay, -- Messrs. W. and J. Pike, whose pits lie in lands belonging to the Rev. N. Bond, at Creech, in the parish of Knowle; Whiteway, Watts, Hatherly, & Co. who work Furzebrook pits, belonging to the trustees of -- Brown; and Kilwood pits, belonging to the Rev. H. F.Yeatman, of Stock House. The clay of these firms is conveyed by the Messrs. Pike, over a railway constructed by them about twenty years since, to a wharf on the River Frome, about a mile below Wareham, near Ridge, and thence in their barges, of from forty-five to sixty tons burthen, towed by a steam-tug to Poole for shipment. Another firm, B. Fayle & Co. have works in Corfe Castle parish, at Norden, belonging to the Earl of Eldon. The clay raised here is conveyed by a tramway, about three miles in length, laid with tram plates (which has been in existence for more than fifty years), to a wharf at Middlebere, to be transferred in sailing barges, of from twenty to thirty tons burthen, for shipment at Poole. The same firm have also a work called Goddens, or Godins, on lands the property of J. H. Calcraft, esq. in the parish of Swanage, and their clay is received into barges at Goathorn, a wharf on an inlet which divides Branksea Island from Purbeck, and with which wharf the pits are connected by a mile and a quarter of railway. Hence it is conveyed to be put on board ship at Poole.

The report concluded with the statement: 'There are about 350 men occupied in the clay-works of Purbeck throughout the year, principally employed at piece-work, and earning from 12s to 17s per week'.

Fayle's old office at Norden was in a thatched building adjacent to the Middlebere Plateway. Also attached were a smithy, stables and weighbridge. The Middlebere line came in from the right and passed in front of the office towards the old tunnels to the left. The 1881 diversion to the new pits at Blacklands, near Matchams, diverged via the curve into the foreground. The horses were standing on the line leading to the main weathering beds beyond the office.
CORFE CASTLE MUSEUM

CHAPTER THREE

The next 40 years, 1863-1903
The Middlebere Plateway and developments at Norden clay works

At the western end of the 1848 tunnel, the plateway made a sharp turn south to reach a new area of clay extraction, just north of Norden farm. This large excavation, about one acre in extent, later filled with water and formed a lake to the west of the A351 road. The tracks through the two plateway tunnels converged a short distance east of the road, and just beyond that point the Company had established offices, stables, weathering beds for the clay and a weighbridge. Charlotte Fayle introduced a wooden paddle tug called the *Royal Albert*, which apart from hauling clay barges for the company, became the workhorse of Poole harbour. It also regularly towed the Poole lifeboat *Manley Wood* powered by oarsmen to rescue shipping in trouble, the first such launch being on 11

February 1866. The annual output of Purbeck ball clay had gone up to about 50,000 tons in 1859 (Hutchins); about half of this still being moved by horses. Fayle's share of the total was about 22,000 tons. Getting clay in the open was still vulnerable to the weather conditions and long periods of rain resulted in less work and poor wages.

On 19 August 1870, a rare occasion was recorded on the plateway, 'when the men of the Norden Clay Works' were conveyed to Middlebere on a horse drawn passenger special. The outing or workmen's treat was initiated in Corfe Castle when the town band started playing at 5am. The men of the clay works then assembled at the smith's shop, where wagons were waiting to convey them to the wharf. The

Norden 1885 shows the Middlebere plateway at the top. Although the 1807 tunnel appears to be still in use the mines it served were closed by 1881 and that section only used as sidings. The diversion following the L&SWR branch led to new workings at New Meadow from 1875 and Matchams about 1881.

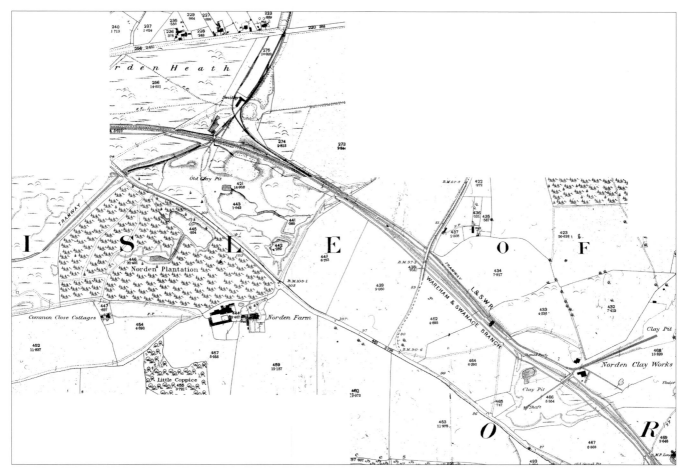

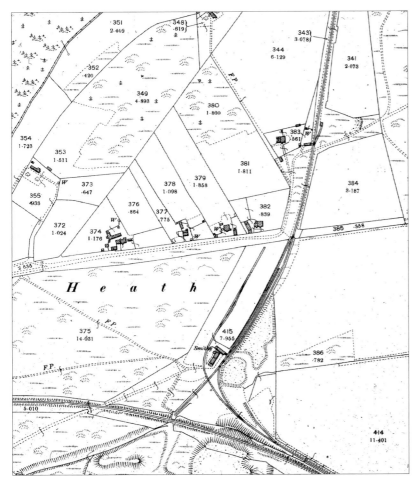

A closer look at the plateway office area on Norden Heath, OS 1907 shows the old line beyond the Swanage branch has been lifted. A single line runs into the old 'Shops' weathering bed area, but most of that work was being transferred nearer to Matchams and a new weigh house. A short siding still remains, perhaps for storing empty wagons.

company's steam tug, *Royal Albert*, then took them on an excursion to the Isle of Wight where two hours were spent exploring Ryde. Returning on board they enjoyed a generous meal of beef, bread and ale. After that the tug steamed back to Middlebere, the men being very grateful for the kindness shown by their employers.

By 1875, the working pits covered an area about half a mile long by 100 yards wide north of Norden Farm but most of the available clay had been taken, and the pits were being worked out. The last pit to be worked out was wedge shaped, being about 60 yards in length east to west, and 27 yards wide at the east end tapering to just seven yards at the west end. The average depth of good clay was six feet. Over a period of six years the company developed a new mining area about half a mile to the south east at New Meadow and Matchams, near the present Norden station. The line from Middlebere was diverted near the weigh house, in the direction of the new mines. By 1881, the workings north of the farm had finished and the old tracks leading

to them converted to sidings. Mining at New Meadow started close to the Corfe River and progressed in stages, moving westwards over the next 10 years. The pits at Matchams developed over the same period utilising a major incline in the excavation. At that time Fayle's were paying the Earl of Eldon a fixed rent of £1,500 per annum.

1876 was a typical year in the life of B. Fayle & Co. At that time the L&SWR main line had not reached Corfe Castle and the Norden mines were still separate from those at Newton, so all clay from Norden had to go on the plateway to Middlebere. Newton's clay output was loaded at Goathorn and had by then the advantage of using steam power to transport clay to the pier. They also had deeper water, which allowed for larger ships and barges to be loaded and all their clay was cut in open pits which avoided the support costs of underground mining incurred at Norden. A regular customer from that period would be the James Stiff company at Lambeth. They used mostly Newton white clay and averaged 2,747 tons per annum from 1876 to 1878. A further 759 tons of Norden clay was also taken in small lots during the three years, mostly best blue but also some pink and yellow clay. For example, on 9 November 1876, the barge *Seven Sisters* took a load consisting of 222 tons of Newton white and 62 tons of Norden blue. The cost of mats to separate the clays was 9s. Norden blue was also the choice of a large pottery in Sweden, Atkie Bolaget Gustafsberg Fabrik. They usually shipped two loads a year amounting to 488 tons in 1883, 417 tons in 1884 and 560 tons in 1885. In those days all the clay was hand cut using picks, whether it came from the pit or mine. Immediately prior to shipment, most of the clay was taken from the weathering beds where it was loaded and unloaded by shovels if in the broken state, or by using a pronged pug if in lump form. Some ships were loaded at Poole Quay, their arrival being telegraphed by the owner or the Harbour Authorities and the clay towed to Poole in lighters to be transhipped. Clay was also being ordered for rail delivery to some customers. This clay was off-loaded from the lighters into railway trucks on the quay tramway, which had opened in 1874. Horses were used to move the trucks on the quayside until 1899, when steam locomotives took over, moving freight to the national system at Poole railway station.

About 20 years after the updated report in

Hutchins, C. E. Robinson was collecting material for his book, *A Royal Warren, or Picturesque Rambles in the Isle of Purbeck* published in 1882. He wrote a description of the pit at Matchams,

> Here is a wide uncovered excavation the rubbish overlying the clay not being many yards in thickness. The steep sides are being cut away in steps by men with spades, and are charmingly tinted, light pink, bright yellow, gray and white, according to the varieties of the clay. As they are cut, the square lumps of the plastic material are slid in a wet state along a smooth plank, towards a truck, into which they are lifted by a man using an iron prong. From the ground level above an engine hauls the loaded trucks up an inclined tramway, and when it has leisure from this employment, is busily engaged in sawing out timber props and sleepers. The whole scene, on a fine day is animated and pretty; but in wet weather there must be pleasanter occupations than the constant handling and treading of slippery adhesive clay. The product of this pit is conveyed to a pier at Goathorn, on the shores of Poole Harbour, by a tramway having a flange to retain the wheels of trucks, and probably one of the oldest in England.

This was an excellent description by Robinson, except for the mistaken reference to Goathorn.

Later in the book he says 'Middlebere, whither runs one of the oldest tramways in England, long used for the clay traffic from Norden'.

By the time Robinson's book was published, action had been taken to connect the main line at Wareham to Swanage, the branch railway being built 1883-5. A railway line from Wareham through the Isle of Purbeck to Swanage had been proposed as early as 1847, mainly to serve the stone trade, but was dropped due to lack of financial support. Early in 1862, a bill was again placed before Parliament for a similar branch line with a proposal for a short branch from Wareham to Creech to open up the Purbeck clay district. It was initially thrown out due to large opposition from Wareham, on the grounds of their amenities being eroded. Later in 1862, a company called the Isle of Purbeck Railway backed by the L&SWR suggested a line similar to the 1847 proposal, passing close to the west of the town. Wareham eventually agreed to the provision of a separate station near the so-called South River or Frome, with facilities being provided for the exchange of goods at the wharves along the River Frome (at that time, freight on the river amounted to 32,000 tons per annum). The bill received the Royal Assent on 22 June 1863. When it was found that the proposed railway company could not comply

The main incline at Matchams, called B, showing the clay excavation just to the east of the main road at Norden, noted by C. E. Robinson in 1882. Originally there were three lines into the pit, the gauge being 3ft, but by that date there were two only. The clay bed to the right had been cut out in a series of ledges and a worker is using an iron prong to lift balls of clay into a wagon.

Clay Pit at Corfe.

The train sweeps by the entrance to Norden siding, showing the protective catch point. 27 February 1968. (taken from LCGB 'Dorset Belle' railtour). GEORGE MOON

with the protection of the fair ground and Wareham's ancient walls, they applied for a deviation of the branch and also for a tramway between the Creech mines and the Frome. Wareham again objected and the powers eventually lapsed in 1868.

The suggested deviation line was intended to cross the Wareham to Corfe Castle road south of Stoborough and run on the east of the road, which it then followed to Corfe Castle. Pike's tramway was to be crossed on the level, but a change was made with regard to Fayle's line. Originally, Fayle's tramway was to be raised four feet and crossed on the level, but in the 1864 proposals this was changed to the tramway being lowered four feet and one arch to be built, 10 feet

Bridge No 15 the so-called skew bridge built 1884-5. This bridge allowed the Swanage branch to go through the original embankment, supporting the Matchams incline without altering the level. The overgrown state occurred very quickly after the line was lifted. AUTHOR

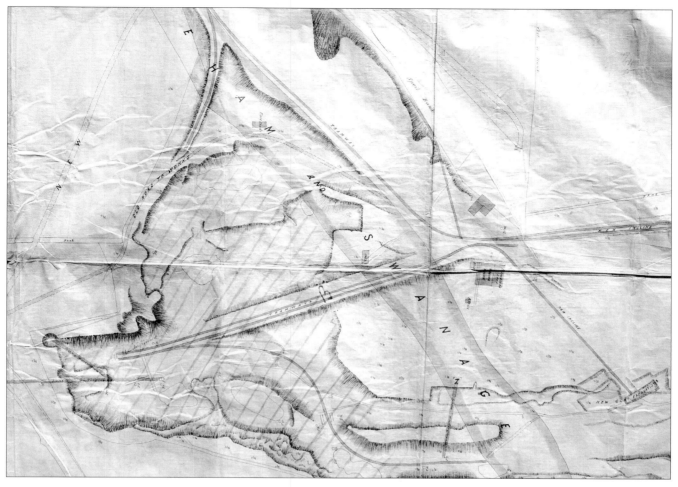

wide and 7 feet high. This would have been to the east of Fayle's offices. The plateway at the Norden end was recorded as being owned by the Earl of Eldon, with the lessees and occupiers being The Rev Richard Fayle, Charlotte Fayle and Benjamin Guy Babington.

Finally, the promotion of the railway line to Swanage came to fruition with the Swanage Railway Act 1881. Fayle's rail extension to the new pits near Matchams had taken this into account when being laid, with the clay line running beside the proposed route of the standard gauge line for about 1,200 yards. The course of the future Swanage branch was again changed, to pass under the main road at Norden and run on the west of what is now the A351, via Furzebrook to Worgret and Wareham, and this was the line eventually built. The clay line to Middlebere was still a flanged plateway, so it could have been assumed that the extension to the new mines at Matchams and New Meadow would be similar. However, instead of stone blocks it seems more likely that timber sleepers,

cut at the company saw mill were used to support the plates on this section, as described by Robinson.

By 1884, when the new L&SWR Swanage branch reached Norden, the railway construction made three main contacts with the clay workings that had to be resolved with B. Fayle & Co., and Lord Eldon's Encombe Estate.

Firstly, the old clay line leading to the road tunnels, in use from 1807-81, but more recently used only as a siding and another plateway branch leading to an open clay pit would have required two bridges under the new railway plan. The clay company agreed with the L&SWR that only one bridge need be built, and the two clay sidings would be brought together at that point, which accounts for the splay under the tramway bridge No. 13.

Secondly, when the Swanage branch was opened to goods traffic on 1 June 1885, a railway siding was built to the clay works, under agreement 1932, between the Swanage Railway and Edward Bell (solicitor) and Lord Eldon. This

The double incline at Matchams showing the engine house and carpenters shop at the top of the 1 in 10 incline labelled B. Extensive workings are shown from the base of the incline. Drawn in 1881 the proposed path of the Wareham and Swanage Railway, which would bisect incline B is outlined, resulting in bridge 15. An old road into the works has been extinguished and a new road marked in to pass under the railway by a bridge later to be called Cattle Creep. Some pools from old workings and tramway remains are adjacent to the present day Norden Station and Mineral Museum.
ECC BALL CLAYS LTD

In June 1952 an open pit at Norden was being worked by an incline a system not much changed from the 1880s. The incline was a single track and near the bottom a small turntable was used to turn the wagons through 90 degrees and send them off towards the working face. The main change by 1952 was using air spades to get the clay. The wagons were the standard side tipping skips on 1ft 11½in gauge. Points of interest were the pit ladder constructed simply by nailing short 'steps' of wood on two longer supports. This type of ladder was also used vertically to access mine shafts. The metal piping, which brought the compressed air to a point above the working clay face, was supported on its way by forked wooden props similar to those used for a washing line. S. W. BAKER

A closer view of the working face in 1952 with Fred Stockley and Bert Stockley getting clay and Cyril Marshallsay loading the wagon. To assist pushing the loaded wagon the line was laid on a slight up-grade to the face and a chain laid across the rail stopped the wagon from running away until it was filled. It was a simple matter then to get the load to the bottom of the incline ready to be winched up to ground level. S. W. BAKER

The tug *Telegraph* waiting for the next job at Poole Quay. POOLE MUSEUM

had facing points for down trains and was laid in on the down side, about a mile from Corfe Castle towards Wareham. It was provided with catch points and worked from a ground frame, operated by an Annett's Key fitted to the Train Staff, without which nothing could enter the siding. The Annett's key was kept at Corfe Castle. The siding was officially known as Lord Eldon's clay works siding and was 410 ft long, with white painted entrance gate. One of the requirements of Major Marinden in the inspecting officer's report was that the safety points at Norden Siding were to be fixed nearer the main line.

And thirdly, south of the clay works siding, the large embankment of earth at Matchams stood in the path of the new branch. This bank initially supported three tracks of 3ft gauge at a slope of 1 in 10 as shown on the Swanage Railway drawings for the bridge. It was decided to breach the bank with a gap wide enough to allow the passage of the branch line and reinstate the clay railway over the gap with a new bridge, No. 15. The incline was reduced to two tracks in 1884, running 173 yards into an open working east of the turnpike road. Shafts were put down in the pit bottom, and underground lanes further extended the mines, some running under the road. The incline was later reduced to one track on the 1887 Ordnance Survey map. The Swanage branch was at an angle to the incline rather than 90 degrees, and the incline into the

pit is still apparent today in the slope of the handrails on the skew bridge. The Matchams winding house at the top of the main incline also served two more open pits, which were excavated within four years of the Swanage branch being built. New Incline No. 1 was built going down to the east, over 170 yards into new workings in Blacklands between 1888 and 1895, and from the foot of the incline several short lines were laid to the new pits. New Incline No. 2, which was 107 yards long, ran into workings south east of the winding house, following a parallel line to the Swanage branch. The practice of winding wagons out of an open pit using an inclined way continued right through to the 1950s. Stationary steam engines first provided the power, but diesel winches were used in later days.

In 1890 a steam tugboat called the *Comet* was introduced to haul barges of clay from Middlebere to Poole for transhipment into larger ships. With increasing trade, the larger flat bottomed barges or lighters were more suited to the shallow channel than the smaller sailing type in use from the 1860s. Also, two or three lighters could be towed on each journey to Poole. Fully equipped the tug cost £700, of which amount the company paid £200, and placed £500 on mortgage to Robert Horne Penney of Brighton. Another steam tug, the *Telegraph*, was purchased the same year on similar terms for £800, and was mostly used at Goathorn and Poole. Both tugs had been used for regular passenger sailings from Poole to Swanage, the *Telegraph* from 1879 and the *Comet* from 1882, but work diminished with the coming of the railway in 1885, particularly in the winter period.

After their purchase by Fayle's, both tugs continued the tradition of towing the Poole lifeboat out to ships in distress and hauling clay to Poole was probably a part time activity for the tug skipper at Middlebere. He had a small-holding on the heath, and for that reason a flag-staff was set up near the Middlebere wharf, so a signal could be made to him when it was time for the tug to depart. It has also been suggested that the flag may have been used to signal trains, so full ones coming down avoided meeting empties heading back. However, it seems more likely, that before the days of easy communications, a timed system would have been operated. With a limited number of passing places time must have been wasted when trains meeting did not coincide. Probably all empties were returned to Norden overnight, or first thing in the morning; full trains to the quay through most of the day and empties back again towards closing time. A telescope was kept in the foreman's office, which may have been used to monitor shipping, or even the railway. Coastal sailing barges were still loaded direct from the pier. A short branch curved away from the main plateway directly on to the pier ending at a tipping stage. A gantry and winches controlled a loading chute, which allowed the clay to slide into the barges. The controlled falling of the clay, about one minute per wagon, prevented any damage which might have been caused by the sudden impact of two tons of clay landing in the hold of the barge. A contract to maintain the lighters was agreed with Chislett and Springett's Shipyard at Poole, which showed that lighters, 1,2,5,7 and 8 were in use during 1891-2. For some reason No.2 had an accident and sank and the cost incurred for raising the barge was £41 15s 6d. Further repairs or work needed on No.2 in 1892 cost another £25.

Company records show that in 1890, 64 coastal sailing barges called at the pier taking loads varying from a few tons up to 340 tons. 63 ships were recorded in 1891, and the total in 1892 was 61. The number of barges fell to 52 during the following year. Cargoes were sent to a variety of ports, recorded by a local clerk at that time as, 'Runcorn, Bordeaux, Westhartlepool, Stockholm, Ellesmere Port, Bristol, London, Keadby, Ferrybridge, Gloucester, Boness, Carthagena, Goole, Glasgow, Llanelly, Hamburg, Leigh (Essex) and Hull for Antwerp'. A record was kept of the condition of each load. Comments varied from 'in good condition and not wet' to 'some of Best against cellar very good looking clay, rather wet, much rain while loading'. Every load was mixed in some way. A good example was on 8 April 1891 when *Princess of Thule* loaded 202 tons for Runcorn. The cargo was made up of three lots of clay, '101 tons from Shops at Norden, dark but well weathered, 71 tons from Mbere, good and 30 tons from opposite cellar, rather wet'.

The monthly wage bill in 1890 varied between £101 and £120 for each works. In November 1890 the Goathorn wage bill was £110 10s and Norden £116 5s 1½. The following month Goathorn pay was £120 10s and Norden £102 4s 8½d. Tom Cattle, the foreman at Norden was paid £3 10s a month.

Also at that time, the total clay shipped at Middlebere in Imperial tons makes interesting reading:

Year	Total clay (tons)
1890	10,804
1891	8,808
1892	11,355
1893	8,361
1894*	7,378.5

* to the end of September.

The estimated average for the 5 years was 9,833 tons per annum on the plateway. By then, an increasing amount of clay was being sent via the L&SWR.

The actual quantity of clay mined in any year did not correspond to that shipped, because the mined clay was distributed around the heaps for weathering. New orders were re-dug and taken from the stock at the clay beds for shipment. The quantities recorded as shipped also varied in type and quality as required by the customer. Records of mined Best blue clay for 1890 show that more clay was mined than shipped. The amount raised that year was 10,480 Liverpool tons (12,631 Imperial tons) the surplus going into stock. In 1892 the opposite happened with 7,003 Liverpool tons raised (8,440 Imperial tons) and 11,355 shipped, the extra being taken from stock.

The lease for clay extraction specified Liverpool tons, which equalled 2,700lb each, and

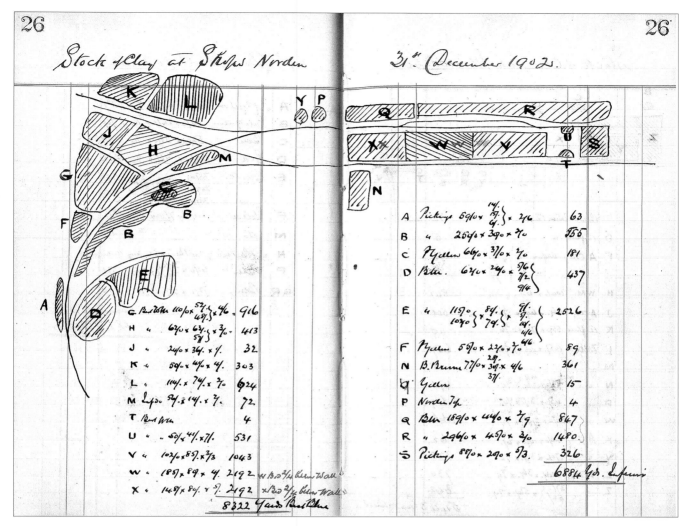

Diagram showing stocks of clay in 1902 in the area known as 'Shops'. The different types of clay are piled in discrete heaps to be weathered. The plateway to Middlebere goes off to the right, with various sidings and loops among the clay to assist loading. The offices were in the gap shown below Y & P. Records of the clay loaded for every customer were kept to ensure a continuity of supply on the next order. B FAYLE & CO

the royalties paid to the landowner were calculated on that basis. There was usually a dead rent specified, say £430 which allowed 4,000 Liverpool tons. The lessor then paid 9d per ton royalty, say up to 9,000 tons and after that 1s 6d per ton. An upper limit that could be taken would be stated, say 20,000 tons per annum.

One of the drivers, who worked on the plateway, G. W. Stockley born in 1874, started work for the company as a horse boy aged 15 in 1889. He helped to pull some of the 3ft plate rails out of the redundant tunnels under the main road for re-use. About 1892, he started as a driver to Middlebere, carting clay that originated from open pits in the Arfleet area. He reported that the clay trains were still the standard 5 wagons, by then pulled by 2 horses in line, instead of using 3 horses as reported in the early days of the plateway. The wagons still had no brakes, but friction slowed them down.

Sometimes a train might overrun the horses and they had to be unhitched for the driver to sort things out! Some clay was weathered at Middlebere, as well as large quantities near the Norden office and weighbridge, and a cellar had also been built at Middlebere to keep clay dry before shipment. The cellar had rubble walls and a wooden roof, the main building being 82ft long and 22ft wide by 7ft 6in. An annexe to the main building, which was open at both ends, was 19ft by 20ft 6in. The company kept diagrams of the weathering beds to show the type of clay and the year each heap had been brought from the mine. The amount of stock clay in each heap was measured in cubic yards, commonly referred to as 'yards' for example a heap of WM best blue could measure 146 x 36 x 3¾ft equal to 730 yards.

In 1898 the L&SWR issued an instruction No. 206 detailing changes to the working of the

The Slepe road bridges looking south from Eldon's Siding, on the left Willsbridge over the plateway, and on the right over the Swanage branch. 9 April 1963. GEORGE MOON

single line between Worgret Junction and Swanage Station. On Sunday, 18 September 1898, the Train Staff and Ticket arrangements, which had been temporary from 27 June that year, were abolished and Tyer's (New) Train Tablet System was introduced. There would be two Tablet Sections, Worgret Junction and Corfe Castle and Corfe Castle and Swanage.

The new working affected Eldon Siding situated 72 chains the Worgret Junction side of Corfe Castle Station, the Points being facing for Down Trains..

The Points (the normal position of which will be right for the Main Line) leading into the Goods Siding are fitted with Tyer's Patent Train Tablet Locking Apparatus, which can only be released by the Train Tablet for the Worgret Junction and Corfe Castle Section, and the Points cannot be moved until the Train Tablet has been placed in the Apparatus and the Points unlocked. After the Points are unlocked the Train Tablet cannot be released until the Points have been put back to their normal position.

The mode of working will be as follows:-

The Station Master at Corfe Castle must provide a competent man to attend to the working of the

Points at Eldon's Siding, and when a Goods Train has to leave any Trucks at this Siding, or bring any Trucks away, the Guard will, after the Train has arrived there, go to the Driver and obtain the Train Tablet, the Guard will then place it in the Apparatus to release the Points, and after the necessary work has been done he will return the Train Tablet to the Driver, and the Train will proceed on its journey.

In the event of any failure a Pilotman is to be used, as sanctioned by the Board of Trade, to be arranged only by the Station Master at Corfe Castle.

At the railway siding, the L&SWR and Fayle's lines were laid at almost the same level, which involved men shovelling clay from the Fayle wagons, and throwing it upwards into the L&SWR trucks. This labour intensive system was to continue after the clay lines around Norden were converted to 3ft 9in.edge railway in 1907, making them compatible with the new Goathorn line. The heavy work at the railway siding may have contributed to the long life of the plateway, simply because until then it was easier to tip clay at Middlebere. Company records show that plates were still being purchased for the

Middlebere tramway between 1895 and 1902. In 1895 and 1896 four deliveries were made by Josiah Guest and Sons of Victoria and Albert Inn Foundries, West Bromwich, a total of 450 rails with an average weight of 49lb each. Two more supplies were recorded. On 19 August 1898, Fayle's received 209 tram rails cost just under £50. The total weight was about 4¾ tons, each rail weighing about 51lb. A similar supply of rails was repeated on 22 May 1900, when a further 204 were delivered, the weight of each rail being 49½lb. It can be assumed these were the standard 3ft long cast iron plate rails. In fact this was confirmed in other Fayle records, when the total length of the plateway was stated to be 5,386 yards from a point at the shop beds near the office to the pier at Middlebere. The distance in 1902 included four turn-outs or passing places, one at the Norden end called the Shop beds 216 yards, another at Langton Wallis and an identical 48 yard loop at the west end of the the deep cutting, near the Slepe road. The fourth was a short 32 yard passing place just before the Middlebere beds were reached. There were also two short sidings, one near Norden 36 yards into a gravel pit used for ballast on the plateway, and the other 69 yards with a 36 yard loop near Middlebere leading to clay beds. A tantalising

note underneath the above record states: '200 yards taken up', but there is nothing to say which 200 yards? This left 5,186yd x 2, giving a total of 10,372 plates and stone blocks. Of these, 1,060 were stated to be new plates, leaving 9,312 old plates. The majority of the stone blocks had a single hole, but some blocks drilled with two holes survived into the 1970s at Middlebere quay. These suggested the use of chairs to support the rails. Perhaps something more substantial, possibly with tie bars to maintain gauge, may have been needed in the soft ground near the shoreline.

In February 1903, some steel flanged rails were bought from W. G. Bagnall. These were longer than the old standard three feet, weighing 41¼lb to the yard. The quantity was 58 rails, and from the total weight it would appear the rails were 28 to 29ft long and when laid would have provided another 280yd of plateway. The purchase was marked for 'M'bere Tramway', although the cost was split between Middlebere and Norden, £40 17s and £14 5s 8d respectively. At that time, some new clay mines were being developed on the west side of the Wareham to Corfe road, where the level crossing leading to them, had been in place since about 1895. This would seem to suggest that the road crossing,

View from *Tiny* looking towards Corfe Castle. East Hill is to the left of *Tiny's* chimney and the castle to the right. The clay wagons appear to be empty, the contents having been shovelled out and thrown up into the mainline wagons.
R. W. KIDNER

Tiny with wagons in Eldon's Siding showing the difference in track level.
R. W. KIDNER

when first built, was a plateway extension. This purchase of rail would explain an eyewitness report of 'lengths of rail' being used, but in fact the lengths were flanged rail and not edge. With only four years to go to the end of its working life, it seemed certain the Middlebere line, the extension to the L&SWR/Eldon's siding and the pits at Blacklands remained plateway until closure. However, some recently discovered Fayle records show the assumption about the road crossing to be wrong, and it is more likely the flanged rail was used to extend the sidings at the clay beds, or other track repairs on the main plateway. The record shows that the railway to the new mines on the west of the Wareham road was laid with edge rail to 3ft gauge. Clay from these mines was transferred using horse haulage across the Wareham road and the Swanage branch, and then reversed alongside the L&SWR branch line to the clay beds at the old offices. Here, at the 'shops', the weathering of the dumped clay took from six months up to three years. It was only after this period had elapsed that the oldest beds were cut according to orders received and loaded on to the Middlebere plateway. For this reason the main plateway which was very outdated did not need a direct connection to the mines railway. It seems probable that the use of track of 3ft gauge started

with the incline over bridge 15, as described by Robinson. Until 1893, the Matchams incline had been left intact with the skew bridge over the Swanage Railway. Back filling of the main excavation then began using waste clay, so that a more level railway could be taken across the road. The new series of shafts across the road were in the field called North Castle, also referred to as Twelve Acres, opposite the old Matcham workings. The miners were getting two veins of clay known as Top and Bottom. No. 1 shaft was working by February 1895 in the top vein but was abandoned in January 1896. No. 2 shaft was sunk early in 1895 working both levels. It followed the bottom vein towards the main road, and about halfway an underground airshaft was built between the top and bottom veins, a depth of 29ft. By May and June 1895 both levels had penetrated back under the main road, almost meeting the old tunnels previously driven from the Matchams direction.

Drawings survive from 1902 showing Twelve Acres, and also the next field, Eleven Acres, with two shafts then working. These were served by the 3ft line using rails that may have been surplus, described as a mixed lot and simply re-used like so many other items on the clay works. A short 3ft system was also in use to convey waste clay at Newton. There was also a separate 48yard branch, which probably served one of the earlier mines, but by then led only to a turntable. Underground, the miners had laid a 160 yard long tramway of 18in gauge and were using five mining trolleys with 15 boxes or cars and five smaller ones. The cars were transported on the trolleys from the bottom of the shaft to the working face and back. At the bottom of the shaft, the railway was extended into a short tunnel so that empty trollies could be pushed out of the way, and several full cars were sent up to the stage before more empties were received down the shaft to go back to the face. At least one steam vertical winding engine was in use, on a cast iron base which carried the boiler and complete with link motion, wheel drum and rope etc, was valued at £70. A new boiler had been fitted in August 1899, costing just over £30. The total length of track from the mining area down to the Wareham road, including two loops at the mines, was given as 641½ yards.

Over the level crossing on the Wareham road, which was a familiar feature for over 75 years, the track continued along the embankment over the disused incline area. It then crossed over the Swanage branch on the 'skew bridge' as far as the old Matchams winding area. Some earth fill was used on the bridge to relieve the gradient and this would lead to problems later when rot set into the timbers. At that point clay trains reversed to continue their journey and the horses, which had been heading the wagons to that point were simply unhitched and walked round to attach at the rear. The track ran alongside the Swanage branch railway, past the new weighbridge loop, under the bridge carrying the Middlebere road, and past Eldon's Siding before terminating at the 'shops' weathering beds. At the weathering beds, a trailing 282 yard siding passed under the L&SWR line, via the old bridge used by the plateway. The length of the tramway from the Wareham road to the point where the beds started with some clay called BM was given as

An April 1963 view of Norden clay sidings looking south through Willsbridge, the Swanage branch being on the right. By that date the mill equipment had been transferred to Furzebrook, the building still being intact beyond the weighbridge in the centre. The points were set to access the clay storage shed. AUTHOR

1,617 yards. The remaining length of tramway, the weathering beds and some other sidings amounted to a further 1,080 yards. The 3ft tramway's mixed lot of rails, averaged 30lb, but in fact, some were 42lb and others 38, 32 and 28lb (some worn lighter). For this reason, no fishplates were used, and the value was given as £180, which was scrap price only for the rails. Twenty-eight wagons were in use, valued at £4 each.

By 1903, change was in the air. The long life of the Middlebere plateway was coming to an end for a variety of reasons. With increasing loads of clay and visiting ship size, larger barges were finding it more difficult to reach the shallow pier

at Middlebere. The channel was gradually silting up. Thoughts turned to the more convenient deep water pier at Goathorn about 5 miles to the east, by that time under-used due to the Newton pits being worked out of the best quality clay. Most ships could be loaded there direct from the pier, without the need for hauling lighters to Poole. The decision was taken to build a new line across the heath connecting Norden to Goathorn, which on completion in 1907 would replace the Middlebere line. The 3ft mines-tramway, which was probably intended to be a temporary construction, would be converted about 1907 to match the new railway when it became operational.

These hand drawn maps of the tramways to Goathorn Pier and the pits at Newton were made during a valuation of the Fayle company in 1902, prior to S. J. Stiff joining. They give an accurate picture of the layout at that time, with measurements and costs included. B FAYLE & CO

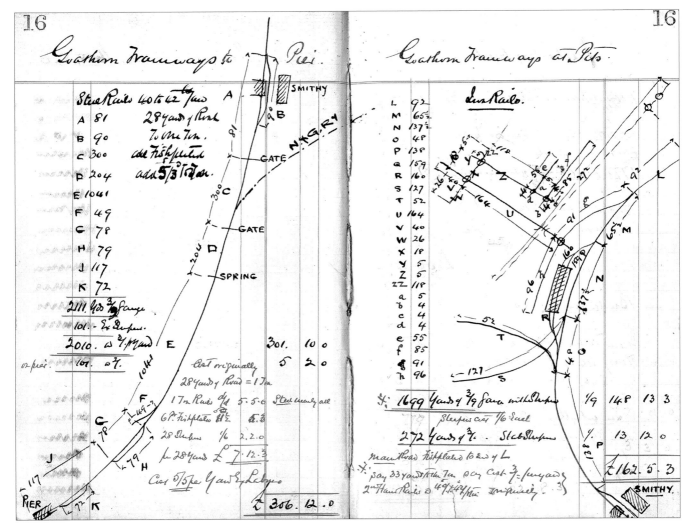

CHAPTER FOUR

Steam power as well as horses
The arrival of TINY in Purbeck, and the works at Goathorn
1860-1902

Until 1865-6, J. G. Picking had been the manager of Benjamin Fayle & Co, based in Corfe Castle. Charlotte Fayle then aged 71 and her nephew and partner, Stephen Peile Babington aged 46, were both resident at Taviton Street in London and beginning to feel the need of someone with new ideas and more energy to be based in Dorset. They decided to appoint a new manager to lead the company, and about the same time Charlotte decided to make a will leaving her share of the business to Stephen P. Babington. Fayle's new manager, generally referred to as their Agent, was a Poole man, Richard Edward Pinney then aged 30. As a family

member he was probably given the opportunity to buy into the company, and went on to oversee the development of the works until 1911, which included the building of the Norden to Goathorn railway 1905-6.

One of the first things that Richard Pinney addressed was the need to speed up the transport of clay from the pits. In 1868, a dramatic change occurred at Goathorn, with the introduction of steam traction to the pier. The decision to use steam locomotive power was taken, partly as the result of competition from the Pike Clay Company, who had introduced a steam locomotive on their clay railway at Furzebrook in

---

RICHARD E PINNEY. Richard E Pinney's father, another Richard, was born in 1804 at Hamworthy, and as he grew up became very active in Poole politics and was elected as Sheriff in 1840, the same year that George Penney became the first Liberal Mayor. The Pinney's at Hamworthy were boat builders, having married into the Adams family, shipwrights of Buckler's Hard, and their friends were all well acquainted with Poole's trading connections and the important business people of the town. Richard also carried on business as a coal merchant in 1833 and was probably influential in his son developing an interest in steam locomotion. It came about this way. By 1835, Richard's business was prospering and he and his wife Mary Ann had seven children, of which Richard Edward was number two. In 1840 he was made Surveyor for Lloyd's Register of British and foreign shipping for the Port of Poole. Probably in 1845, the family moved to Moresby on the west coast of Cumberland, when Richard was appointed Lloyd's Surveyor for the Ports of Cumberland, the west of the county being a narrow heavily industrialised belt whose wealth was made from coal and steel.

High-grade haematite iron ore was extensively mined around Whitehaven, Workington and Millom and from a very early time this encouraged the development of a local rail network. The Lowca works were founded in 1763, and started as a general foundry and engineering company with products including a range of brass cannons for ships. In the early 1800s they were making heavy plant for the local steel works and from 1830 sold a novel hydraulic system for lowering wagon loads of coal into ships' holds at Whitehaven Docks. The manufacture of locomotives started from 1840 and by the time Richard Pinney was in post, they had built several types of engines for the Maryport & Carlisle Railway Co., one of which was floated on a raft up the coast, because of the state of the roads. Richard Edward was age 15 when the Whitehaven and Furness Junction Railway was developed to the south using locomotives built by the Lowca Works. Three years later in 1853, his father died, but the family continued to live at Moresby into the 1880s. Richard Edward, however, returned to Poole, possibly influenced by his uncle, George Anthony Adams, who had been Sheriff of Poole 1846-7. In 1865 Richard was appointed Manager of the Fayle Clayworks. There was another Cumberland factor in the later Fayle story. The next small town to Moresby was Distington where Joseph Longmire was the Chemist. His son Walton married Richard Pinney's youngest sister Isabella in 1881, and it was their son Frank Longmire who was destined to join B Fayle & Co., as Managing Director in 1935.

Goathorn pier showing Brownsea Island in the background. The clay chute at the end of the pier was pulled up through a pulley system attached to the timber gantry; the hand winch can be seen outlined against the water. A point was installed very close to the end of the pier, which allowed each wagon to be emptied and switched straight into the loop, allowing another full to be shunted forward, the locomotive having run round the train before shunting started. R. W. KIDNER

1866, and partly influenced by his experience as a young man in Whitehaven.

Sadly his first year in office was marred when a boy was killed working on the Newton tramway. In July 1866, Alfred Jerrett age 16, in the employ of Fayle & Co. at Goathorn, was killed near there. A report on the accident concluded Alfred was engaged in moving clay on the railway from the pits to the pier at Goathorn, when he attempted to get on a loaded wagon while in motion, and fell underneath, the wheels passing over him. He was taken to his home, where Doctor Delamotte found that his left leg and arm were very severely injured. He decided to amputate the injured leg, but after lingering about two hours, Alfred died. F. Filliter, Coroner for the Isle of Purbeck, opened an enquiry into the circumstances the following day. This was held at the office of Fayle and Babington, and after hearing the evidence a verdict of 'Accidental death' was passed.

Despite this setback Richard Pinney pursued the development of the tramway and turned to his hometown on the question of steam working. William Pearce, who was born at Stretton, Herefordshire, in 1810, had migrated south and started the Poole Foundry business, making all kinds of factory and domestic hardware and agricultural implements. By the 1850s he was widely known through exhibitions for the quality of his products, such as portable and fixed steam engines, and boilers of every description. Stephen Lewin took over the works in 1863, when Pearce retired, and appointed as his manager, William Wilkinson who had been a partner in a similar company in Boston, Lincolnshire (Lewin's home town). The Boston firm had been started by William Howden in 1803, and was testing marine steam engines by 1827, and demonstrating portable steam engines for agricultural work in 1841. With a combined history of steam boiler and engine building of at least 65 years, the Poole Foundry was in a strong position to respond to Fayle's enquiry for a locomotive. Pinney had seen the Lowca locomotives, built in Cumberland by a company with a very similar background to the Poole engineers, and he had no doubt that Lewin could build a small loco suitable for the clay works. The Poole Company became only the third or fourth private manufacturer of steam locomotives south of the Thames when the engine, nicknamed *Tiny* emerged from the works in 1868.

Richard Edward Pinney was listed as a ship owner operating from the quay at Poole, which no doubt cemented his friendship with George Robert Penney, whose company manufactured rope, twine, canvas and sacks not far away. In 1878 George had lent Richard the sum of £2,000, on the strength of assets and estate which had been left to him and his brother and sisters by their Grandfather when he died on 30 October 1830. George also acted as Fayle's agent in Poole. Some significant changes occurred in the ownership of the company, when Charlotte Fayle died unmarried in 1882, having willed her interests to Stephen. Stephen Babington, as Managing Director, then decided to will half his interests to his twin brother William, who was the Rector at Staunton-on-Arrow, Herefordshire. The rest went to Richard E. Pinney and Richard Woollcombe (lawyer) held in trust. As it happened, Stephen only outlived his aunt by 4 years, dying in 1886. He had remained a shareholder and partner in the company until his death, and for example, in 1885, received payments totalling over £400. Rev. William P. Babington received payments of over £300 in 1885.

After the deaths of Charlotte Fayle and Stephen Babington, Richard Pinney became Managing Director of the clay works. His brother-in-law Joseph Hughes joined Richard as Company Secretary in 1888 and his experience resulted in excellent borehole records in the search for more clay. Joseph Hughes was born at Stourbridge, Worcestershire, and trained to be a civil and mechanical engineer. When Joseph married Richard's sister, Susan Eliza, at Moresby in 1887 they were both aged over 40 and their move back to Dorset must have seemed like coming home to Susan. They settled at The Old Vicarage in Kingston for some years, and Joseph became very absorbed in his work with Richard, who at that time was living at West Bucknowle. Joseph was lucky to survive one dark night when he was almost knocked down by a passing train on the Swanage branch. He fell against some wire fencing, which resulted in the loss of an ear!

The company had a lease with John, Earl of Eldon, to take clay for the next 21 years from 24 June 1887, at the rate of 9,600 tons of 1st quality clay for which the certain rent was £1,200 yearly. If all went well they could take up to 12,000 tons at 2s 6d per ton, or over that quantity 2s per ton up to 20,000 tons. By 1895, the shipping of the clay at Poole and from Middlebere was co-ordinated from an office run by B. Fayle & Co., clay merchants, on the Quay at Poole. In 1896 a report by Joseph S. Martin, H.M. Inspector for the South Western District, said that B. Fayle & Co., employed 24 workers underground and 8 on the surface.

After moving to Arne House near Wareham,

Drawings of *Tiny* by GORDON HATHERILL/GEORGE MOON.

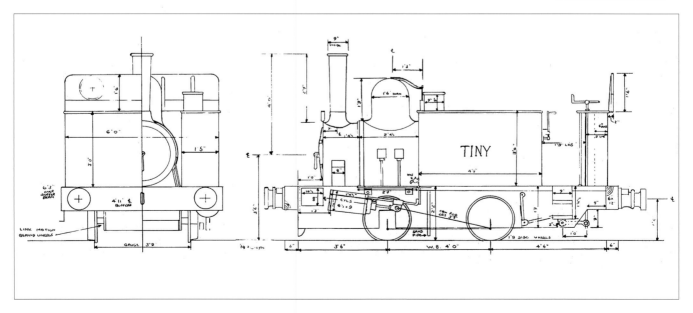

School house and engine shed for *Tiny*, Newton. REMPSTONE ESTATE

William Tubb, on the left, about to operate the water pump at Newton while his son-in-law Fred Surface uses a bucket of water to prime the force pump. The water was mostly used for the locomotives as well as drinking. William's father George, who died in 1905, was also foreman of the Goathorn Works before him. ELSIE TOMES

local issues were taking more of Richard Pinney's time and the decision was taken to appoint a younger man to carry the business forward; by 1900 Richard was age 64 and Joseph 55. At the same time it was decided to reorganise the business and in preparation for that and the start of a new 21year lease, a survey of the company value was undertaken at the end of 1902.

The main items of tramway interest at Norden were details and drawings of the mines in Eleven Acres and Twelve Acres and the rail connection through Matchams to the office and weathering beds. Also details of the Middlebere

plateway at that time. At the Newton works drawings illustrated the tram and mine layout in 1902. The tramways at Goathorn, from the pier to the pits at Newton, totalled £468 17s 3d. Because of the layout of the pits, several turntables were in use. There were four 3ft 9in gauge turntables valued at £33 6s 8d, and also one 3ft 9in turntable large diameter which cost £14 new, valued at £9 6s 8d. Two turntables were also used on the rubble line, which had cost £6 10s each when new, but by then valued at £8 for the pair. At the Goathorn loading point, the timber pier on piles, complete with tip, winch, ropes and blocks was entered at £125. Also at the pier was a pile driver, 4 tons of steam coal and 2 tons of small coal, a shunting chain and a water cask and a trolley valued at £1 12s 6d. The engine shed at Goathorn was valued at £4 13s 6d, and two pumps were situated beside the railway at Newton, to provide water for *Tiny* and for local use; a 4in pump was valued £9, and a 7in pump was £8.

The appointment of a new manager was also an opportunity to involve other close family members and friends as shareholders in the company. These included Charles Anthony Ellis and Henry Pitt Ellis, both brewers of Millbank House, Wimborne, Thomas William and Julia Maria Pinney, Isabella Longmire and Henry

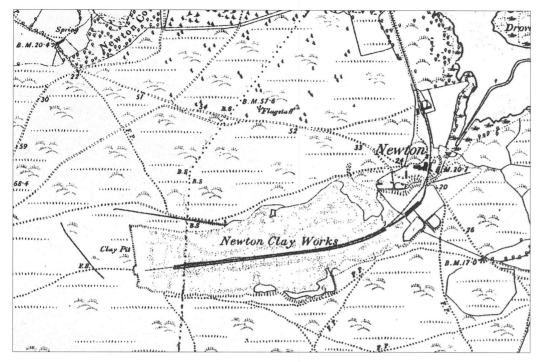

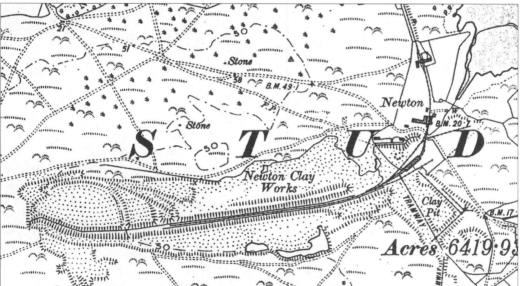

The Ordnance Survey of Newton in 1889 (upper) shows an extensive clay pit served by a long branch of thetramway. Between the Works and Newton hamlet a long building for keeping clay dry is shown built over a loop in the tramway.

By 1901 (lower) a new clay pit has been opened up with the tramway running in to it with several turntables in use. A short 3ft railway for disposing of rubble is carried on a timber bridge over the tramway where it enters the pit. More detail is shown in the drawing on page 50.

Pocock, of the Pinney family, soon to be joined by members of the Stiff family. The only outsider was G. C. Filliter, a Wareham solicitor, who had a £1,500 stake in the company. Richard Pinney was aware that the ideal man to lead the company after his retirement could be Sydney James Stiff, of London. He was well known through their customer network. Aged 37, he was a potter living in Lambeth and was sold a third share in the company for £5,796. A valuation taken at the end of 1910 saw an increase in the third share to £6,856 16s. The involvement with Fayle's from 1903, may not have been full time to start with, because Sydney still had commitments at their pottery in Lambeth until 1911 and while still living at 57 Greyhound Lane, Streatham, travelled back and forth to Dorset by train, to oversee the clay business. Regular letters were exchanged with Joseph Hughes as the train passed Corfe Castle Station, Sydney having a residence in Swanage called Amberwood, until at least the end of 1913. Eventually Sydney Stiff and his family settled at Norden House, quite close to the clay works.

THE LONDON POTTERY in Ferry Street, Lambeth had been started in 1840-2 by Sydney Stiff's grandfather James Stiff. James was born in Rougham, Suffolk on 9 November 1808, where his father Robert was Master of the Workhouse. In 1826, James who was a plasterer's assistant engaged in the building of Rougham Hall, left home with a sovereign in his pocket, to seek his fortune in London. In 1830, he entered a famous Lambeth pottery, on the strength of improving their moulds and continued for 12 years. In 1842, having saved some money, he started on his own account in Ferry Street and having no pug mill trod the clay by foot! After a year he moved to the High Street, Lambeth, and acquired a pug mill worked first by horsepower and later steam, where the property and business gradually increased over the years. At the beginning the pottery consisted of just two small kilns, but as it grew along with James' family it became known as James Stiff and Sons. By about 1880, the works comprised of 14 kilns, some of them more than twenty feet in diameter, and covered two acres with an extensive frontage on the Albert Embankment, overlooking the River Thames, employing about 200 hands. Through their private dock, they carried on a very extensive export trade and were able to import the fifteen thousand tons a year of coals, clay and other raw material used in the production of brown and white stoneware and terracotta. They also made high quality plumbago and fireclay crucibles for every conceivable purpose and were one of Fayle's biggest customers.

Richard Pinney valued the input by Joseph Hughes and decided to recognise his loyalty and great knowledge by giving him full charge of his interests, should Richard pre-decease him. This was set out in a letter from Corfe Castle, dated 11 May 1906, to his solicitor, Mr Woollcombe.

Referring to your letter of 28 Nov last, and a subsequent interview I had with you, it has escaped me until now to carry out my intention of writing a letter to be left with my Will expressing my earnest wish that my Brother-in-law Mr Joseph Hughes of Kingston, Wareham should be my acting Executor, and that the other Executors should consult him on all matters connected with the Executorship more particularly with regard to any matters connected with my business as Clay Merchant, he being thoroughly conversant with the business in all its details, and therefore most capable of protecting the interests of my family, in connection with the Firm of B. Fayle & Co., in the event of my decease.

I further desire that an allowance of Fifty Pounds a year should be made to Mr Hughes out of my share of the profits of the clay trade, as a slight appreciation of kind and ready assistance rendered to me for many years and as some compensation for the trouble involved by his undertaking the acting executorship. This allowance to continue so long as Mr Hughes continues acting executor.

Kindly place this letter with my Will as expressing my desires,

Yours sincerely, (signed) Rich. E. Pinney

Lily Surface (nee Tubb), was born 1901, daughter of Mark William (Bill) Tubb, later to follow his father George as foreman at the Goathorn clay works. *Tiny*, being driven by her father, became a familiar sight to Lily, before being displaced by *Thames* in 1909. This view of *Tiny* shunting a wagon, (taken at a later time with Tommy Stockley in charge) was a reminder of her young days living at Goathorn.
ELSIE TOMES (Lily's daughter).

CHAPTER FIVE

S. J. Stiff in charge and the new rail link.
The Corfe to Goathorn Railway (Fayle's Tramway), 1907-48

Soon after 1885, as noted above, some clay was being dispatched at the Norden siding on to the L&SWR Swanage branch, but there was still a substantial seaborne demand for loads up to 500 tons. It was decided the Corfe to Goathorn Railway would be built to utilise the deepwater pier at Goathorn, using most of the capital put in by S. J. Stiff. Although the railway press generally referred to the line as Fayle's Tramway, the company called it either the Corfe to Goathorn Railway for any publicity material or more usually in their records as 'The Norden to Goathorn Railway' or more simply the N&G Railway. The new line would connect the Norden mines to the Newton Tramway just over five miles across the heath to the east. In addition, as noted above, the best clay at Newton was coming to an end and a branch line going south from the N&G Railway, just east of the Corfe River would reach new pits and mines being opened up at Arfleet. This would help to make the new line viable.

One of Sydney Stiff's first jobs on joining the company was to oversee the building of the Norden to Goathorn Railway. He enlisted the help of his brother-in-law, Henry Coleman Head, to draw up the plans, the first drawings being ready in 1904. Henry had also helped with the 1902 valuation of Fayle's plant and other assets. The land for the new railway was estimated to be four acres, and at 8s per acre from 24 June 1905 added £1 12s rent cost per annum. Construction of the new railway was carried out using 40lb rail, supplied by Bolling & Lowe, spiked to wooden sleepers, laid in earth ballast. The rails were of various lengths from 6 metres but mostly 9.6 metres. At that time pit sawing of planks and timber was still common and proved to be convenient in the construction. Every sleeper on the line was hand-cut; the sawpits being dug at random along the railway as building of the track progressed. Building commenced in 1905 and on their balance sheet for 30 June that year Fayle's recorded, 'Work done on the N&G Railway £1,417 18s 4d.' And by 31 December 1905 the 'Total cost of Goathorn Railway to date, £2,569 13s 2d.' Their records show that by 30 June 1906

the cost to date had gone up to £3,695 4s 6d and by the end of the year the amount spent was £4,622 0s 10d. Similarly in 1907 the cost had risen to £5,113 7s 8d on 30 June and the line was virtually completed by 31 December 1907, the asset being valued at £5,229 11s 4d. A few extra jobs took the final cost to £5,252 16s 11d by the end of 1908. It was said the cost of the railway was shared equally between the company and the Rempstone Estate, as was the recovered scrap value when the line eventually went out of use and was lifted by a contractor at the beginning of the Second World War. However, that rumour was not borne out by the company's books. Some work on the line was contracted out, partly to save time. For example, in April 1905, a culvert had to be built at Claywell. The clay company called in George Pond, a builder in King's Road, Swanage, to do the job, which cost £20 7s 6d. The extent of the overall work was well illustrated in the official set of nine photographs taken by the company to celebrate the day when an inspection train ran over the new formation in 1907. These were titled 'The Corfe to Goathorn Railway, Commenced 1905, Completed 1907, B. Fayle & Co.,' and sets were given to selected friends such as Dr Dru Drury of Corfe Castle. Norden clay could then be transferred to Goathorn for shipment and after 101 years the Middlebere Plateway became redundant. The Ordnance Survey maps, which the company used to plan the railway are still among the mining records at Furzebrook and show the projected route drawn on them. They also recorded the cutting and filling that would be necessary to produce reasonable grades, although some of these being 1 in 66 proved to be quite steep in practice, especially for *Tiny*'s limited power. It had been intended that *Tiny* would assemble loaded trains at Eldon's Siding, hauling them to Goathorn, but it soon became obvious that at only 7 tons the engine was struggling to cope with heavier loads.

The main features of the new railway could be summed up as follows. At Eldon's Siding, a short spare track was laid between the two tracks of the loop and a wagon shelter over part of the east track. The new line to Goathorn started as a

The Corfe to Goathorn Railway, 1907. The single wagon inspection train was run over the new line so the proprietors could see the result of two years labour. Richard Pinney surveys the scene from his temporary seat in the wagon and Sydney Stiff stands with one leg resting on a step attached to the wagon waiting for the photographer so driver Tubb can get under way. The engine had probably been refurbished to coincide with the opening of the new railway. The sandboxes had been removed and two large lumps of coal were being carried on top of the right hand water tank. The right hand tank was divided in half by three vertical lines of rivets, the rear part being used as a coal bunker and the front for water. There was still no weather protection for the footplate crew, but other additions included a pair of Salter safety valves, a toolbox behind the front buffer beam and a running plate over the cylinder and motion. The front end had received quite a lot of attention, the main change being the smoke-box now longer with different riveting and the door hinged on the left hand side which may have been original. B FAYLE & CO

View of the 1ft 11½in line looking east. The shed for *Russell* and the diesels can be seen through the tree on the left. The building about to fall down was the shed to house *Tiny* in 3ft 9in days, the line running right through to weathering beds. It was the custom to leave the school coach in the shed during the day and it was taken round to Arfleet to pick up the children when they came from school.
19 May 1966.
GEORGE MOON

Corfe River Bridge. The new railway ran from the sidings at Norden across the heathland, much of which had been surface mined by clay getters for generations, to a connection with the Newton tramway just north of the village and thence to the pier. Soon after leaving Norden the Corfe River, although just a stream, was a sufficient barrier to justify a substantial wooden bridge to carry the railway; it had a wooden handrail along each side. B FAYLE & CO

branch off the existing sidings south of Willsbridge and the tramway then curved away heading east, before passing a shed for *Tiny* built on the south side of the track. The shed was also used to house the school wagon during the day while the children were at school in Corfe Castle. A short distance further on the railway crossed a substantial timber bridge over the Corfe River. This small river was known as Wicken Brook in Saxon times and its name still survives locally in Wych, near where the river falls into Poole Harbour. Leaving the river behind, the course of the railway continued north and east to Bushey and Newton. The line went through some quite deep cuttings, eg. Blackdown, through several gates at Thrasher's Lane (south of the pit), Meadus's Lane, Fir Glen and Churchill's Green,

Blackdown Cutting. The inspection train passes through the cutting with the over bridge in the distance. B FAYLE & CO

Sydney Stiff waits on the Goathorn side of the bridge for the photographer to get his record of the new line. B FAYLE & CO

Claywell embankment. The inspection train pauses on the highest embankment on the line, about 18 feet at the deepest part, and shows the considerable excavations that were done in some places before the railway could be laid. B FAYLE & CO

The junction with the old line. The new line from Norden came curving in to join the Newton Tramway on a straight section just north of Newton Works.
B FAYLE & CO

and across some embankments of which Claywell was prominent, until Newton was reached. Here the new line connected to the Goathorn section on a curve of 17½ to 18 chains, just north of Newton hamlet and clay works. The tramway then continued along its old course, until the pier approach was reached. At this point onwards in 1902-3, a short siding 49 yards long went off to the right, followed by a 79 yard loop on the left, followed quite quickly by another 72 yard loop, also on the left, just before the pier was reached. The cost of building the N&G Railway at over £5,000 had been an expensive commitment and severely tested the owner's finances for some years.

Sydney Stiff made some meticulous calculations to compare the running costs of the

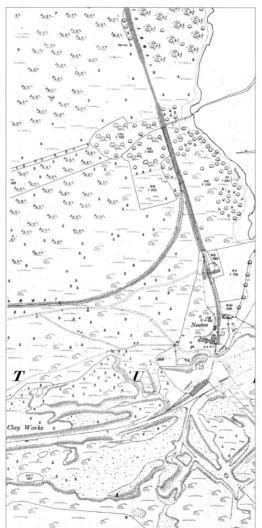

The 1928 map of Newton shows the clay pits extinguished. The tramway from Norden is shown coming in from the left with a curving connection to the Newton tramway, north of the village.

Goathorn pier on the south side of Poole Harbour was over a mile from the clay pits at Newton. It was largely due to the pits being worked out at Newton that the tramway connection was built to transport Norden clay to be loaded at Goathorn.

new Goathorn line to the old Middlebere plateway, which make interesting reading.

Cost of plates Middlebere tramway	
1900, 1901, 1902	£58 5s 9d
	(supplied by Josiah Guest, 204 rails on 22 May 1900)
1898, 1899	£49 12s 11d
	(supplied by Josiah Guest, 209 rails on 19 August 1898)
1896, 1897	£43 3s 10d
	£23 16s 4d
1895	£28 15s 7d
Total	£203 14s 5d
	? £12 15s 5d
	£216 9s 10d
Over 8 years, the average cost of plates was £27 per year.	

Middlebere tram, cost to maintain per year	
Plates average over 8 years	£27
Wages of 1 man	£45
Blacksmith	£8
Total	£80 = approx. 1.92d per ton
The corresponding figure for the N&G Ry is £200 = approx. 4.8d per ton	

At first glance the N&G railway maintenance was much more expensive, but he then calculated the cost, including extraction through to loading the clay, taking the above repair costs into account. The rent paid to Bankes (Middlebere) had reduced over the years, giving an average of £150 per annum or wayleave of about 3.6d per ton, say 3½d to Middlebere. By comparison, the wayleave payable to Goathorn was about 2½d per ton. Taking other factors into account such as the tipping of clay and in the case of Middlebere, the cost of towage to and from Poole 7¾d, and

loading to ship 2d, the total cost on the old plateway was 1s 11½d per ton.

The haulage to Goathorn, based on the 1909 figures was 6¼d per ton plus tipping costs, wayleave and upkeep, a total of 1s 2¼d per ton on the new tramway. The difference was a saving of 9¼d per ton on the new line, which for 10,000 tons clay gave an overall saving of £385 8s per year, a substantial sum in those days. Nearly all of that saving was made by the loading of ships directly off Goathorn Pier, instead of incurring towage costs to Poole.

More research revealed the amount entered by S. J. Stiff as £12 15s 5d with a question mark. On 24 July 1901, Lott and Walne Ltd, of The Foundry, Dorchester had supplied 201 tram plates weighing 5ton 1cwt 2lb the average weight of each 3ft plate being 56.3lb. At the same time Fayle's were clearing out a lot of scrap iron about 15½ tons, which Lott and Walne received in two deliveries, crediting a total of £30 3s 3d. This left the balance of £12 15s 5d to be paid on 22 Dec 1902. These local plates made by Lott and Walne were probably made to a pattern supplied by Fayle's, as it was unlikely they had any other customers requiring them. The price was also right, being two-thirds the price of rails supplied the previous year by Guest of West Bromwich.

Between 1900 and 1906 the mines railway was extended across the next field, Peaked Close, also referred to as Eleven Acres, following along the main road direction towards Norden farm and eventually serving at least six new mine shafts. The extra rent for Eleven and Twelve Acres, amounted to £23 11s 6d per annum, on top of the lease. These shafts were given numbers

By 1907 the 3ft 9in gauge tramway had reached the fence between Peaked Close and Dandy Hayes. A number of mines had been worked along the line since crossing the main road, and the work would continue just south of Norden Farm and into Five Acres, 1909-13. In 1914, a new branch was made towards Little Copse, and the mine shown at the end of the tramway on the map was christened Railway Junction shaft.

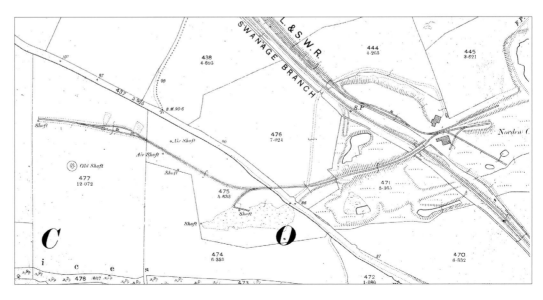

in a new series, extending across the next field called Dandy Hayes and into Five Acres by 1908. No. 3 mine on the edge of Dandy Hayes was also known as Railway Junction Shaft. The name arose because when the mining in Five Acres finished after a few years, a branch was built in 1914 going southwest to some new workings in Little Coppice, thus forming a junction with the original line.

Sydney Stiff had a lot of experience of the properties of clay as a material and enjoyed running the Dorset business, but it was said he was less interested in the underground work. However, he was quite a disciplinarian, and forward looking if he thought it would benefit the company. From 1907 he had virtually sole control of the works, subject to shareholder agreement.

Working conditions underground had improved somewhat; picks were still used for getting the clay, but the use of small wagons to move the clay by rail speeded up the transport to the surface. Each gang of miners was made up of three men, two miners and a runner, mainly because the working faces were limited to 6ft high x 6ft wide. Only one or, at most, two men could work up at the production face. Usually, one miner was on the pick excavating clay, the other shovelled clay back from the face and loaded wagons. The runner trammed the clay to the shaft and brought empties back. The miner driving the tunnel kept a straight line by following the shadow of his pick thrown by a candle. The candle was stuck to the side of the lane in a lump of soft clay known as slub, just behind the shoulder of the miner. As the face advanced, the miners laid more rails to extend the haulage. In order to keep the slight upward gradient a 5ft rod was used, with a small square of wood tacked on ⅛in from the end. Using the rod in the lane, with a level, the rails were laid to the face giving a gradient of ⅛in in 5ft, which helped full wagons to run out well. This made life a bit easier for the runners to push loads of clay to the shaft bottom, and small amounts of water entering the workings also ran to the lowest point, known as the mine sump or well. Being near the shaft bottom, the water could then be lifted or pumped out of the mine. Where the gradient was steeper, the runners soon learnt they could save time by jumping on the rail each side and use the track as a slide down the slope. This was not allowed officially for obvious reasons, but time was money when pay depended

Miners driving an underground lane using short handled picks, the marks of the blade being very clear on the clay face. Illumination was by carbide lamp, which must have been a help to the photographer. The usual lighting was by candles longer and thinner than the domestic variety. The 22in gauge railway, which served the face, was built and extended by the miners as the work advanced. Each wagon was weighed on the stage using old bar scales at that time. They were set for 11½ cwt and recorded as 1, 2, 3 or 4 light or heavy. The numbers 1, 2, 3 and 4 referred to quarters of 1cwt, 2 meaning 2 quarters or ½ cwt light. The miners were paid less if the wagon was light, but never any more if the load was heavy. This was often a bone of contention. AUTHOR

on results. As the working area enlarged several working faces would have been opened up allowing more gangs to be underground. In some cases the mine could accommodate up to seven gangs, but as the clay was worked out there was less space and the number of gangs would gradually reduce to two, or possibly just one.

In the late 1800s and early 1900s the underground track had been 18in gauge. On 6 February 1903 the company records show they bought 100yd of 10lb rail, portable railway 18in gauge from W. G. Bagnall for £14 11s 8d and repeat orders for this track were a regular feature over some years. In later years the wagons were designed to carry 11½cwt, running on track with a gauge of 22 inches. It was a Fayle tradition to sink shafts directly into the clay lens. The disadvantage of this method was that when the mine was eventually worked out, it was impossible to get all the clay surrounding the haulage without compromising the shaft.

In open pits the surface railway track was laid right up to the clay face and with a suitable board structure to direct the clay, lumps could be dropped or pushed from the working area into the wagon. Other lumps were picked up using a pole with a curved spike on the end called a pug and thrown into the wagon. The railway was

Clay pits at Goathorn in
1907. B FAYLE & CO

extended to keep up with the face as mining proceeded and more clay was uncovered. This method continued in use for generations and large uncovered workings were to be found on Fayle's property at Newton, Arfleet and Norden.

The first shaft in Five Acres was quite close to the Norden farmyard and became known as Rickyard Shaft. It was working by 5 August 1908 and was about 340ft from the Dandy Shaft, as shown on a drawing dated 11 February 1909. Several more shafts were to follow in that area, which by then were sending clay via the newly opened Norden to Goathorn Railway, hauled by *Thames*, see below. The dangers of mining in a sand and running water situation were intensified on 8 February 1909, when two men were killed working in a Dandy Hayes mine shaft. They were Walter Bennett age 33 and George Burden age 27, both married men. They were removing timbers from the redundant shaft, perhaps without being sufficiently experienced and filling in properly below, when suddenly sand and the rest of the shaft collapsed on them. Desperate attempts to dig down to them were to no avail. Bennett was almost uncovered, but before foreman Cattle renowned for his strength could get to him, another 15 feet of sand fell into the shaft. It would be another two bitter days and nights before the bodies were brought up. A poem was written in memory of the men and the attempted rescue. The men most involved in the work were Levi Stockley,

who wrote the poem, foreman Cattle, Lawrence Stockley, Seth White, Charles Jeffries, William Cattle, William Stockley and George Morris.

About the same time, changes were being made at Goathorn. A three-track layout was built at the pier approach, where the 49yd siding went off to the right. Instead of using a normal bladed point, the three tracks were accessed by a stub point. This type of switching mechanism involved moving a complete section of the approach rail sideways, so an end on connection could be made with any of the three tracks going toward the pier. A short distance further on, the three tracks became a double track on to the pier, and finally a short single line near the end of the pier leading to the loading chute. When a loaded train arrived on the pier, the leading wagon was detached and tipped. It was then pushed back through the point on to the second track making up a train of empties. Tipping of the heavy wagons was achieved using a hand winch, and a chain attached to the rear of the wagon prevented any tendency to over tip. Eventually, tree planting by the Forestry Commission grew up to surround much of the tramway formation.

Some records have survived of the clay tonnage carried on Fayle's tramway (N&G Railway) from the time it opened in 1907. The records were kept separate from Arfleet for royalty purposes and the ledger page is headed, 'Norden Clay sent to Goathorn for shipment via the Norden and Goathorn Railway.'

Rempstone Estate photographs showing the rear view of the Goathorn/Newton cottages, a row of eight built beside the 3ft 9in track.
REMPSTONE ESTATE

Various buildings were erected on the other side of the track from the cottages, the stables for the horses on the right and granary on the left. In the background can be seen the large clay storage shed.
REMPSTONE ESTATE

In this view, taken in 1938, looking towards Goathorn pier the old school house is on the right. In the shed with the right hand track running to it is the tank wagon that was used to bring water to the house from the pump at Newton. The centre track ran straight to the pier with the gantry in the background, but not in use at the time. The loop on the left enabled the locomotive to run round its train. In the foreground, a triple stub point was in use; both rails of the running track were moved bodily across by the lever to engage the three-way junction. R. W. KIDNER

The terminus at Goathorn
with Sydney Stiff.
B FAYLE & CO

Accidents did occur and this
photo taken on 28
September 1971 shows a
fisherman at Goathorn,
doubtful oblivious of the old
3ft 9in wagon chassis lying
on the foreshore, where it
probably derailed from the
pier. The axle boxes are still
attached to the main side
members of the wagon and
the wheels still look capable
of use. GEORGE MOON

The very first load of 220 tons to traverse the new tramway was taken by *Island Maid* on 15 May 1907. The next load of Norden clay was 95 tons taken by *Lady of the Lake* on 11 July followed by 161 tons on *Baltic* on 19 July. Between these cargoes were 'Ships loaded with Arfleet Clay at Goathorn pier.' The first was *Vindex* on 28 May, which loaded 312 tons of A (Arfleet) clay followed by *Richard Fisher* on 4 June, which took 305 tons of A clay.

The following chart shows the success of the tramway, which was unfortunately cut short by the Great War.

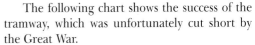
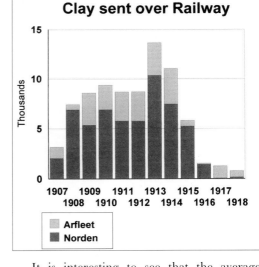

It is interesting to see that the average tonnage per annum, for the 7 years, 1908-14 was 9,636 tons. As expected, some of the individual loads taken by ships at the Goathorn deep-water pier (up to 500 tons) were considerably more than at Middlebere in the 1890s. Any larger vessels were loaded at Poole Quay using lighters hauled from Goathorn and a maximum 720 tons was loaded by the *S.S. Countess* on 4 September 1914. But much of the clay was still being taken in smaller loads by coastal barges, so the overall amount 9,636 shipped at Goathorn was slightly less than the previous average of 9,833 tons a year shipped at Middlebere.

The Arfleet clay came from another new mining area. At a point where the railway crossed the bridge over the Corfe River and continued across the heath, about half a mile north of Arfleet mill, a trailing branch was built. The branch came south before dividing into two sidings to reach the middle of the mill complex, serving a large open pit and also transporting clay from a series of vertical shafts. The timber shafts were generally short-lived mainly due to flooding, which also affected the Norden mines in Peaked Close and Dandy Hayes being worked at the same period. Probably because their life was short no photographs seem to have survived, except of the open pit where a Ruston excavator was used for a few years before being transferred to the Norden pit. The open pit at Arfleet, or 'Arflit' as Eli called it, was in production from about 1910 until worked out in 1926. It was customary to use a stationary steam engine winch to pull wagons out of open pits, but in this case the train of 'fulls' was brought to level ground using a wire rope hooked on to *Tiny*. Eli said, 'the loco ran on back down the Goathorn line' as the wagons came up. These would have been the 3ft 9in gauge wooden wagons, probably too heavy for horses to manage up the incline. Because the ground at the top was reasonably level the

wagons stopped without the need for sprags. The wire rope was then discarded and *Tiny* connected directly to the train for haulage to the weigh house.

The series of shafts at Arfleet were numbered from 1 to 10 and on average, each shaft was in use for about two years. From the records, No. 1 must have been sunk soon after the railway was laid, probably in 1907. The underground 18-inch

The view in 1968 looking east from the entrance track to the West works. On the left Tiny's cab back plate is used to retain a heap of gravel. The main tramway runs past the skip and descends bearing right towards the catch point and the A351 road. Above the skip can be seen a timber ramp built for clay transfer from lorry to rail. It was not very successful and little used. MICHAEL MESSENGER.

The open pit at Arfleet. AUTHOR

Steam navvy originally used at Arfleet about 1925, then for some years in the Norden open pit from 1926. On the left is William Tubb the foreman, helped by Marshallsay in the white shirt and Seth White. Side-tipping skips were used in open pit workings long before their introduction on the 1948 1ft 11½in gauge. Tubb was followed as foreman by his son Frank, then 'Midge' Welsh and George Allingham. Seth White was born about 1880 and from age 15 worked as a driver on the Middlebere plateway. One day he was riding towards Middlebere (in fact he should have been walking with the horses holding back), when he fell off. This resulted in him being dragged over two miles with a broken arm and various injuries. Photograph taken about 1932 by Mrs Guy, daughter of Seth.

track was again supplied by Bagnall's, 100yards of 10lb rail then costing £15 17s 6d. Arfleet No. 2 mine was open shortly afterwards. It was mentioned as working on 9 March 1910 and was recorded as just filled in, on 23 July 1912. By that time shaft No. 5 was new and No. 1 was said to be 'old' the usual expression to mean disused. The working shafts were situated all round the mill, and as recorded on 20 September 1911, there was a mine in the garden plot and a mine near Arfleet Mill. The corn mill had been on the Corfe River since the 1700s and probably before, but because of the mining it was gone by 1920. Fayles were blamed for the damage and the landowner brought an action against them for compensation, (see chapter 7). Over the years other cottages and property have been demolished to allow clay mining. It has also been surmised that the branch to Arfleet was extended through a tunnel under the Studland road to pits south of the road. In fact, these pits were a quite separate mining operation by Pochins, a Cornish company at a much later date. The tunnel was used by Pochins to tram waste clay from their works to be dumped in the old Arfleet mining area.

Richard Pinney realised he was very fortunate to have working for him two or three families that were adaptable and capable when the change over from horses to steam took place. Their experience and long family connections

with the firm helped preserve the historical record of the railway, with the oral tradition passed between generations such as the date of *Tiny*'s introduction. In 1910, when he was writing his will he remembered two in particular of his faithful workers.

He wrote, 'I give the sum of one hundred pounds to Thomas Cattle, my foreman of Clay Works in recognition of his valuable services in that capacity during many years. And the sum of twenty five pounds to William Tubb the foreman at Goathorn Clay Works for his valuable assistance in connection with the construction of the Norden and Goathorn Railway and the working of my pits at Goathorn.'

Tom Cattle, born in 1840 and a claygetter all his life, had a reputation for fairness and great physical strength. He was obviously made up to foreman of the works, 'many years' before 1910 according to the will, and was still foreman in 1915 and continued at work until the age of 80. The Tubb family was heavily involved at Goathorn clay pits, George being foreman from 1872. William had followed his father into the clay works and became the regular driver of *Tiny* for several years, before becoming foreman himself at the age of 36 in 1902. He lived with Ellen, his wife, in a cottage near the pier at Goathorn. One of their children, Frank, who was born on 28 June 1898, had learnt at an early age how to manage *Tiny*, and was just waiting for the

Cattle Creep showing the level crossing across the Swanage branch. The clay line was on the embankment in the background and a large shed structure was built over the bridge at this point. The shed offered some shelter to the bridge structure, which was mostly timber, and also to the men when tipping clay.Cattle Creep allowed animals and farm machinery to reach the fields beyond, and also clay company workers to the stables and sawmills from 1885 onwards. The new access replaced a previous cart track. 29 May 1969. GEORGE MOON

day to leave school. Nobody could guess then, that Frank was destined to live for driving, and eventually to die on his footplate.

Near the present Norden station on the restored Swanage Railway can be seen the remains of a bridge that used to carry the clay railway over a farm track. This cart track crossed the adjacent L&SWR branch on a level crossing, the clay line being on an embankment at this point. The cart track had been a new 'road' in 1884 and gave agricultural access to fields. It also carried traffic to the Matchams works and the later clay mill, replacing an earlier cart track that

approached the works through the present station site. The bridge which was known on the works as Cattle Creep had been built to carry horse hauled trains of 2 or 3 wagons and was not strong enough to support *Tiny* when the engine was transfered from Newton to begin work on the new tramway. Full wagons were allowed to run by gravity from the mines down the gradient toward the Corfe road, usually stopping where the line levelled out before reaching the road. A catch point was in position in case any wagon over-ran. From here the horses took the loaded wagons across the main road and the Swanage

Eli is moving a train of full skips towards a line of empties with No 18 visible and No 20 among the empties. On the right side of Cattle Creep bridge can be seen the covered chute where the wagons had been tipped into a lorry below. The empties would then be shunted along to the sidings loop by the small Ruston and exchanged with the full wagons brought by Eli.
3 July 1969. GEORGE MOON

Catch point at the Corfe road. This was about 50 yards from the main road; if any wagon or train ran away from the works it would be derailed and prevented from causing an accident. The point was of very simple construction. The rail on the left, looking towards the road, was cut through and one end moved out of line using the point lever. For trains to pass safely the lever was thrown restoring the continuous track. On one memorable day even the locomotive came off the road here. AUTHOR

Tiny with wagons piled high with clay at Eldon's Siding, 27 June 1932. In the foreground can be seen the wire rope used for hauling wagons on a parallel track to the locomotive.
H. G. W. HOUSEHOLD

branch line, to the new weighbridge area established south of Cattle Creep. The new weigh house measuring 8ft x 8ft x 6ft 6in with its prominent pointed roof, had been set up at Norden in 1881 or 1882, on the plateway extension near Matchams. It was of course built to withstand the weight of horses and wagons only, about 5 tons maximum. After recording the clay tonnage, the horses pulled the loaded wagons across Cattle Creep for *Tiny* to take over. Likewise, *Tiny* with returning empties would fly shunt them against the grade over the bridge.

The wagons were then made up into short trains and taken on by the horses up to the mines.

Between looking after the company horses, Eli Kitcatt did some rope running for Milton Riddle, who was a relief locomotive driver in the late 1930s. The original concept of rope working or running was of the rope being used to move or haul wagons on a parallel line to the one the locomotive was travelling on. The driver of the loco had a 'rope-runner' working with him whose job it was to control points where the levers had to be held over in position, due to rough running. The runner also controlled road traffic at the level crossing and checked the lubrication of wagon wheels. Axle boxes had to be filled with grease about once a week, but some wagons had no boxes, and the grease was put straight on the axle using a stick. Needless to say, after about one journey, it was mostly gone. The practice probably started when wagons were horse hauled and it was convenient to use a wire rope hooked

Tommy Stockley standing on *Tiny* in characteristic pose. As usual the locomotive has a well-polished dome and boiler. AUTHOR

into a ring on the side of a wagon, the coupling up being done by a young lad. The habit was then extended to include locomotives and eventually several mines also used a variation of rope haulage.

The horses were also used to fetch timber for the mines and much of that used at Norden in Eli's time came from Hethfelton woods near Wool. Eli often used to do this trip using the company's timber carriage. With the horses to be got ready, it was quite usual to make a 3am start, to be through Wareham by 6am and to return by 4pm. Alfie Brinton and Bill Talbot then cut the wood to the required lengths in the sawmill. Pitwood was also delivered to Eldon's Siding by the L&SWR. During January 1900 five deliveries of pitwood were made from Ringwood, just over 24 tons. Another job for the horses involved trips to Poole with items for repair, the most obvious being steam boilers from winding engines to be re-tubed at Poole Foundry.

When it was found that *Tiny* was unable to cope with the heavier loads on the new tramway, the company decided to purchase a larger locomotive. In a memo dated 11 January 1908, Stiff wrote, 'Buy a new or second hand engine'. He also wrote, 'Either get more miners at Norden, or if unobtainable, the Arfleet men must

just work in their one shaft and go over to Norden until stocks have increased there'. Henry Stockley was already employed on the clay works, a reliable stationary engine driver. His son Thomas James Stockley, who was known as Tommy or 'Trulo' started work for Fayle's on line maintenance about 1907. A year later William Tubb approached Tommy, and said, 'We are having a new locomotive (*Thames*) and I think you ought to be able to drive it'. This would mean a small increase in wages from 18s a week to 21s, so Tommy decided to become a driver, and eventually took on *Tiny* for the rest of her working life. During the 80 years that *Tiny* worked in Purbeck she had just 4 regular drivers, the first having been Mr Short.

It was 1909 before *Thames* arrived, but at 14 tons the locomotive seemed ideal for the haulage from Norden to Goathorn and from then on *Tiny* would be used to work Eldon's Siding and the Arfleet branch. In fact, *Thames* was unable to work at Eldon's, or Norden siding as it became known, because Willsbridge on the approach was too low for the locomotive to pass until 1938, when the track under the bridge was lowered by 4 inches. There was a good reason why the bridge was too low. Originally, the 1881 plateway diversion to the new mines near Matchams had

Tiny driven by Short, an early view of the engine showing the lining out on the side tanks. There was no cab protection or obvious safety valves at the dome and the smoke-box appears to be short with a single line of rivets where it joined the boiler. There was no running plate extending over the cylinder. AUTHOR

Tiny at Willsbridge illustrating how close the fit was. Tom Stockley leaves the engine for a few minutes to talk to his family who were walking along the Slepe road. It also explains why *Thames* the larger locomotive was unable to reach the siding beyond the bridge until the track under the bridge was lowered about 4 inches in 1938. AUTHOR

crossed the road to Middlebere and Slepe by a level crossing. When the Swanage Branch was built the road was taken up over the branch line on a new bridge, and a small bridge to accommodate the plateway had to be made in the approach embankment. This small bridge, called Will's Arch but more generally Willsbridge, was constructed with just the horse drawn plateway in mind, which explains why it was such a tight fit for *Tiny* to pass through and impossible for *Thames*.

For the next 28 years until 1937, *Thames* continued travelling between Norden and Goathorn, doing an efficient haulage job. Clay output, as noted above, was from two main areas, the pits at Arfleet served generally by *Tiny*, and the newer mines established south of Norden Farm, on the west side of the A351 road served by the horses. Substantial quantities of clay were weathered at Norden, the beds being near the old office at first, and then at Matchams from 1907-37. Any surplus clay was taken to Newton and treated in the old weathering beds there. For many years there was no telephone on the works, so messages regarding mining and loading were sent around the area by train. Customer's orders usually came in the post and Poole Harbour used telegrams to inform the company of shipping arrivals. Sydney Stiff often travelled on the footplate to Goathorn or any other area requiring his attention. On return trips to

Eli looks out from the footplate of *Thames* at Norden, while some fellow workers get into the photograph. On the left was Bert Reed who was working as rope runner and next to him was Bill Selby the works foreman. Leaning on *Thames'* running plate was Fred White who operated winding engines in the mines or open pits and was also a foreman. *Thames* had received a bump on the front resulting in a dented smokebox door. AUTHOR

Norden trains were often made up using old clay wagons, some still numbered, but in a fairly dirty state and no longer used for clay. These were used for the transport of peat, cut by Jack Burgess at his business in the woods near Goathorn. Over the years, thousands of tons were brought to Eldon's Siding, but the quantity was never weighed, and was shipped to various nurseries about twice a week.

Thames with a load of peat about to leave Goathorn plantation in September 1936. The picture was taken by Sydney Stiff and sent to Tommy Stockley at Christmas, with the message, 'Remembering many good trips!'

Thames about to leave Goathorn with another load of peat for Jack Burgess. No weighing was done and the peat was shipped from Eldon's Siding about twice a week. The older peat wagons were kept separate from the ball clay transport. To avoid any contamination of the clay, main line wagons coming to the siding to be loaded were carefully examined and thoroughly cleaned out and washed. AUTHOR

In 1938-9, both Cattle Creep and the skew bridge were upgraded to enable *Tiny* to work trains to and from the mines. It was first proposed to hold up the deck on one 18in x 6in rolled steel joist under the centre section of the bridge. This was then revised to use two 22in x 7in joists supporting the tramway sleepers directly, all the soil being cleared away and the space between the new tramway 'deck' being filled in with timbers. *Tiny* could haul four loaded wagons up the gradient over the Swanage branch, whereas a horse could only pull two. The driver then had to remember that the engine was too heavy to drive over the weighbridge. This was a good reason for retaining the dead-end siding to the east of bridge 15, so that the wagons when reversing were always leading as the train approached the weigh house. One dark afternoon, after 4pm, Milton Riddle was driving *Tiny* past the transfer siding when a loud rasping noise and scraping of metal occurred, which upon investigation proved to be one of *Tiny*'s side-tanks fouling a Southern Railway wagon, which was quite a bit wider than usual. This resulted in a broad white mark on the side of

Tiny. Milton had allowed Eli some driving practice and he became regular driver of *Thames* after 1940 when Frank Tubb was promoted to foreman in the Norden cutting pit. In the meantime Milton had joined the Royal Air Force and, sadly, was later killed in action over Germany. The loss of his driving skills contributed to the quicker promotion of Eli.

Fayle's were paying three different landowners annual rent under lease, which affected the status of the railway. The main area at Norden was owned by the Earl of Eldon, of Encombe House, the rent being £1,200 per year plus royalties. Back in 1885 the total amount paid was £1,342 17s 4d. In 1886 the payment was £1,347 14s and in 1887 £1,164 16s 3d. At the same time Fayle's were paying the owner of Rempstone, W. M. Calcraft, £525 per annum rent for Arfleet mines, and W. R. Bankes of Kingston Lacy, £300 for Middlebere. Stiff acknowledged they should be paying double rent for land used for clay getting compared to agricultural use, but he felt sure the land at Arfleet was not properly designated. He thought it might be right that the double charge also applied to land actually used

Tiny shunts the Norden sidings, showing the scrape-mark on its tank, 27 June 1932. Tom Stockley with shovel in hand was about to get some coal out of the bunker nearest him. The other half of the side tank was filled with water and the white mark along the side of the tank was caused by accidental contact with an extra wide Southern Railway wagon at the siding. The cylinder lubricator ahead of the chimney had to be kept topped up with oil. AUTHOR

for the railway, but expressed his doubts. W. R. Bankes had agreed to a reduction in rent when the Middlebere plateway was lifted. As a railroad it was costing £200 per annum, but after 26 December 1907 the area previously occupied by the line, reverted to clay lands at £50 per annum.

In June 1903 Lt Marston, who had inherited Rempstone Estate, allowed a rebate of £50 per annum because the clay trade was so depressed. It was agreed for the present as a private arrangement and not altered in the lease, but on 22 July 1912 Marston wrote a letter announcing the withdrawal of any rental concession. Stiff wrote to Hughes suggesting an appropriate response, with the note 'we ought to go on to point out that the railway was rendered necessary and the mines opened at Arfleet largely because of the partial failure of the best clay at Goathorn. We could therefore, I think, legitimately ask for a remission of a further £100 a year rent, or asking £150 in all, or a dead rent of £375. Of course I don't think we should get as much as this but we might get another £50, especially if Marston thought we might give up the Arfleet mines if he proved too obdurate'.

The tramway to Goathorn traversed land owned by the Rempstone Estate and a wayleave was payable by B. Fayle & Co. for the privilege of carrying clay from Norden over the new tramway. The charge started at Arfleet where trains entered the Rempstone property and from 1907 to 1918 was 3d per ton. This was paid twice, if for example, clay was taken from Norden to

Newton Hill for stock to be weathered and then returned to Norden; the cost was 6d per ton for both journeys. The record for 1915 showed £54 4s 9d to be paid for 4,339 Liverpool tons carried from Norden. Needless to say, the weighing of clay was an important matter, partly to see that the various teams of miners were fairly paid, but also to have a complete record of the quantity of clay being mined. Also to make sure the extraction process conformed to the terms of the lease in force at any particular time and the royalty to be paid. The clay company had to keep fair and legible books of account with true, regular and exact entries of every ton of clay, a further copybook being kept for the landowner. The returns were normally dealt with through Eldon's solicitors as far as Norden clay was concerned; they were Bell Steward, May and How of 49 Lincoln's Inn Fields. In March 1909 a query arose over a difference between the (annual) figures submitted by Richard Pinney and those held by Bell's. Their letter of 12 March was short and to the point, 'We think it is best to make up the Returns to Christmas in accordance with the terms of the Lease, instead of to the 31 December'.

In 1912 following the death of Richard Edward Pinney it was decided to form a limited company and from then on the business was known as 'B. Fayle and Company Limited', with a nominal capital of £18,000. This was divided into 9,000 cumulative preference shares of one pound each and 9,000 ordinary shares of one pound each, with a view, amongst other things, to the acquisition of the original Fayle business. In the agreement made on 14 December a clause was inserted which allowed the Messrs Stiff, if desired, to erect a new pottery works at Goathorn on land already under lease not exceeding 10 acres. The rent due would be £100 per annum and they would receive an extra discount of sixpence per ton in respect of clay used by them in the Goathorn Pottery. They would also need the permission of the superior landlord to carry out any building on the site.

The agreement stated,

…the pottery if erected, would pay the Company three halfpence per ton for the carriage of all pottery-ware, coal, merchandise or goods belonging to them, which should be conveyed over Goathorn Pier and the railways connected with it with a minimum charge of two shillings and sixpence for each journey'. It was also agreed, 'In case the proprietors of the pottery wished to construct any tramways or sidings connected with the tramway of the Company or to alter or improve Goathorn Pier by extending the same or erecting a crane thereon in connection with the said pottery works, they could do so at their own expense. If boats or vessels arrived at the pier together for loading or unloading, those involved in the clay works would take precedence over the pottery, except for any extension to the pier that may be built by the proprietors of the pottery.

Eventually the proposal lapsed and the pottery

remained a dream for the Stiff family and any possible extensions to Fayle's Tramway that might have served the pottery remain a pleasant conjecture.

Some very serious mining accidents in the coal industry in 1910 and 1913 had resulted in hundreds of deaths. Fayle's early shafts were lightly constructed using timbers of 3in square section, and were said to be not much better than holes in the ground. The wood was sometimes assorted which led to weakness so shafts often needed righting. On 23 September 1913, the change to 4in timber was made in a company memo, which incorporated new rates of pay for construction.

The shafts now are 62in x 62in outside the boards, instead of 60in x 60in as formerly. This is an increase of 7%. The old rate of pay in 1911, commencing at the surface was 3s per foot, so 3s plus the 7% increase = 3s 2½d. But the timber now being 4in thick, as against the old 3in is heavier to handle. Therefore, in future the price paid for sinking is to be 3s 4d per foot, instead of 3s. (Depth is the same sliding scale as formerly, plus the 4d per foot).

Apparently the old scale of 3s per foot applied to the first 36ft, then 1d per foot was paid extra for all over 36 (37ft would be 3s 1d; for 38ft, 3s 2d was paid, and so on).

A further note said, 'These prices include fixing the stage and gear (windlass) and are taken from the top of the stage.' This was changed in

This map about 1920 shows the tramway diverted in 1914 slightly south from its original course closer to the farm and into Little Copse. The main tramway runs through the copse to a shaft and a short branch to another shaft in the copse. The names of these seem unrecorded. The Norden to Goathorn tramway can be seen top right going off toward the pier, and the trailing branche(s) into the Arfleet mining area are far right beyond the Corfe River.

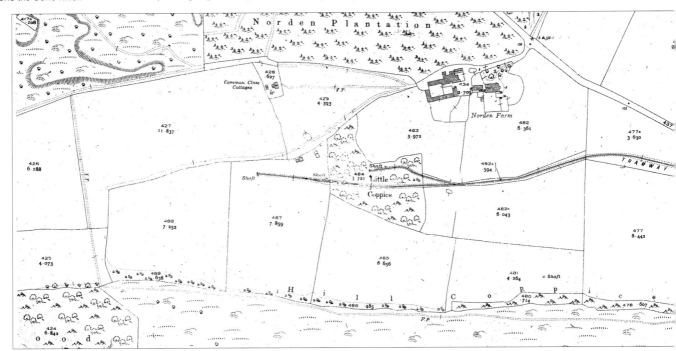

1913 to read, 'These prices are taken from the top of the stage, when sinking.' From this information we can see that prior to 1913, the hole was dug 5ft square, and the shaft constructed using 3in timbers, 5ft long, alternating with 4ft 6in spans, to form the working shaft 4ft 6in square. No access ladders were provided at that time, so men had to ride up and down in the boxes; there was just enough room for 2 men in a box. This also made it more balanced. With one man only, the box would swing around and bang the sides of the shaft giving a very uncomfortable ride. From September 1913 onwards the shaft hole was dug 5ft 2in square, and using 4in timbers, 5ft 2in long alternating with 4ft 6in spans, the size of the working shaft remained 4ft 6in.

It was about this time, as mentioned earlier that mining again changed direction. In 1913-14, a new branch of the tramway was built from Railway Junction Shaft in a south west direction across Dandy Hayes and into Little Coppice where two shafts, No. 7 and 8, were opened up and were working from 1915 to 1917. This extension eventually became the 'main line' after the shafts 4, 5 and 6 were worked out in Dandy Hayes and the original line going to Rick-yard shaft and the workings in Five Acres was lifted. The new area south and west of the farm would be extensively mined over the next 85 years.

In March 1914, the *S.S. Gustafsberg* arrived at Poole Harbour to collect clay. This large steam

The *Gustafsberg* heavily loaded with clay was approaching its homeport in Sweden. AUTHOR

ship from Sweden caused quite a stir when it first came, as it was said to be the largest ship calling at the harbour at that time. The *Gustavsberg* as originally named with a 'v', was built in 1910 by Oskashamn N/V Ack. at Oskashamn and registered at the port of Stockholm. The ship was later acquired by the pottery owned by the Odelberg family, and they changed the name to *Gustafsberg*, probably in 1914. Her original tonnages were gross 1,379, net 1,109, and her registered dimensions were 230ft x 36.5ft x 15.6ft. Stiff had taken soundings at Goathorn toward the end of 1912 and sent them to Odelberg, with the size of the new steamer in mind. Until then the Gustafsberg Pottery had used any available steam ship. The *Gustafsberg* took cargoes limited to a maximum of 1,200 tons, in order to leave the harbour through the shallow entrance or bar. Annual visits, sometimes twice a year, went on for the next 20 years.

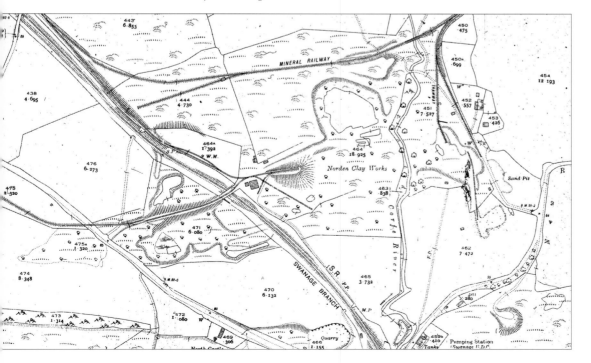

In this picture taken about 1920 by Churchill of Wareham, Eli Kitcatt is standing with Prince on bridge 15 with East Hill in the background. As they move forwards they will approach some works buildings, first the sawmills, which were later burnt down, and the stables a bit further on. Teddy Riddle was the clerk and can be seen standing forward from the weigh house with its pointed roof. The weigh house was in use for 40 years from 1907 to 1947 and huge piles of clay can be seen in the weathering beds surrounding it. Also to be noted are the trestles or other supports for wheeling boards. The clay was dug out and brought in wheelbarrows to be tipped into the wagons. CHURCHILL OF WAREHAM

CHAPTER SIX

Horses, Locos and wagons before 1948
Called 'Broad Gauge' by the mining community

For generations, the working horse was the lifeblood of the clay mines and railways that served them. As noted, the original Fayle's plateway to Middlebere was worked entirely by horses for a century, as well as the shunting and marshalling of wagons at the mines and on to the pier. Richard Pinney loved horses, which no doubt contributed to their long use on the plateway, and he used to hide behind bushes along the route to make sure the drivers handled the animals kindly. Their patience and strength helped to grow the industry and their intelligence was legendary. Likewise at Newton, horses operated the plateway before *Tiny* came and they continued to work in the open pits for many more years. Eli Kitcatt, from the age of 3, when running off to school at Corfe with the older children, remembered seeing horses pulling empty clay wagons across the main road on their way to the mines. Eli was unaware that for this privilege Fayle's were being charged one pound a year for rent of the level crossing by the Dorset County Council. He started working for Fayle's in September 1917, when 12 years old, leading the horse picking up barley at Norden Farm. In 1923, Joe Stockley who was in charge of the pit horses went on to tipping clay at No. 8 mine. Stiff asked Eli to be in charge of horses at the mines and he worked with them for the last 16 years they were in regular use. Each horse would be hitched to a couple of empty wagons at Cattle Creep and moved on for assembling at the weathering beds near the weighbridge. *Prince* was so good, he could do everything needed except hitch himself on. *Punch* and *Betty* were other long serving horses. The three horses together in trace harness would then pull the six wagons up to the mines. They could manage up to eight empty wagons, which would be divided at the mines into two sets of four.

The horses also worked the weathering beds where clay was stored and turned in the open. The weathering period could be several months, and for some clays up to two or three years, the purpose being to increase the plasticity of the clay. About twelve men were employed on this part of the works, re-cutting clay and loading trains to customer's orders. When any new horses were required they were bought by Stiff, and usually came from farm use age 8 or 10 years, with an average working life of 25 years. For example, on 3 March 1899 Pinney had paid Stephen Green of Puddle Mill £16 for one bay horse, 8 years old. Nelson Bird, the company blacksmith, shoed the horses regularly, this being more often than the usual 6 weeks in agriculture because their shoes were dislodged by rough sleepers.

In the opencast pit at Newton, Billy Green was in charge of the horses, with usually two or three in use. In 1902 these were listed as, *Champion* aged 14 years, *Prince* aged 8 years and *Captain* aged 20 years, valued at £80. An empty wagon weighed about 15 to 20cwt and if derailed it was quite a tricky process using the horses to get it back on the line, because the collar could choke the animal if too much pressure was applied while pulling the wagon upright. In the 1920s and 1930s, rerailing was completed using wedges and a very large crowbar wielded by Eli. By 1938, Longmire was looking at every possible way of increasing clay output, from re-driving lanes underground to the capacity available from each shaft. He then wrote 'It seems quite unnecessary to employ horses' and described a time trial he had carried out using the small locomotive. After years of faithful labour the horses were finally made redundant with the coming of the war and were sold at Dorchester sheep fair market on 21 September 1939.

PLATEWAY WAGONS, 3FT 6IN GAUGE.
By 1890, using photographic evidence, the wagons in use were basically oblong wooden boxes with an upward hinging door at the end facing Middlebere. The patent axletrees on the plateway wagons were very noticeable, extending several inches beyond the wheels. The wheels were typical cast iron plateway type with 8 dished spokes and varied in size from wagon to wagon. On some wagons, one axle had different size wheels to the other, so the wagon sloped down at one end, usually the end opposite the door. By

1890, most of the earliest wagons, presumably numbered from 1 originally, seem to have been scrapped, or to have been out of use for other reasons, such as accidental damage. The following wagons were listed as in use, and perhaps because of their age or condition, were carrying inferior clay, or yellow clay, via Middlebere. Wagon 6 and 10 to 19 inclusive, had an average tare weight 15cwt. The tare weight was important of course, as this was deducted from the gross weight of each wagon recorded at the weighbridge to give the true weight of the clay load. The following wagons were in regular use from 1 January 1890 for loading best clay, numbered from 56 to 77 having an average tare weight of 13cwt, except for 77 at 15cwt which was first recorded in 1890.

In 1892 six wagons numbered 56 to 61 were added to stock with tare weights of 14 to 15cwt. These appeared to be replacements for the original 56 to 61 with lower tare weight. This was probably to facilitate heavier loads of clay, the average amount increasing as follows: 1890, 30 to 35cwt, 1891, 35 to 42cwt, and 1892, 38 to 42cwt.

Six years later, in November 1898, loads of 44, 46 and 49cwt were recorded. To achieve a load of two tons the wagons were piled high with clay. It is probable that the earliest wagons from 1807 recorded as carrying 2 tons were built with higher sides than the later model. It seems likely that the company carpenters constructed all the wagons, including the original 30 in daily use. This tradition continued until 1947.

From the nomenclature of the time it seems likely the rail road wheels were for use on the plateway to Middlebere and the tramroad wheels to be transferred to Newton for the 3ft 9in line. The Middlebere wagons were very similar to those used later on the 3ft 9in Goathorn line and some may have been converted to the new gauge to save cost.

In 1902, the wagons at Goathorn were valued at £261 10s. There were 48 wagons of which 44 had cast iron wheels and iron axles, and were valued at £5 each. Four of the wagons had steel wheels and axles valued at £7 each. One tip wagon was £4 10s, and three 3ft gauge rubble wagons were valued at £3 each. The 3ft gauge was only a limited run for waste clay at the Newton pits. The contents of the carpenter's shop was interesting because it included 12 rubble pedestals, 16 clay wagon pedestals, sundry wagon iron work, 8 new clay wagon wheels (£7), a pit saw and one clay wagon partly made (£1 15s).

TINY, LOCOMOTIVE, 3FT 9IN EDGE RAILWAY.

In later years, some authors have questioned the capability of Lewin's company to build what was a fairly basic locomotive by 1868 and claim *Tiny* was built after 1870. In fact the current research shows there was plenty of experience and a strong verbal tradition that the 'loco' was introduced in 1868, which cannot be dismissed lightly. Eli Kitcatt's maternal grandfather had been a cutter in the 1848 tunnel pit, and it was well known among the men that *Tiny* arrived 20 years after the dating of the tunnel. Stephen Lewin said in his catalogue that orders for locomotives were executed to individual purchaser's requirements. He made two kinds of tramway engines, *Tiny* being a simple form of direct-acting contractors' locomotive, to draw weights from 40 to 150 tons on gauges varying from 2ft 6in to 5ft.

The Lewin engine was brought on a flat barge across the harbour from Poole to Goathorn, but from the time it arrived at the works, it was always referred to in the clay company records simply as the Loco and no nameplates were ever fixed. The Newton plateway was chosen for the steam experiment because the line would have to be converted to edge railway to accommodate *Tiny* and a shorter length of track and therefore less expense was involved. Rumour suggested that *Tiny* was built for a line in Spain and was surplus at Lewin's works. It was also said that the 'Loco', at first called *Corfe*, had been tried on the line while still a plateway, using flange-less wheels, but she was too heavy and broke a lot of the plate rails. This seems very unlikely, because by that time it was generally accepted that the action of a steam locomotive was damaging to a cast iron road. If the locomotive already carried nameplates, no explanation has ever been given why the appropriate name *Corfe* should have been removed. Whatever the truth, the line which had been re-laid using inverted U-section, or bridge rails in 1854, was up-graded using flat bottom rail, and the 'Loco' was soon running as a standard locomotive on normal edge rail to 3ft 9in gauge. *Tiny* continued working at Newton hauling clay from the pits to Goathorn pier for the next 39 years.

Maintaining a locomotive was quite an expensive business and most of the time Dorset Iron Foundry, West Quay Road, Poole, carried out the work on *Tiny*. Records show a selection of items bought from them and repairs carried out

A picture of *Tiny* in the early 1930s, taken by a member of the Fayle family. It appeared in the *Locomotive* magazine 15 November 1934 with a brief history, which proved accurate and reliable. It stated for example that the year Fayle started operations in Dorset was 1804 which was correct, and also referred to the mineral as ball clay when most writers erroneously refer to the china clay workings!
H. FAYLE

over the period 1891 to 1902. These items were charged as 'Goathorn Loco Repairs' to smokebox, valve gear and also a wide assortment of supplies including fire bars and copper pipe feed, a new chimney and ashpan, injector pipes and one loco water tank, the total cost for the period being nearly £200.

The December 1902 stocktaking confirmed some of the costs for *Tiny*. The book value of the locomotive engine, under Goathorn was entered as £130.

The entry read:
    1 x 6¼ Loco
    Nearly new boiler, 30 Sept.1897 cost £150 for boiler;
    1 set spare valve gear used.
    2 spare cylinders used.
    1 set old wheels and axles.

These notes would suggest the original cylinders, stated to be 6¼ in 1902, had later been bored out to 6½, and the other parts marked used had

Tiny, seen in the 1930s, with different rivets to the smokebox and the door hinged on the right side. The lumps of coal have gone and the sandboxes re-instated. The side tanks have been renewed with a single line of rivets down the centre of the divided tank and closer together on the water section than the coalbunker. From measurements taken by Gordon Hatherill the left hand tank took 14.25 cu ft of water, plus 7.125 in the front section of the right hand tank, a total of 21.375 cu ft giving a capacity of about 130 gallons. The coal carried was 7.125 cu ft, about 4cwt. The right hand tank had a drain cock fitted and ahead of the chimney a cylinder lubricator had been added. AUTHOR

Tom Stockley stands proudly beside *Tiny* at Norden. The locomotive was well polished and perhaps recently refurbished following the fitting of a new cab, made up at the shops by the blacksmith, Nelson Bird. AUTHOR

probably been replaced on the Loco. and the old retained for possible further use. In their books, the company usually marked purchased items G or N, meaning they were allocated for use at Goathorn and Norden respectively.

At a later date *Tiny*'s boiler pressure was advanced to 160lb. Tank capacity was 130 gallons and coal 4 cwt making a weight in working order of 7 tons. Coal came from various sources over the years, but on 13 December 1898, Peter Stewart and Co.of Southampton supplied 19 ton 4 cwt at 20s per ton to Goathorn. Other railway items such as wheels, axles, boilers, rails and fishplates came from W. G. Bagnall & Co.the Castle Engine Works in Stafford. On 31 July 1895, engine wheels were received, 'as tendered' for £29, almost certainly for the 'Loco.' Another significant item in 1897 was a locomotive boiler for £150. (probably Bagnall order No.318 5/1897, which covered a boiler + firebox, smokebox, regulator and safety valve).

Some years later a report re-iterated the build date as 1868. G. G. Woodcock reported on various narrow gauge railways in a number of magazine articles. In August 1938 he wrote in the *Railway Magazine*, with reference to *Tiny*,

> This engine is now exactly 70 years old. The principal dimensions are as follows: Type, outside cylinder 0-4-0 side tank; cylinders 6.5in x 9in, working pressure 120lb, coupled wheels 1ft 9in diameter on tread when new, now 1ft 8in, wheelbase 3ft 10in, boiler diameter 2ft 4in, 46 x 2in tubes. The motion, which is Stephenson's link, is outside the frames and between them and the

wheels, an eccentric is fitted on the leading axle for a feed pump, but this is now displaced and an injector fitted. The engine was fitted with a pair of new cylinders in 1916 at the Dorset Iron Foundry, West Quay Road Poole. [Bagnall order 4636 for spares would suggest the date was April 1917.] The old cylinders are to be seen at the back of the shed and bear the name on the steam chest covers of 'S. Lewin, Engineer, Poole, 1868.

Another Bagnall order in November 1924 stated, 'Repair motion of loco Tiny', at a time when new wheels were recorded fitted. In the 1930s *Tiny* was fitted with a cab so the driver had more protection in bad weather.

THAMES, LOCOMOTIVE, 3FT 9IN EDGE RAILWAY

Thames was built 1902, by Manning Wardle and Co.of Leeds, their records stating, 'This is a special 9½in dia. x 14in outside cylinder saddle tank engine on four coupled wheels 2ft 6in diameter. Wheelbase 4ft 6in. Heating surface 242 square feet viz: 27 square feet in box, and 215 square feet in 55 tubes 2in outside diameter. Grate area 4¾ square feet. Capacity of tank 250 gallons. Boiler plates of mild steel, slide valves of cast iron.'

In July 1903, they sold it second-hand for £500, which included delivery to Plaistow, to the works manager of the London County Council (LCC). The locomotive was required by the LCC to operate a 3ft 6in gauge temporary railway for the duration of sewer laying works. The Northern Outfall sewer Enlargement Scheme

The maker's photo of *Thames*. GEORGE MOON

This picture of *Thames* first appeared in the *Locomotive* magazine 15 November 1934 in an article on Fayle's tramway, 'A Dorsetshire Narrow Gauge Railway'. It is still the most accurate account to be found in the railway press and reported, 'It (Thames) had been built for use in the construction of the Barking Sewer Outfall to run on a 3ft 6in track. As the gauge of Messrs. Fayle's line is 3ft 9in the L.C.C. engine was adapted to suit this wider gauge by using stepped tyres on the wheels.' These can be clearly seen in the photograph. H FAYLE

was begun in 1902 and eventually completed in 1908. At that time the locomotive was fitted with a special cab made to suit tunnel. It also had special block buffers (no spring buffers), Manning Wardle & Co's No. 4 injector, also feed pump and railwashing gear. Following completion of this work, *Thames* and some other equipment surplus to requirements, including wagons, were offered for sale but not cleared at the first auction for lack of bidders. It was reported that eventually the purchasing agent was J. Stiff & Sons, who acquired *Thames* in May 1909 and sold it on to Fayle's.

Before working in Dorset, *Thames* had to be re-gauged to 3ft 9in. Other repairs were probably due and the locomotive was returned to

Thames brings another load of clay down from the mines and crosses the Wareham to Corfe Castle road. It was this level crossing that the Council had to dig up in preparation for the change of gauge from 3ft 9in to 1ft 11½in. The date of the picture was between late 1937 and late 1939, as the Ford model Y car behind the flagman carried a London registration mark –DYE, but did not have masked lamps or white edged mudguards that were required by the black out regulations from January 1940. AUTHOR

Manning Wardle's Boyne Engine Works, Leeds. Manning Wardle & Co's records state, 'When this engine was sold by the London County Council to B. Fayle & Co, we supplied special tyres under order number 64234 to alter it from a 3ft 6in to a 3ft 9in gauge. See special tracing (No. 13523 marked for B. Fayle & Co., Corfe Castle), and print of tyres 4 June 1909'. The change was achieved by using stepped tyres on the wheels, meaning the tyres were fitted over-width, with the flange about one third of the way from the inner edge.

So, although *Thames* became available in 1908, it seems the locomotive did not arrive at the clay works until the following year, and *Tiny* was kept busy on the new line for the first two years. One obvious change to *Thames* was the addition of a front wooden buffer beam, fixed 5 inches below the original level to suit the Norden wagon buffers. However, the name of the locomotive was kept the same, as a reminder of its early days in London, its livery remaining dark green. *Thames* was displayed on cast plates either side of the saddle-tank, with the number 48 on the cab side. The basic measurements of the locomotive taken from the Manning Wardle drawing showed it to be 8ft 10in high over the

cab and 6ft 1½in wide over the cylinders; actually 6ft 4in width over original buffer beams and footplating. The engine had a working pressure of 140lb per sq in.

On 31 July 1915, Manning Wardle supplied a chimney barrel and cast iron top, the barrel being 1ft 8½in long and ¼in thick, to order number 73414. Later the same year on 25 November, a special mud plug 2¼in diar, 9 threads per inch was supplied to order number 73905.

On 17 January 1924, a mild steel driving axle was fitted to wheels, under order number 84058.

The last item in Manning Wardle's records is dated 29 October 1926, when a new copper fire box, made by Kitsons was supplied under order number 86174.

WAGONS 3FT 9IN, EDGE RAILWAY.

Eli said the wagon design originated at Norden and probably developed from the plateway wagons. This has been confirmed in the ledger used to value the company in 1902. At that time Middlebere had 33 clay wagons, which were valued at £3 each. A note was made that, '23 had been broken up to N&G Ry'. Although at that stage the Norden to Goathorn line was only just being planned, it seems a start had already been made on wagon conversion. Two rubble wagons at Middlebere were also valued at £3 each. The number of wagons required in use was controlled by the demand for clay, and when business was bad, building soon stopped.

On 18 August 1912, Stiff replied to a query from Hughes,

> Wagons ... I agree stopping building new wagons and I think we ought at once to get rid of one carpenter and the men Cottrell, Bartlett and Stockley, who were the last three engaged at Goathorn. If they go it will leave Tubb, and 8 rubblers and this I think will be sufficient for a long time to come.

The clay wagons were of simple construction in wood, with a short length over the body of 6ft 6in. They were unsprung, running on four wheels with 6 curved spokes each, with a 2ft 7in wheel base. Hefty 10in deep timbers formed the main frame, which was 8ft overall length. The axle boxes were bolted to the frame, and each side member of the frame extended 9in to form dumb buffers at each end of the wagon. Some photographs show clearly why *Thames'* buffers had to be altered to match the wagons. The low planked sides were supported by 3 outside frame members called strouders, and these were often damaged, or pulled out by forcing the hook behind them when the rope was used to pull

wagons on an adjacent line. Metal rings were then fitted to the wagon sides for this purpose. The fixed end of the wagon had a metal tie rod for rigidity, but the other end facing Goathorn pier had a door, which could be dropped over the buffers for loading clay into barges. The number of each wagon appeared twice on each side, stencilled on the planks between the strouders, No. 104 being the last. Many of the wagons were constructed during the 1930-40s by the company's carpenter, George Day, assisted by Jack Talbot. The top edge of each side was finished with an angled piece of wood called a

A redundant frame from a 3ft 9in wagon, showing the substantial side-timbers, measuring 10in x 6in and the diagonal metal cross tie to give the wagon extra rigidity. AUTHOR

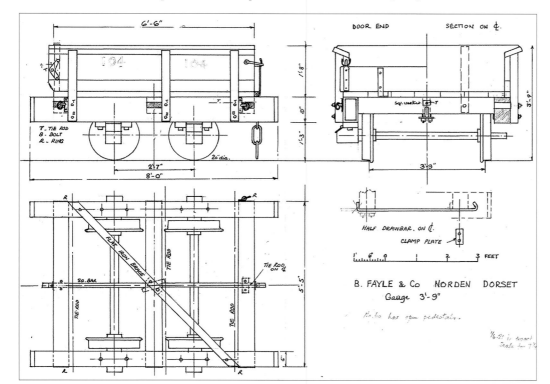

Drawings of 3ft 9in wagon. DRAWING BY GORDON HATHERILL/ GEORGE MOON

Thames passes Claywell crossing with the school wagon in 1934. Taken by Humphrey Household who said the passing of the train caused a lot of interest among his group of young pupils.
H. G. W. HOUSEHOLD

rave and the wagons were joined together by loose 3-link couplings. The terms used such as strouders and raves were the names applied to similar fittings on farm wagons.

Only a few of the wagons were fitted with brakes and for one reason or another none of them worked efficiently. So in effect there were no brakes and the wagons were slowed down by spragging, a common method on early industrial railways. A sprag consisted of a length of metal pipe or rod pushed through the spokes of the wheels, thus locking the wheel when the sprag came against the wagon frame. Some of the wheels had holes through them instead of spokes, but Eli became expert at 'throwing' a sprag into one of the holes while the wagon was moving. However, because of the skidding effect the practice caused a lot of 'flats' on the wheels, which resulted in rough riding and heavy wear and tear on the track. Eventually the wheels became worn out and, Eli said, with a grin, it was quite common for a wheel to fall in half! Part of George's work was to fit new wheels to their axles in a process known as 'boxing' using the wheel tub. The tub consisted of a large section of trunk from an elm tree, with a groove cut across the top, to hold the axle horizontally. Each wheel was designed to be wedged to the axle, and George would do one first using wooden wedges

followed by metal. Then the second wheel was positioned on the axle, using a wooden or metal 3ft 9in gauge to get the correct distance from the first, and likewise fixed by wedging. The wagon would then be weighed empty and recorded, the usual being about one ton, and this amount would be deducted from every load at the weigh house to give the correct weight of the clay, up to 4 tons per wagon.

THE SCHOOL COACH, 3FT 9IN GAUGE.
In 1932, the Dorset County Council negotiated with the Clay Company in an effort to get the Newton children to school. The clay company agreed to convert a clay wagon, which was roofed over for the children to ride in, and in this way they were brought by rail to Arfleet, walking the last half mile or so to the school in Corfe Castle. The school train consisted of *Thames*, pulling the 'passenger' coach made up of clay wagon No. 78 fitted with a brake and covered in by a wooden structure with a corrugated iron roof made up by George Day. A window, fitted with curtains, placed high up near the roof provided light rather than any enjoyment of the view and the interior was fitted with narrow wooden seats, covered with leather, around three sides of the wagon. At the end facing the locomotive a sliding door allowed entry.

CHAPTER SEVEN

The first shadow of war, 1914-18, and the aftermath

During 1913, S. J. Stiff opened a correspondence with L. G. Pike with a view to getting co-operation between him and the much larger Pike clay mining operation at Furzebrook. Over the next eight years they discussed everything from wages, trade unions, disputes with landowners and the price of clay, which included manipulating the asking price in favour of the other producer. This eventually led to the fixing of prices to compete with Devon clays and agreement to vary charges depending on the destination country. Although Middlebere had closed, some clay stocks remained there and Pike agreed to lighter this to Poole, some 200 tons or so. In October they agreed the freight rate for clay should be fixed at 7s 6d per ton. Stiff had been experimenting with mixes of Fayle and Pike clays and was ready to approach new customers. He asked Pike if he would send to 'Eldon Sidings' about one ton of Twoball clay for testing with a view to having 1,000 to 2,000 tons in 1914. This arrangement was probably cut short by the war. In February 1914, Fayle's made a request to explore Arne for clay but this was turned down by the landowner.

Fayle's had been operating at Arfleet for seven years when the coming of the 1914-18 war had a disastrous effect on production, with many men joining or being called up. This was noted in the quantities of clay being shipped from Goathorn. Despite the fall in tonnage, the clay industry remained an essential part of the war effort and was designated a reserved occupation. However, the declaration of war on 4 August 1914 did not stop the *Gustafsberg*, which continued calling to take clay from Poole quay. On 6 July 1915, 300 tons of type WM clay was loaded at Goathorn railway pier. On 11 September 1916, Fayle's had 100 tons of clay lightered from Middlebere to Poole, but after that most of their clay was taken by rail to Poole Quay and loaded into ships from there. The *Gustafsberg* made her final departure on 11 June 1934.

In 1916, the company was required to make a return of men of military age and this was completed on 23 May. The return recorded if the men were single or married and if between the ages of 18 to 25, 25 to 30, 30 to 35 and 35 to 40. Men aged under 18, or 41 and over were not of military age. The totals were compared with March 1914. In 1914, B Fayle & Co. Ltd had employed, 3 Foremen, 23 clay miners, 9 clay cutters in pits, 26 men working weathering beds, 4 uncovering and removing overburden and 2 stationary enginemen. There was 1 loco driver (age 35), 1 loco stoker (runner under age 18), 3 carpenters, 6 men repairing tram and railroad, 3 carters and 2 clerks and timekeepers. All together, a total of 86 men were employed in 1914, and this had dropped to 45 in 1916. By 1917, the workers had dropped to a third of pre-war; the engine men and foremen were the same but many less clay 'getters'.

On 2 June 1917 a report submitted by Company Secretary, Joseph Hughes, showed that two railway locomotives were in use, one loco-type portable engine, and one multitube vertical engine, all hand fired, using coal as fuel, with natural draught. A coal-fired boiler was also used for 9 hours a day. The company's business hours were given as 10am to 6pm. The name of the coal used was Dowlais Merthyr, Admiralty Welsh smokeless large Steam Coal, unwashed. It was supplied by Bradbury's and arrived by rail, and the present stock was 10 tons, with about 15 tons of inferior coal. About 2½ tons were burnt each week. Hughes made the telling point that, 'it was very important they should use best Welsh smokeless steam coal as inferior kinds make smoke which dirties the clay and renders it unsuitable for Government use'. Onward transport of the coal was 'by our tramway wagons from railway siding'.

At the end of the year Stiff asked for Pike's support in a dispute that had arisen between Fayle's company and the Rempstone Estate over the mining at Arfleet. The Estate claimed some 'wilful and unnecessary damage and waste' had occurred, and Stiff wanted Pike to agree and support that they had worked the mines in the best and most approved manner. Pike was asked if he would come and look at, 'our mine at Arfleet and at the worked out mines and give me your opinion thereon with a view to giving evidence on our behalf if necessary. The mine is close to the Corfe River at North Castle, just through the arch where the railway crosses the Studland Road. I know of no one who could help me as you can with your experience'. Pike was rather loath to get involved.

In January 1918, Fayle's made a return to the Ministry of Reconstruction detailing the business and work force and how soon they might return to full production following the war, stated to be six weeks depending on adequate labour. Apart from the main line rail siding, they could load ships to 500 tons at their pier on Poole Harbour, 'connected to works by our own 3ft 9in gauge line'. The hands then employed were 23 skilled men, 10 unskilled and 2 boys. The number of hands to produce maximum output was stated as 30 skilled men, 10 unskilled and 2 or 3 boys. There had been 86 men at outbreak of war, but some went to munitions work and about 25 were serving with the forces. The unions were demanding an increase for engine drivers of 10s per week. The Ministry was hoping for brick and tile manufacture, but Fayle's said it was some 25 years since they were made and it did not pay because of freight charges. They could start again for a big local demand, as there was a considerable quantity of clay suitable for brickmaking. No other records of the brickmaking by Fayle's have been found.

By 1921 there was a long discussion with Leonard Pike on the prices being charged for clay and any discounts given. The price to Italy was 40s and in some cases 42s 6d per ton, but Sweden were claiming they could buy Best blue for 35s when Fayle's wanted to charge 41s. Stiff wanted to know if this was the same as Pike's price and could it be Devon who were offering clay at 35s? In April, Fayle's were cutting clay from an open pit, which was below sleeper level of the railway. Stiff wrote to Pike wanting to know what rate of pay they were on per yard and per ton in open pits. If the cutters were three feet or more above sleeper level they were paid 1s 8d per yard and if from three feet down to sleeper level, 2s per yard. Below sleeper level the first three feet was paid at a rate of 2s 3d per yard. An extra 5d per yard was paid for 'heaving' for every yard of depth. At the end of November Stiff said they were not barging any clay to Poole at present as no barges were available and the landing stage at Middlebere was practically washed away. This was followed in December by another round of wage reductions. Back in July, 'runners' underground who manhandled the tubs of clay had suffered a reduction of pay from 60s a week down to 52s 6d. They were now reduced again to 47s per week, the same rate as 'men repairing the tram line (platelayers) and tippers at top of mines'. One of the reasons for the reductions was the L&SWR freight charge for clay, which had been revised in July. Ball clay in bulk was now being charged at 20s per ton (4 tons minimum) and the same in bags approx 36s 3d per ton. Stiff was insensed at the preposterous difference in the two rates writing,

It is actually more advantageous to the Railway Company to carry clay in bags as the trucks are then kept quite clean; and trucks can readily be loaded to their full capacity with clay in bags.

The correspondence record ends with another round of price manipulation. Stiff wrote,

Thank you for allowing us to give J. & G. Meakin a slightly lower price than yours. If you like I will gladly reciprocate by quoting Johnson Bros. a slightly higher price than yours. If you will say what net price you want to quote them I will put ours 1s or 1s 6d higher, whichever you like. -- We are like you, no orders and I do not think we shall open the works at all next week. Please keep this letter as confidential to you. All good Christmas wishes to you.

CHAPTER EIGHT

Mechanisation underground, but still working by candlelight.

For several years following the 1914-18 war, the recovery of the clay business was very slow, mainly due to the depletion of the work force and a slack demand. The shaft at the end of the tramway branch, just beyond Little Coppice was started about 1920 and remained in use for many years. It was later re-numbered becoming No. 12 in the final series of mines at Norden (1 to 16). There was no shaft 13 because the miners thought it unlucky. The tramway also divided to give a short branch into the copse to reach Oak Tree shaft on its northern side (1920). About that time the workers were taken on a day out by char-a-banc to Weymouth, which was due reward for continuous short staff working through the war years.

The company decided that mechanisation underground would make mining more attractive to the local workforce. About the beginning of April 1924, a demonstration, using compressed air equipment was made for one of the Directors of the Company; subsequently reported to a management meeting and recorded in the minutes book by the Chairman, S. J. Stiff on 28 May 1924.

A small air compressor is now fixed at Norden Old Mine and about 3 weeks ago, Mr C. A. Ellis witnessed a demonstration of pneumatic clay diggers by the Ingersoll-Rand Co. Ltd. The Chairman reported that he had since worked the diggers himself for a period of two hours and twenty minutes and had dug in that time 2ton 5cwt 1qr of Blue and Black from a clean new face. He reported that it would cost about £1,100 to install engine compressor, receiver, pipeline and tools for working 7 or 8 diggers in the mines. With this equipment, he estimated the output of clay should equal that which 16 miners could win by the present method. Mining is heavy labour and there is increasing difficulty in obtaining enough men for this work. At present only six miners are working in the Norden Mines.

It was agreed they should proceed and the original shed to house the Ingersoll Rand compressors was built 1924-5. This was on the edge of Little Copse near the cart track leading west from Norden Farm. The shed was quite close to the haulage, which contained the steam winch for operating No. 8 and 12 mines. The Ingersoll compressors were diesel driven, and were basically all one unit. The fuel was brought by tanker from Southampton and transferred in two loads to Fayle's oval shaped portable tank, which was mounted on the frame of an old 3ft 9in wagon. This job was usually done near the saw mills, the first load being taken up to No. 12 mine, and the engines used to pump the diesel into a storage tank. The second load of diesel was kept in the wagon, to provide a mobile supply of fuel. The wagon was of course horse hauled and a sprag was used to lock a wheel, and keep the tank stationary while filling. On one occasion, about 1942, someone pulled out the sprag to move the wagon on, but before it could be replaced the wagon ran away and was thrown off the line by the catch point spilling 200 gallons of diesel. Norden was now able to offer powered digging and better pay rates, both of which attracted miners from their competitors at Furzebrook. For example, a runner was paid 50% more at Norden, where his wage was £3 per week compared to £2 at Furzebrook.

In 1927, following a major breakdown, the Ingersoll compressors were replaced. Two Belliss & Morcom machines, Nos.733 and 974, were obtained, apparently second hand and installed in a new compressor house built under Stiff's direction in Dandy Hayes field. The compressor installation to power spades, pumps and underground winches was the beginning of a new centre of operations, known to some as the West Works, which would continue in use with some internal changes until the mines closed in 1999. The west works would eventually consist of various buildings most-

The main compressors for many years were a pair of Bellis and Morcom's built in Birmingham and driven by two large Ruston diesel engines. One day the engines caught fire and were burnt out, but the compressors were saved and converted to run by electric power. AUTHOR

View of the west works with Knowle Hill in the background. Small diesel No 175413 was recorded on a short siding leading to a lean-to shed in the angle of the blacksmith's shop and the main workshop. Beyond the posts carrying the power line was the compressor house with three large water tanks outside. The furthest building was the carpenter's shop. 29 May 1969.
GEORGE MOON

ly clad with corrugated iron, with a road access from the A351 road just south of Norden House. Included among the buildings was a blacksmith's and spares shop, carpenter's shop, various storage and mess huts and the foreman's office. The carpenter's shop was just to the west of the compressor house and Arthur (Art) Marshallsay was the resident carpenter for many years. The weighbridge, clay drying sheds, clay mill and tranship shed remained located at the so-called East works where the clay sidings ran adjacent to the Swanage Railway near the present Norden Station.

The Belliss machines were dated 1913 and 1916, the 1913 machine being at the south or Corfe Castle end of the house and the 1916 unit at the north or farmhouse end. They were two stage air compressors, the first cylinder compressing up to 30p.s.i. the second up to 90p.s.i. the output being 220 cubic feet of free air per minute, the machines being lubricated with sump oil. Both cylinders had a 6in stroke, the first stage being 12½in diameter and the second stage being 7½in dia. When first installed the compressors were driven by two Ruston and Hornsby 47hp diesel engines at approximately 375 revs per minute, but later changed to electric. The large drum like tanks outside the shed contained water for cooling the Rustons, and in later years long after the engines had gone, visitors often wondered what these tanks had been used for. Cooling of the machines was absolutely essential of course, as temperatures up to 160° F were usual in the first and second stage and remained 38° F at the inter cooler outlet.

The Rustons were horizontal engines, Nos. 168607/8 with single cylinders and 12in diameter pistons, and had 8ft diameter flywheels running in channels cut in the concrete floor of the house. They were started using compressed air at 200p.s.i. stored in a bottle in the corner of the shed. After starting the first engine, the bottle was back charged to start the second engine.

As well as clay, peat and children, the railway was also used to transport stone. From about 1924-1928, trains loaded with Purbeck stone were run from Norden to Goathorn pier for use in the building of the Poole Harbour training bank. Sir Alexander Gibb and Partners were the contracting engineers and they had already constructed the base of the bank using blocks of stone, each weighing 10 tons. More stone was brought from Langton Matravers, up to 20 loads a day hauled by steam Foden lorries. It was then loaded on to the tramway in the timber yard at Norden and transported on the railway in 30ton loads, using 10 to 13 wagons. At Goathorn it was transferred to barges and towed out to the bank by the tug *Maudie S* to be dumped and form the middle core of the bank. Completed in October 1928, this structure extended about a mile out to sea south eastwards from the east-end of Shell Bay and was designed to use the power of the tide to scour silt and sand from the entrance to the harbour. Because of shallow waters in the area, nearly all vessels had to use a pilot when entering or leaving the Haven. The extra income generated by stone haulage was mentioned in Fayle's annual report of May 1929, which said they had been deprived that year of substantial profit previously earned in 1928 by the transport of stone from Arfleet to Goathorn pier over the company's railway. Stone had been previously carried on the railway in 1920 following the demolition of the farmhouse and mill at Arfleet, when Jack Gale helped in the transfer of the stone to be used at Rempstone House. It should be mentioned in passing that Fayle's also sold a quantity of sand, which was sent on the railway from Arfleet to Goathorn between 1932 and 1936. For example, in 1934 the total amount carried was 375tons.

By 1924 some of Fayle's clay was being despatched via Eldon's Siding onto the national rail system by regular timetable. When the Swanage Branch line was opened in 1885, freight traffic was inaugurated on 1 June and it became possible to send clay direct to some customers via the L&SWR. After the grouping in 1923 the branch became part of the Southern Railway and they provided two goods trains per weekday. One was a general goods that left Wareham at 6.50am arriving in Swanage at 7.35am. The return working left at 11.30am arriving back at Wareham at 12.38.

The second freight train, which was mostly dedicated to the clay traffic, left Wareham at 12.58, and arrived at Corfe Castle at 1.19pm. It began its return journey by leaving Corfe at 3.00pm. Shunting at Eldon's siding took 10 minutes from 3.03 to 3.13pm. The full wagons were drawn out, and any empties left in the siding. The train then proceeded to Furzebrook siding where 32 minutes were allowed between 3.23pm and the leaving time 3.55pm. In the meantime the 3.25pm passenger from Swanage passed by and arrived at Wareham at 3.52pm. Also, the 3.02pm from Wareham passed the freight at Furzebrook, and crossed the 3.25pm from Swanage at Corfe Castle, (3.39pm) reaching Swanage at 3.51pm. Eventually, the clay freight train arrived back at Wareham at 4.07pm and departed onwards at 6.20pm. There was no Sunday service. Trains were forbidden to leave Furzebrook siding for Wareham with a maximum load, unless prior assurance could be given for a clear run past Worgret Junction.

Wilf (Robert) Stockley was born at Corfe Castle on 26 April 1911, and was able to give an account of the works in 1927. Mr Salmon, the manager, offered Wilf a job at Norden so he started work for Fayle's, age 16 for £3 a week. Wilf's job was runner to his father Laurie Stockley and Charlie (Jaffo) Jeffries, who were both senior miners working at No. 8 Shaft. Clay getters at Fayle's were paid about 70s a week (a piece work wage average of about 12s 6d a day.) This depended upon a variety of extras such as the installation of rails, and the building of jumps, slides or cages. One Saturday about 1929-30, Stiff gave everyone the sack and then told them they could come back on Monday at a reduced wage, runners for example being offered 58 shillings a week instead of 60. The way in which the piecework rate of pay was calculated also changed at the whim of the employer. Frank Longmire who took over in 1935 at first based the payment on tonnage, for example 2s 6d per ton. Later, he decided payment would be based on the distance or the number of feet per week advanced along the tunnel. A measuring mark was cut with an axe on one of the timber sets near the working face. In weeks when the miners needed more money they made sure that on the day the mark was made, the lane was timbered as close to the face as possible!

When Wilf joined the company mining was at low ebb with just two mines working, No. 8 shaft, and No. 12. At No. 8 shaft, Wilf was needed as a second runner to join Cyril Cottrell. Cyril was working the first lane that ran from the bottom of the main shaft, about 70ft from the surface, to the top of a 20ft underground shaft, where he used a tugger and pulley to winch boxes or cars up and down to a lower lane. Wilf was employed at the lower 90ft level where he attached loaded boxes going up and received empties from Cyril, which he then trammed to and from the miners at the

A box for hauling clay to the surface, known locally as a car. In early coal-mining practice, the coal was conveyed in a corf or box on a tram to the pitshaft, where the corf was wound to the surface by means of a windlass, a very similar operation to the early system at Norden. The name may have been a corruption of Curr, because John Curr was the first person to use angled rails, which revolutionised underground transport at a colliery in Sheffield about 1778. Curr was often called Carr by mistake, even in letters from friends, such as the engineer George Overton. AUTHOR

At Furzebrook, the spares department had just fitted a new blade to a Holman spade. AUTHOR

working face. The cars held about 2cwt clay and were transported on trolleys and hauled up the main shaft by Joe Stockley. About 52 boxes a day were expected, about 104cwt or 5.2tons. Joe used a water hose to keep the stage wet for sliding the cars across to be tipped into the railway wagons. Both mines produced best Norden Blue clay, with some pink stained, but at that time all other clay was considered rubbish. The tippers were asked to pick out lumps of the very best blue clay and were paid an extra shilling to save it in a separate wagon for orders from car-plug manufacturers Lodge, who used it in making the insulator.

Lodge & Sons were also Fayle's agents for selling clay in the Potteries. Oliver Lodge had applied for the agency and was appointed by Charlotte Fayle. Stephen Babington would call on Lodge to see how the agency was going and drive around the potteries with him. When that generation died out, Oliver's son (another Oliver) continued the selling of clay for Fayle's under Richard Pinney and S. J. Stiff. In 1912 Stiff was trying to get a complete revision of the terms of the agency, noting that the arrangement had never been an exclusive agency. Another dealer called Buckley was now offering an order for 5,000 tons of clay hoping to get their business.

Stiff thought he might offer an extra 3d per ton on the account, increasing the usual 9d to 1s per ton and give 6d each to Lodge and Buckley. Part of the agent's agreement was that while Lodge & Sons continued to sell Fayle's ball clays, they should not handle or deal in any other English ball clay. Stiff made the journey to Staffordshire to see Buckley and in a conversation with him found that some cancelled orders and lost customers were probably due to some slack work by Lodge whose main interest by then was his work as principal of Birmingham University. Despite that, the company were loath to change after so many years, and on 24 October Sydney Stiff wrote to Joseph Hughes, 'I quite agree that the *S.S.Alderney* had much better go to Ellesmere. I note Lodge has 375 tons at Runcorn, and will have 544 at Ellesmere or 919 tons in all. If he sells this amount in the next 6 weeks he will do well, and we ought to obtain another vessel in that period'. After all that, Lodge managed to retain the agency and its lucrative income. A sample payment was the £45 19s 3p received by Lodge for sales of Blue Clay in the quarter ended 30 June 1928. Lodge had obtained orders from 18 customers totalling 727 tons 6 cwt. It was his sons, Brodie and Alec who created Lodge Plugs Ltd, their father having received a knighthood in recognition of his scientific work in physics and radio.

Bill Salmon, son of the clay works manager, was responsible for some light relief from all the hard work. He was a good shot with an air rifle and his favourite trick was to creep up a working lane, take aim and shoot out the miners' candles. They could not understand what was happening, the sound of the gun firing being drowned out by the noise of the pneumatic spades. Over the years many types of spade were used, but all the miners the author spoke to were in agreement that the Holman 101 machine which became the standard, was the best for the job. Because it was a fast stroke spade, 3000 strokes per minute, it would bite straight into the clay and helped take the weight off the arms when using the machine above the head.

The compressed air system had two main advantages. Although the exhaust from the spades was not exactly fresh but somewhat 'oily', it did help to counteract bad air at the face. The other advantage was the introduction of air powered winches, commonly known as 'tuggers' for pulling wagons up gradients underground. Tuggers became a vital piece of equipment

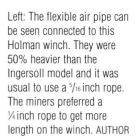

Left: The flexible air pipe can be seen connected to this Holman winch. They were 50% heavier than the Ingersoll model and it was usual to use a ⁵/₁₆ inch rope. The miners preferred a ¼ inch rope to get more length on the winch. AUTHOR

Right: On the floor of the workshop, an Ingersoll-Rand air winch or tugger was in for repair. The miners kept them well oiled to prevent breakdown delays, a serious issue when working at piecework rates. On the top can be seen the brake lever. The Ingersoll's had a dog clutch to take them out of gear, but later they had to be constant drive to comply with the law. AUTHOR

underground and some gangs would have up to 3 air winches depending on the situation. Sometimes a tugger was fixed at the bottom of a slope and pulled the wagon up by having the wire rope running over a pulley, which was welded to a girder at the top. Others were a straight pull up. When going down a gradient, sprags were used in the wheels the same way as above ground, and sometimes two sprags were needed to brake a wagon on a steep slope.

A disadvantage of air tools in confined spaces was that many of the miners at first suffered deafness from the noise. Spades were the least noisy machinery at 110 decibels, but two working together soon affected the ears without protectors, which were used in later years. Tuggers generated 130 decibels, but pumps were worse at 140 decibels, which was enough to induce giddiness. The pumps were mounted on a type of wagon frame, 22in gauge, so they could

be hand-trammed around the workings. An unexpected occurrence with the spades was the formation of ice. Because of the moisture in compressed air and its rapid passage through the machine, the exhaust ports could freeze up and it was not unknown for a piece of ice to shoot out. A good spade had shields over the exhaust! The temperature in a mine, such as No. 6 at Norden, varied from hot and humid in one place to a cooler more even temperature in another. This could be due to lack of oxygen or the presence of bad air, but most mines were generally constant, being cool in the summer and comfortably warm in the winter. Before 1950, headgear was usually only a beret and clothes were kept to a minimum, usually just trousers and a vest. If possible, a ventilation or air shaft was sunk in ground on a higher level to the main shaft, so that a difference in air pressure would cause some circulation of air around the mine.

Bottom left: Compressed air water pumps tended to be very noisy, a common one being the Mono. They were generally fixed to a frame with wheels fitted so they could be moved around more easily on the underground 22in gauge system. AUTHOR

Right: Tom Dorey was a miner with a reputation for safety and meticulous mining procedures. Tom was using an early type of spade in the 1950s and was wearing a beret, which was popular headgear in those days. Tom's beret was also used to sweep out wagons before loading to avoid any contamination of the clay. Miners were prone to deafness due to the high level of noise in the working environment. THOR TOOLS

In this 1920 photograph a group of people are joining a special train hauled by *Thames* to Goathorn for the dedication of the new church. AUTHOR

The education of the miners' children living near Newton and Goathorn was addressed by Fayle's, from about 1830. Over the years the number of children fluctuated and this influenced the provision made for their education. No records exist of the earliest days, but Fayle's had set up a private school for the workers children before 1880. This was at Goathorn near the pier, and held in one of the large sheds near the weighbridge, the company clerk being the schoolmaster. The children from Newton would have walked the mile or so by following the track, or had a ride on the train. When a loaded train arrived at the pier, the schoolmaster/clerk would give the children some work to get on with, and jump out of the classroom window to resume his clay weighing duties! The railway also ran an unofficial passenger service on Saturdays after work finished at 1 o'clock to enable the families to travel to Corfe Castle for shopping, and to visit a local public house.

However, by 1903 there was a different teaching arrangement for the children. Fayle's were then paying a rent to the Rempstone estate for the schoolhouse, cottage and garden of £10 per year. The pupils totalled 25, of which 9 were the children of Fayle employees. The schoolmistress from 1901 to 1912, possibly longer, was Miss Joyce, who received a salary of £26 5s per annum. Ellen Joyce started life in Fordingbridge, and by the 1901 Census was living at the schoolhouse at Goathorn. She was

then age 40, single and listed as the Governess at Public School. Her nearest professional colleague was Elizabeth Desallioud age 41, the schoolmistress at Bushey. When Ellen Joyce left, Miss Hart joined as teacher, the company paying her travel expenses of £1 2s 8d. Joseph Hughes, writing to Stiff about clay business matters on 18 June 1912, mentioned there were 12 children at the school, with 3 away sick. Miss Hart's salary was paid monthly, £2 18s 4d. She submitted a list of the 18 children attending Goathorn School on 30 June 1914, of which 12 had fathers working for Fayle's. The rest were farmers' children and one whose father had died. The Fayle children had familiar surnames, Cattle, Churchill, Tubb, Green and Parker. However, Miss Hart only stayed three years and was gone by June 1915, when the school prizes cost 14s. By then Miss E. Willett was schoolmistress.

A few years later in 1920 a large group of people were taken on a Fayle passenger train to Newton to celebrate the opening of a new Mission Church, fully reported in the Swanage Church magazine. In 1927, a new Rempstone clay lease gave Fayle's some valuable concessions. They were given free right of transport over the Norden and Goathorn Railway for all clay worked by the company, whether obtained on Capt Marston's land or at Norden. They could also carry over the railway without paying royalty, coal, bricks and cement for any persons and/or goods or any materials for the use of tenants of the Rempstone or Norden estates. The lessor (Marston) was anxious that the whole of the Norden to Goathorn railway should be maintained and handed over in good condition at the end of the lease. The lessees pointed out that, 'if at the end of the lease any portion of the railway were not then useful or necessary for the then existing clay business the landlord would be able to take over such portion without payment'. It was finally agreed that the lessees should accept a covenant to maintain the railway in proper working order throughout the lease, and the landlord should accept a covenant to pay for the whole line at the end of the lease.

By 1930, the children at Newton were walking to Studland to attend school, often in the dark, and all weathers. In 1932, the children had been kept off school for several months following complaints from the parents, and the Dorset County Council negotiated with Fayle's in an effort to get the children to school in the dry. The company agreed to convert a clay wagon, which was roofed over for the children to ride in, and in this way they were brought by rail from Newton to Arfleet, walking the last half mile or so to the school in Corfe Castle. So began a daily task for *Thames*, which went on for some years. Sometimes the children were dropped off near the trestle bridge over the Corfe River and had to

walk the remaining mile. By 1934 the train to Arfleet had been noticed by railway enthusiasts and was said to cost the Education Authority 7s 6d a day, which on average worked out at one penny per mile for each child, (i.e. 10 children x 9 miles). The train consisted of *Thames* pulling the 'passenger' coach made up of clay wagon No. 78, fitted with a brake and covered in by a wooden structure with a corrugated iron roof. Sometimes, if the sliding door was left open, 'Uncle' Frank surprised the children by letting steam from the engine blow in to fill the coach. The train reached Corfe Castle at 8.50am in the morning and returned at 4pm in the afternoon when the miners came off work, taking about 20 minutes in each direction. When *Thames* was out of service, Tommy, instead of finishing work at 4pm was expected to take the children home using *Tiny*. The children left school 15 minutes early to get to the train, and one or two of the workmen went home this way as well. Sometimes, when they got to 'Newton Nap' before the junction, Tommy would unhitch the train and shunt them on down the gradient and make a hasty retreat back to Norden. The school journey home was completed by gravity, the men applying the brake on the wagon as needed and also any pushing where the line levelled out. At

Thames with converted wagon No 78, which made up the school train from Goathorn to Corfe Castle. Four of the children were sisters from the Surface family, whose mother Lily was sister to Frank Tubb. The two girls standing beside the train were June, the eldest, and Joyce. The group between the coach and the locomotive consisted of Elsie on the left and Eileen on the right by the chimney. The boy's name was Fennel, and Pam Foot next to Eileen was a cousin. 1934. S. B. CORBETT

Thames and *Tiny* shunting at Norden sidings. The photographer, Roger Kidner, said of this photograph, 'As the Lewin engine propels a loaded train to Eldon's siding in August 1932, the Manning Wardle, which had drawn clear of the points with empties comes forward to take them across the road to the west pit.' Roger later agreed the date must have been his visit in 1938, the locomotives being too heavy to cross the bridges before that date. The large hut had been brought from Swanage, where it had seen use in the Great War and then used at Norden for some years as a mess room for the men.
R. W. KIDNER

the junction with the Newton tramway, a gate was put across the Norden line to stop cattle straying and one of the children used to jump out to open the gate for the train to pass. Not quite a 'slip coach' but certainly fly shunted. In 1936 the amount of clay being moved to Goathorn reduced considerably and the school train stopped running.

There was a small cottage at the pier occupied by the foreman. Drinking water for the house at the pier had to be delivered by train and a large barrel labelled 'Oporto' transported on a flat trolley was used for this purpose. There was a pump in the village, a short distance south of the engine shed, which supplied water for the locomotive, and also the residents.

Another group of adult visitors to the heath travelled on a special passenger train. On Wednesday 11 June 1930 about 70 people attended a visit to Fayle's clay pits, which was organised by the Dorset Natural History and Archaeological Society. Following their visit, a report in the annual proceedings said that the members had arrived by train at Corfe Castle station at 10.45am, and W. R. G. Bond led the assembled party to the clay pits, where S. J. Stiff welcomed them. He pointed out the clay in the pit face and stated some facts concerning the company. After the talk, the members took their places on a clay-wagon train arranged by Stiff, and set off on the light railway for a trip to Goathorn Point. They were the largest party to travel the line. After lunch various groups set off to study the birds, plant life and insects of the area. After an enjoyable afternoon the group took their seats on the train and steamed back to Corfe Castle for tea with the Stiffs at Norden House.

On 24 November 1930, Sydney Stiff reported to the shareholders that the year 1929 had been very unfortunate for the company. Recession was still affecting business world wide, and in order to get out the remainder of the clay at Arfleet it had been necessary to divert the Corfe River for a short distance. This diversion proved very expensive as the cutting of the new channel proved to be through old made ground formed of the rubble excavated when the pit on the Norden side of the river was worked in about 1870 to 1880. This ground slid into the cut as it progressed and a very large amount of material had to be excavated to complete the cut. However, the cost of diverting the river paid off, when close to and underneath the old riverbed, 5,000 tons of best blue clay was raised during 1930.

A ride on the train was always a novelty, many trips being made by the family, the adults mentioned above and children when on holiday.

The Stiff's photograph albums showed the happy outings en route and at Goathorn Pier. Some local cubs had an interesting time during a visit in 1930 and also one holiday in 1935. A memorable picnic at Goathorn took place on 2 August that year when a party of Wolf Cubs from Oldfeld School, Swanage were granted a ride by S. J. Stiff. The cubs joined the train at Claywell level crossing, during a special camp for 10 days on Rempstone Heath. The trip to Goathorn was offered instead of a visit to the clay works. The teacher in charge was Humphrey G. W. Household, an enthusiast of narrow gauge lines and we are indebted to his exceptionally clear photographs of the train that day. Humphrey later wrote to the author, 'the happy memory remains very vivid still, but alas, some of those cubs lost their lives in the 1939-45 war'.

The remains of Middlebere pier, seen on 1 August 1930. The only activity was that of the scouts from Oldfeld School, Swanage, on a visit from their Round Island camp to have a picnic. Apart from seabirds, the pier had seen few visitors in 23 years and its decking had rotted away. The timber frame that would have supported the clay chute for loading the barges still pointed defiantly skyward, but it was a vain gesture, as the clay by then was travelling on another route. In a few more years, the timbers were gone, claimed by the incessant tides. H. G. W. HOUSEHOLD

Tiny at Norden shed with the Wolf Cubs, on Thursday, 1 August 1935. Humphrey Household who was in charge of the 10-day camp in wonderful weather wrote, 'examining *Tiny* at the shed near Corfe before going along the line to Norden, and then across the heath to Blue Pool'.
H. G. W. HOUSEHOLD

Thames is standing at Claywell crossing waiting for the Wolf Cubs to get on board. A fine day has been chosen for the picnic at Goathorn, on Friday 2 August 1935, and the train is made up of clay wagons, No 87, 104 and 89. *Thames* always ran with bunker towards Goathorn, and like *Tiny*, had to run round trains before shunting at the pier The iron rings attached to the wagons were used when shunting wagons on an adjacent line to the locomotive. A wire rope on the engine had a hook, which engaged with the iron rings, and attaching them was one of the jobs of the 'rope-runner'.
H. G. W. HOUSEHOLD

Preparations are being made for the return run to Claywell. The cubs have begun to board the train and Frank is making a last check. A steamer is waiting in the right background to load clay. H. G. W. HOUSEHOLD

Entrance to drift mine, East Holme. AUTHOR

After some 30 years in charge, Stiff was feeling the need for more assistance in the management. Frank Pinney Longmire, (Richard Pinney's nephew) had been working as a metallurgist for the Rio Tinto Company in Huelva, Spain, and the family shareholders insisted he should retire and take over the management of the Norden company. He and S. J. Stiff continued to work together until after the Second World War, when it was agreed that Cecil Ellis, a descendant of the Adams family should enter the business, but he stayed only to 1948. It was Frank who introduced the use of inclines or drift mines, the first being started soon after he arrived in August 1935. The main advantage of the incline, or tunnel as they were called locally, was that several wagons of clay forming a train or rake could be pulled out of the mine at once, instead of a single wagon as in a shaft. The safety aspect was also increased, because the miners could walk out of the workings in case of an accident, instead of having to climb ladders or exit via an airshaft. Over the years seven tunnel mines were recorded at Norden none of which had names, being simply numbered 1 to 7. The image of the mine had not changed much but the sound had. The quiet of the countryside was now broken by the intermittent thumping of the compressors and the singing of wire rope on steel rollers as sets of small wagons disappeared at speed into the bowels of the earth.

The incline No. 1 tunnel was built of timber similar in construction to a vertical shaft, except for the angle it entered the ground. In error, the tunnel was angled down too steeply, so at the bottom a vertical shaft had to be built up 20 feet to bring the miners to the required clay working area. At a later date lanes were driven off at both levels. The incline was on the south side of the tramway, near Little Copse, and because it was close to the railway, the clay was loaded direct from the mine stage into the 3ft 9in wagons. In effect the waiting wagons were blocking the main line, so Eli with the horses would shunt the loaded wagons into the nearby siding leading to No. 8 mine. This allowed him to go up to No. 12

A Warwick was a device projecting upwards between the track, its purpose being to derail any runaway wagons in a drift mine. It was usually fixed just below the top of the incline. When wagons were ready to go down the mine the winch winder pulled a lever, which through a connecting wire lowered the Warwick and allowed free passage of the empties into the tunnel. AUTHOR

In this photo of miners at No. 12 shaft, taken in 1933, Gordon Lillington, who lent me the photograph was kneeling on the left, age 16. The others in the group from the left are Jim Best, Bill Foot, Bill Tatchell and Harris Griffiths, with Charlie 'Mama' Welsh (born 1900) standing with hands on knees. Gordon was runner for Charlie and Harris for 6 or 7 years until he was called up. Bernard Penney, who took the photo, was runner for Jim Best and Bill Foot. Bill Tatchell was the mine tipper and he had previously worked in the Arfleet cutting pit.

Runaway wagons were not uncommon and the miners remained fairly tight-lipped when reporting such accidents. Wagons that came to grief presented quite a major repair job for the carpenters. AUTHOR

shaft to do any other shunting and then pick up the full ones at No. 8 on the way back. Wilf Stockley said the haulage at No. 1 was wound using a large compressed air tugger and larger wagons than usual were used carrying about 1 ton of clay. The men also rode down in the wagons, but this practice was later banned because of the risk of a run-a-way train. Wilf recalled one occasion when the empty wagon, held back by the rope, was pushed over the top of the slope by the winder, Charlie Brinton. Just as the miners were about to get in, the rope parted allowing the wagon to run away down the tunnel, (In some inclined mines there would be two drives, one for men movement and one for materials, but in Purbeck the practice was a single

incline per mine.) Little account was taken of safety in those days, but post-war, more stringent rules were introduced, such as regular measurements of wire ropes, and earlier replacement times.

In a survey of working methods carried out in 1938 by Frank Longmire, on the question of haulage on the surface he said, 'It seems quite unnecessary to employ horses'. This was the conclusion from a time study he had carried out, showing how rapidly the work could be done using the small locomotive.

> Started from weigh cabin with 10 wagons at 10.15am pushed these ten without difficulty to mines. Side tracked empties and got out fulls leaving them in loop, pushed up empties and started back with full at 11am. Came down on brake of loco quite easily, shunted out 2 wagons of bad clay 11.08am, arrived with full and put on weighbridge at 11.12am. Round trip 57 minutes.

To do the same work three horses would be needed and two men, while the damage done by the horses' feet to the track added to repair costs. 'Using the locomotive we should at least economise one man if not two. How soon can we get rid of the horses?' No. 1 incline closed by 1946.

Changes were also being made to improve clay transport underground. In 1936, a 70ft shaft had been sunk in Little Copse, which became No. 10 by 1938 and worked all through the war. From that time on, new mines had ladders installed in a small shaft adjoining the main haulage, and heavier timbers became standard, 6ft long and 6in square section, giving a working shaft 5ft square. The cars or clay boxes remained in use after the shafts were enlarged, but being unguided they tended to swing around causing possible damage. The cars were then enlarged, because in 1938 in a letter to the Divisional Inspector of Mines, they were referred to as a box 26in square containing approximately 3¼ cwt. Frank Longmire took the decision to replace the trolley and box system with larger box shaped wagons complete with wheels. These were hand-trammed as before, and the whole unit winched up the shaft. Each wagon had a metal strap round the centre of each long side, pierced with an eye both sides, which could be clipped to a spreader bar on the main rope for the lift up the shaft. The lifting mechanism was guided up and down the shaft by two vertical fixed wire ropes, which gave much better control of the movement. The tension on the fixed ropes could be adjusted at the pithead.

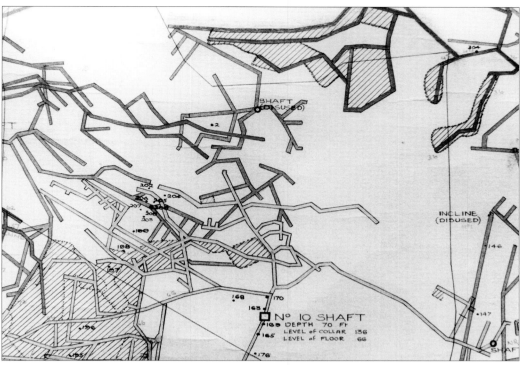

Underground works map of No 10 shaft. The drawing maps the working lanes radiating from the shaft, often dated to show the mining progress. The direction of underground roadways was plotted using a mining compass or dial, applying a correction to the magnetic reading to find true north. Apart from the natural magnetic variation, known as declination, which changed gradually from year to year, the magnetic readings could be influenced by the presence of steel or rails in the mine. Distances had to be measured accurately. Steel rules were in common use, but traditionally the Imperial chain was used, made up of 100 links. A chain, made of the finest mild steel measured 66 feet, so each link was 7.92 inches long. In case of accident underground, an accurate map could pinpoint the position from the surface. ECC BALL CLAYS LTD.

A Norden wagon of the clip on type, known as shaft wagons they were smaller capacity to the standard underground type. They were the same gauge 22in, but the load was 7.5 to 8cwt instead of the 11.5cwt standard. AUTHOR

An empty wagon with eye and clip fastenings attached, about to return underground. JOHN LOAKES

Because subsidence in the area affected the surface tramway, No. 10 shaft when built was not directly connected to the 3ft 9in system. Clay at the pithead was transferred into wagons that were horse hauled to the clay main line, adding 2d or more to a ton of clay. It was decided to save these costs by laying new track to the mine and shunting the wagons using the small locomotive. This made it possible to eliminate the horses and also two men. No. 10 shaft eventually flooded, and was closed in 1958. It was also decided to bring the blacksmith's shop alongside the compressors where he could carry out small repairs quickly and attend engines in case of emergency.

By 1940, No. 2 incline was working to the south of No. 10 shaft and going towards West Hill, but no records have been found. Just to the west of No. 12 shaft a new incline No. 3 was built having the main haulage tunnel in a westerly direction. It was unusual because the haulage was later extended round a bend, and on down another incline in a north west direction to a second bottom. When empties were being let down, the wire rope ran round the bend on rollers set in the side of the tunnel. To haul full wagons out, one of the runners had to rush up the tunnel to the bend and loop the rope around another set of rollers between the railway lines. This enabled a smooth pullout for the wagons. Incline No. 3 was driven during 1944-5 by Bert Tubbs and Sonner Dorey according to George Fry who helped to sink it, the spoil being brought to the surface using a compressed air winch operated by him. It became the second mine where wagons were hauled using a rope attached to the locomotive. Eli said that No. 3 tunnel was situated between 12 shaft and No. 6 tunnel, which came later. The tunnel was all timber construction, and done in rather a hurry because the company needed the clay. Tommy Stockley used to pull the wagons out and tip them into the old 'broad gauge' wooden wagons. The filled wagons were allowed to run down towards No. 12 mine into a dead end siding. At that time *Thames* was the locomotive in normal use. Eli reported, 'There was a lot of mucking about at No. 3'. A wire rope was attached to the train of full wagons, taken round a wheel in a frame, and attached to *Thames*. While the engine was going down the main line towards 12, the wagons were pulled up and out of the siding. When they got up far enough, Eli's runner had to put a sprag in the wheel to hold them there, so the train could

be attached direct to the locomotive. 'That was a job.' The working described here was reminiscent of what happened underground where wagons were pulled up a gradient, when the winch was situated at the foot of the gradient and the wire rope ran round a pulley at the top. No. 3 tunnel survived into the narrow gauge era to be worked by *Russell*, and presumably with the re-laid track the rope working described by Eli was then eliminated.

Until those happy memories of 1935, described by Humphrey Household, several loads of clay were taken daily to Goathorn, depending on shipping arrivals, but this gradually reduced until 1937 when the line saw little use. Roger Kidner said he visited in Easter that year, and found *Tiny* doing its usual chores between the Norden pits and Eldon's Siding, with *Thames* and the school coach in the shed (the coach being redundant by that date). It seems likely that this was actually Roger's 1938 visit after bridge 15 had been upgraded and is born out by his photographs. In the same year all the clay workers from Newton and Goathorn were moved to jobs around the Norden Works, and Frank Tubb later became the foreman of the open pit, and when that finished he was made foreman at the east sidings. The tradition of small coastal trading vessels under sail was coming to an end and with another war imminent the line to Goathorn was sold back to Major Dudley Ryder (then owner) of Rempstone and was lifted in 1939. The Admiralty requisitioned Rempstone House for use during the war and any remaining residents on the heath were evacuated from the area by 1942. This action allowed defence experiments to take place on the beach at Studland and war practice across the entire heathland east of the Wareham to Corfe Castle road. Much of this was a prelude to the D-day landings. Since that time, the formation of the old railway has been slowly obliterated by encroaching nature. The Newton section of the line to Goathorn was the second clay railway in Purbeck to celebrate its centenary, having been in use for at least 107 years.

Tiny needed repairs in 1938, carried out by the Dorset Iron Foundry. On 5 September, Hunslet had quoted the foundry for a copper fire box, loco unknown. This seems to have been rejected, because the record of spare parts supplied by Bagnall's to Fayle's of Corfe Castle included a copper firebox, invoiced on 20 September 1938. F. H. Wood, who had become

Chief Draughtsman at Bagnall's kept a spare drawing, No. 24193, of the box in their records. The overall dimensions of the box were 1ft 11¹/₈in long, 1ft 6½in wide and 2ft 4¼in high and it was supplied un-drilled. If the 1897 boiler had been looked after, it should have been in good enough condition to fit the new firebox in 1938.

While *Tiny* was out of action, *Thames* carried out shunting duties to Eldon's Siding, but only after the track had been lowered about four inches under Willsbridge. Between 1937 and 1947 both locomotives were kept and used at Norden, but as mentioned earlier, *Tiny* could only manage 4 loaded wagons up the grade over the Swanage line. Both engines began to suffer from lack of maintenance during the war years. By 1941, bridge No. 15 was upgraded again so either locomotive could be used over it and the working roster could be more flexible. For example, in 1943 the steam boiler at No. 12 mine failed and a special line was laid in so *Tiny* could be positioned as a stationary steam generator operating the winch hauling wagons to the surface. *Tiny* was fitted with a 10ft high chimney, but the 'Loco' only steamed efficiently while moving in normal use, so the change over to electric haulage at the mine resulted. *Thames* did all the clay haulage while *Tiny* was stationary. After 1945, when the line to Goathorn might have been re-instated, it had become more cost effective to send clay by the Southern Railway, or by lorries direct to the consumer. Following the closure of the pier at Goathorn, clay for export was sent via Norden siding. Trucks of clay departed from the siding on the short journey by rail to Poole Quay and from there it was loaded into ships to Italy, Beirut, Finland and many other countries.

Tiny, bringing a short train across bridge 15, August 1938. Eli Kitcatt and Ernie Petter are on the footplate and the first wagon is filled with picked clay from underground. There are two wagons loaded with lumps of cut clay, probably from the open pit. R. W. KIDNER

Looking over Willsbridge, this was the view of the east works and sidings with Corfe Castle dominating the scene. The mill and Cattle Creep can be seen, with a small diesel and wagons near the new weighbridge and the Swanage branch on the right. Beyond Cattle Creep, and in front of Castle hill, can be seen the wooded section that the clay trains passed through on their journey to and from the mines, situated off to the right. The track in the foreground went under the bridge to Eldon's clay siding. Just to the left of the weighbridge can be seen the line curving away leading to the engine shed, which was originally the start of the line to Goathorn. DENNIS CULLUM

CHAPTER NINE

Post-war, a new era begins
1946 and a slow return to normality

During the Second World War, production of ball clay in the UK came under the jurisdiction of the British Ball Clay Federation, formed in May 1941. Their function was to co-ordinate clay output to meet Government needs while the war lasted. Ball clay mining at Fayle's relied on the existing shafts 10 and 12, and the incline No. 3. There was also a short-lived shaft numbered 11 (about 1941 to 1947), of which little record seems to have survived. The shaft was situated up under the hill, like the later No. 16, but opposite the compressor house. George Allingham had worked there for two years before being called up, but it was closed on his return in 1949. When the war ended, there were delays in returning to full production due to the clearing of land used for war practice and for it to be released from requisition by the Admiralty. The Norden clay washing beds were not declared clear of unexploded ammunition until a letter arrived from the Admiralty Surveyor of Lands dated 25 May 1946, allowing their release from requisition on 1 June 1946. The letter emphasised the possibility of strange objects coming to light at a later date. Fayle's workers were instructed not to touch any such objects but to mark their position and report the matter to the police or the Commanding Officer of H.M.S. Purbeck, at Rempstone Hall.

Most of the stimulus for future production as far as Fayle's was concerned came through Frank Longmire who had by then nearly ten years of experience at Norden. John Cooper, the son-in-law of Frank Longmire, also became available. John had been doing some quarry development work in the chalk industry near Basingstoke, using Atritor plant to pulverise the chalk. He had been expecting to take up a job in South Africa, but was persuaded to join Fayle's in April 1948, on a salary of £50 a month. Stiff died shortly after John joined the company. Clay getting and processing was about to change dramatically from traditional methods and the movement of larger amounts of mineral demanded a more efficient internal railway.

Before the industry could get into production following the disruption caused by the war, there

Prospecting at Norden, near No 6 mine. AUTHOR

was a need for more prospecting. A program of test core drilling was initiated to determine the extent, quality and configuration of any new clay deposits to be extracted or deep mined. By 1953, after the merger with Pike Bros., the company had three hand-operated rigs in use, which were considered to give the best results, but the process was slow. By 1960 the hand drill had been partly mechanised. In later years, tractor driven drills followed by purpose built power rigs arrived, with a total of 6 rigs in 1982. The cost of drilling, which was calculated per foot of hole drilled, had increased significantly and became an important factor when calculating overall costs. Each hole drilled could normally be completed in 10 to 14 days and the borehole data covered an area of 40 square miles.

According to the workers, the L&SWR. and Southern Railway had not allowed clay to be tipped into their trucks at Eldon's Siding, all clay having to be shovelled between wagons. When British Railways was formed in 1948 the practice of tipping was allowed. Longmire decided to build a high level tranship shed at Eldon's siding to make the transfer of clay to the mainline easier, but realised that the existing 3ft 9in wagons would be too heavy to manhandle. It was decided to convert the remaining track around Norden to the more common industrial gauge of 2ft or to be more exact, 1ft 11½in (60cm). Clay could then be

The weighbridge is unoccupied for a few minutes waiting for a clay train to arrive from the mines. A few empty wagons, including No 56 stand in the loop. Above the left side of 56 can be seen the entrance to the mill in the background, which was accessed via a turntable in the loop. Showing over the top of the wagon is the timber structure built over the line at Cattle Creep. 31 August 1964. GEORGE MOON

In the line of wagons at the siding the two next to No 56 appear to be fairly new. They had probably been repainted to improve their appearance after refurbishment. The train was made up of wagons, 56, 14, 26, 92, 93, 27, 20, 19, 101 and 6. 31 August 1964. GEORGE MOON

Another view of the clay mill, with wagon 56 and Cattle Creep showing above the wagons. It was quite common to see discarded wagon bodies, in this case No 118 and 108 on the left. AUTHOR

tipped directly into the main line trucks using V-shaped steel skips. By December 1947 a new weigh house was being built nearer to Willsbridge and this remained in use until the railway closed in 1972. Designed at first for 3ft 9in and then converted, it retained both sets of rails in position on the weighbridge until the line closed. John Cooper said a considerable amount of rail was purchased for the line conversion and Frank Longmire had ordered about 50 1½ cu yd skips as well as a small Simplex locomotive to propel them. The company records state the size of wagon as 1½ cu yd but in reality the wagons were all invoiced from various suppliers as 36 cu ft or 1.33 cu yd.

During March 1948 a delivery was made to

Norden, by C. & L. Barter of Waddock, Dorchester of 429 yards of railway line, and two sets of points. Eliza Tinsley & Co. supplied about a ton of rail dog spikes in several orders during 1948 and as an example, 5 cwt of 2½in x ⁵⁄₁₆in genuine Clyde Dogspikes cost £10. However, progress was halted when John calculated that the main problem with the locomotive was likely to be the brake power needed for the heavier loads of clay then being moved, particularly at the main road crossing which was becoming busier with traffic during the summer. A small diesel did not have enough adhesion to cope, and a heavier steam locomotive might be needed, so Longmire said to John Cooper, 'You can find the loco!' After a scan of sales of war surplus equipment, John found just what was needed at a Ministry of Supply auction, held at Weyhill, Andover between 21 and 26 April, 1948. *Russell*, Ministry of Supply property No. 157215, located at its last place of work in Oxfordshire, was quite a substantial engine of its type and John was able to secure it for £100. On 26 May Coupar Transport completed the delivery of the locomotive to Norden, and *Russell* was then kept on a short length of track until the gauge was changed. The cost of haulage from the Brymbo Co. Ltd, Hook Norton, Banbury to Wareham works was £42 10s.

On 13 April, George Cohen delivered a further 8 tons of rails, consisting of 60 30ft lengths of good second hand, 30lb rail at £17 per ton. In June 1948, Frank made another crucial

purchase for the works. In another Ministry of Supply sale, organised by the Directorate of Disposals, he noticed and was able to acquire a Bailey Bridge for £270. In Fayle's ledger it was marked, 'For Siding' and the bridge would be ideal for converting to the new transhipment shed. They had recently erected another shed at Eldon's Siding, Corfe Castle, which required a railway flagman to be present, and the Southern Railway invoice dated 5 May 1948 for £18 8s 1d was to cover expenses in connection with the safety provision. Looking at Southern Region charges, it is of interest to see how much Fayle's were paying in 1948 for clay despatched from the Norden siding. The amounts paid for 'carriage on clay' were February £1,954 0s 1d, March £1,903 17s 11d, April £1,616 14s 11d, May

The weighbridge still carries the rails from the 3ft 9in era. The new lines set to a gauge of 1ft 11½in were fastened to sleepers laid between the original track. 19 May 1966. GEORGE MOON

Russell arrives in 1948, stored on a short piece of track at Norden. It was a dull day on 12 June and the evening light was nearly gone. J. H. ASTON

£1,384 11s 8d, June £1,565 19s 11d and July £1,722 7s 4d, so this was valuable income to the railway company. Fayle's paid £1 5s per quarter for the rent of the siding at that time. They also paid £1 1s for a Christmas gift for the staff at Corfe Castle station and on 9 February 1949, had 50 sleepers delivered at the siding for a cost of £17 10s. The Dorset Ironfoundry were invaluable in the railway maintenance department. In July 1948, they had charged Fayle's £34 19s 2d for

cutting 8 own axles, removing ball races and pressing off wheels on one end of axle. Machining axles to suit wheels ball races and nuts. Pressing on wheels, fitting races and nuts, new slit pins, greasing bearings and fitting caps.

This would appear to have been for re-gauging the axles, probably for wagons to be used on the new line.

While all the changes were being implemented to the railway system, John Cooper was considering future clay sales and the appointing of agents. Commission was usually paid on a quarterly basis, and the rate had gradually increased over the years being 1s 3d per ton for most of the 1930s. Fayle's again came under pressure to change their agent to P. E. Hines who acted for Pike's and were already selling more clay for Fayle's than Lodge. Frank Longmire was also loath to leave Lodge after so many years, so he decided to split the selling and commission due to Lodge between the two

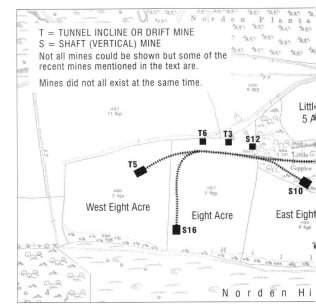

T = TUNNEL INCLINE OR DRIFT MINE
S = SHAFT (VERTICAL) MINE
Not all mines could be shown but some of the recent mines mentioned in the text are.

Mines did not all exist at the same time.

agents and continued sending cheques to Lodge until 1949. At that time the rate paid for Best blue clay sold was 1s 9d per ton and Lodge received cheques for about 60% of the amount they had sold and P. E. Hines had the balance added to their sales.

In the early days of ball clay mining, very little processing of the raw material was done. Apart from the weathering process, which was supposed to increase the plasticity of the clay, customers bought their clay in lump form direct from the beds, dried in heated sheds, or purified in wash ponds. Dorset clay straight from the

Russell arrived at Norden 12 June 1948 awaiting refurbishment. This view was looking toward Corfe Castle, with East Hill in the background. J. H. ASTON.

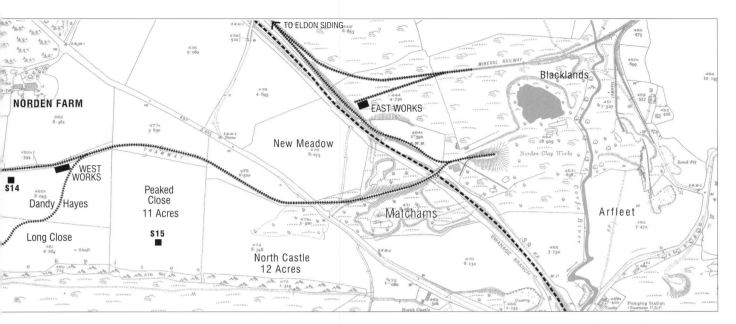

This photo shows the turntable near Cattle Creep which led into the high level section of the mill and the girders left from demolition of the mill. The mill came into use after the war when customers' requirements changed. Previously, clay was just weathered and sent out in re-dug lump form, but at the mill it was dried and shredded. After blending, the clay was powdered and bagged. Also visible are three of the flat wagons used for the transfer of bagged clay to the weighbridge. AUTHOR

Below: Inside the old mill were some of the flat wagons with loads of heather. Back in the 1890s it was cut on the heath by local small holders and sold to the clay works for a pittance. 3 July 1968. GEORGE MOON

Below right: The turntable showing its origin in 3ft 9in days with the 'broad gauge' rails still attached. It was made locally at the Poole Foundry and converted to 1ft 11½in for use at the mill entrance. AUTHOR

The mines shown in the area below Norden Hill are No 5 incline in West Eight Acres, No 16 shaft in Eight Acres, No 10 shaft in Little Copse and No 4 incline in East Eight Acres. The clay works were situated beside the main tramway in Dandy Hay until the branch to No 4 was built, when its situation was in the fork of the tracks. The east works and sidings near the Swanage branch has the mill building shown near Cattle Creep. The powdered clay was bagged and shipped via Eldon's siding. AUTHOR

Frank Longmire was standing on the right, with *Russell* and other friends. SHEILAH COOPER (NÉE LONGMIRE)

would be easier to handle. It would eliminate the weathering process, which had never been proved essential in maintaining the clay's plasticity. These changes in processing the raw material resulted in a clay milling plant being built in the summer of 1948, near Cattle Creep just before the change to 1ft 11½in gauge. A small turntable was built into a loop on the clay siding which was on a convenient embankment at that point, so wagons of clay came straight from the weighbridge and were turned into the upper part of the mill. A Ferguson tractor with a power lift was used to load the shredder and to blend or mix the shredded clay, which was then transferred on a conveyor to the mill. The average moisture content at this stage was 17%, and after heating and milling this would be reduced to 3%. A fan was used to blow hot air into the Atritor, which consisted of two revolving notched wheels, interlaced and moving at high speed in opposite directions and very close proximity. The atritors were very powerful machines manufactured by Alfred Herbert of Coventry, originally used to pulverise coal but adapted for clay. About 3 tons of clay an hour could be powdered in this plant to 300 mesh, or finer for refractories, depending on the type of clay. A small service railway about 18in gauge was used to bring bagged clay out of the mill, where it emerged at the lower level and was loaded onto flat wagons. The loaded wagons were hauled away toward the engine shed(s), and then up to

mine would have a moisture content of 10 to 15% and from an opencast pit, 10 to 20% moisture. At 18 to 20% some clays became sticky and difficult to handle in the loading of wagons, lorries or the hold of a ship. At Norden a large drying shed was erected near Willsbridge, where clay was subjected to natural drying by the current of air passing through louvre windows, the time taken depending on the velocity and initial dryness of the air and also the time of year. Dorset clay would only dry naturally between late May and September. The tramways were kept busy transferring clay around the works and to loading points for customers.

In 1948, it was decided to adapt machines used in the agricultural industry such as the turnip cutter to develop new machinery for shredding ball clay. The shredded product would become the primary material, which could then be blended using clays from different mines. The clay could then be dried further to a controlled moisture content, or milled to a fine powder to produce a more standardised product which

The track at Norden showing signs from the change of gauge. The conversion was achieved by moving one of the rails inwards to the new position on the sleepers. GEORGE MOON

Bridge 15, showing the decking, which illustrates how the line was built up to make it more level using a mat of sleepers with extra strengthening. The new level can be compared to the gradient of the original incline over the bridge, which was about equivalent to the sloping handrails. Despite this work, the 1ft 11½in track was still on a fairly steep gradient and it can been seen on the other side leveling out to a dead end near the power line. The train reversed at that point and ran off to the left, running parallel to the Swanage line towards Cattle Creep and the transfer siding. 19 May 1966. GEORGE MOON

the weighbridge for recording, before being loaded on to the main line. Bagged clay was also stored in the railway siding shed, up to 1,000 tons stacked under cover for future shipments via the Swanage branch, each bag stamped with its lot number and the 'Made in England' legend.

Frank Longmire, who had been used to an extensive railway system at Rio Tinto, was quite excited about *Russell* and used to show the engine off to all his friends. The change of gauge was put in the diary to be carried out over the August Bank Holiday in 1948, but August was not the ideal time from the road traffic point of view, so the re-gauging was put off until October. It was a fairly easy task for most of the track. One of the rails was simply detached from the existing sleepers and moved inwards to the new gauge position of 1ft 11½in. Balancing the track and making the sleepers even was done later. Various problems arose, which had been forseen by the clay company and were dealt with before the date reserved for the gauge change. Firstly, the 3ft 9in rails on the skew bridge over the Swanage branch had been laid on longitudinal supports. For the narrower gauge the bridge had to be decked with oak, with occasional steel girders and sleepers

Tiny with *Thames* behind after the two engines had been withdrawn. They were stored temporarily on a length of track near the main road at Norden. AUTHOR

Tiny and *Thames* awaiting disposal. R. T. RUSSELL/ NATIONAL RAILWAY MUSEUM

ground as waste clay was tipped or moved. A merger with Pike Bros. was imminent. *Tiny* was dismantled in November 1948 and the boiler, which was in good condition was later transferred to Furzebrook, to replace the old boiler of *Tertius* one of the locomotives on the Pike's 2ft 8in system. John Burgess, who was a fitter at Pike's, assisted Charlie Tubbs with the boiler work in 1951. The remains of *Tiny* were scrapped about April 1949 and *Thames* was reported sent to Cohens for scrap about the same time. However, one of the company ledgers records that Pollock Brown & Co. Ltd, paid £55 5s for '*Thames* Loco' on 27 January 1949.

With the increasing post war demand for clay, three more vertical shafts were quickly sunk, Nos.14, 15 and 16, which were all rail served. Most Purbeck clay mines employed individual direct haulage to bring the wagons to the surface. Norden was unusual in having two pairs of mines, and at a later date, four mines with a shared haulage. As noted elsewhere, the two mines that were first operated together had been Nos. 8 and 12, and their winding house was close to the original Ingersoll compressor house in Little Copse. However, after No. 8 shaft closed it was decided to connect No. 10 shaft with 12, and these two shafts were operated in tandem from a new winding house situated beside the clay railway, just to the east of No. 12 mine. Because of its position in relation to the winding house, wagons from mine No. 12 had normal direct pullout. The wire rope to No. 10 was taken around a horizontal pulley wheel, 3ft diameter, in a wooden frame fixed to the top of a rail driven into the ground. The pulley wheel directed the rope up over the clay railway and toward No. 10 shaft, a short distance away, then over the vertical pulley above the mine stage and down to the wagon lift. It was a single shaft mine, with ladders installed beside the shaft and was in effect, a mirror image of No. 12 mine. *Russell* was higher than the older Norden locomotives and it became necessary to cut out part of the galvanised cladding at mines such as No. 12 so the locomotive could pass under the loading stage.

The extra height of the loco also caused an amusing incident, one day in 1952, which Eli related with some relish. The haulage rope from No. 10 mine, over the tramway was only just high enough to clear passing traffic. One morning, Eli was passing and noticed the rope seemed lower than usual and actually caught on *Russell's* cab. Thinking to have some fun he went on slowly

between, the decking preventing any lumps of clay falling on the Swanage branch trains. The rails were then laid to 1ft 11¼in gauge on the 6in timbers. The Southern Railway eventually submitted their charge for attending the work on 15 October; expenses incurred in re-decking of Bridge 15, for supervision, and flagging, wages £14 10s 11d, plus 5% general superintendence 14s 7d, a total of £15 5s 6d. Secondly, where the clay line crossed the Wareham to Corfe Castle A351 road, the track bed had to be dug up with co-operation of Wareham Town Council, starting about 3 or 4am one day. Under lighting, a new bed of oak sleepers was laid to support the rails and the check rails. The Council's charge for the work, invoiced on 18 October was £43 1s 5d. When the line closed in 1972 the crossing was covered over with tarmac and, probably because it was no longer visible, remained in position as late as 1997.

Tiny and *Thames* were then retired and laid up on short lengths of track for a final decision on their future. The wagons were scrapped by being run away down one of the old pit inclines towards the Corfe River to be covered by waste clay. When they realised what had happened Newbery (Pond), the Wareham blacksmiths, obtained permission from the company and made regular visits to recover iron fittings for re-use at their forge. It seems likely that some of those fittings were re-forged and used on 12 wagons then being built for Pike's railway. For some years until 1970, wheel sets from the old 3ft 9in wagons would re-appear from the burial

Russell in a siding near the west works. The blacksmith workshop is the building in the left background. AUTHOR

Russell receiving attention outside the engine shed at Norden. The front bogie had been removed and left beside the track because it was thought to be contributing to the many derailments suffered by the locomotive.
HUGH BALLANTYNE

Russell steams past the old No. 3 mine with No. **12 shaft** in the background. J. I. C. BOYD

which had the effect of raising the box in No. 10 shaft. The result was shouts of surprise and a few expletives from 'Wibble' Welsh, the tipper on the stage.

At first the dual operation was steam powered, the two mines being wound together using a continuous wire rope, one end serving No. 10 shaft with some turns of the rope round the drive shaft, and then back to No. 12 mine. The signal to operate the winch was either a shout or a hammer blow on some metal piping at the mine. If no tipper was available, the winder, who for a long time was Hubert Coffen, had to leave the winding house and go up and down to the stage to empty the clay, which was tipped straight over the edge into the waiting railway wagons. The empty was then returned underground. When one of the mines had a wagon at the surface, the other was at the bottom. The system was later changed so that each mine had its own rope.

When the haulage was later converted to diesel and then electric power, about 1948, the layout of the winding shed was changed so that four mines could be accommodated, and for some time No. 3 incline and No. 14 shaft were wound from the shed, as well as 10 and 12. Before being added to the system, No. 3 incline had been using a winding engine driven by compressed air. To facilitate the change, a single

drive shaft, running the length of the shed was installed, powered by a 12½hp electric motor. The shaft was turning continuously and was fitted with four pairs of fixed gear wheels, facing four winch units. Each winch unit was able to travel in its main bearing, so at one end of its travel it could engage the main drive shaft and at the other extremity a brake system. The movement of each winch was controlled by a five-sixteenth inch wire connecting the unit via a hole in the roof of the shed to its appropriate mine stage. The tipper could then operate his mine without leaving the stage, simply by pulling a lever. When a wagon was ready to be wound up the shaft, the wire was operated to bring the winch into gear with the constant shaft and thus bring the clay to the surface. At this point, letting off the control wire allowed the winch to return to the brake position. After tipping the clay, the winch was partly disengaged from the brake system using the wire control, which allowed the wagon to return to the bottom of the shaft, or incline. The mine haulage ropes from each winch were ½in diameter and passed through holes cut in the side of the shed, or around low level pulleys, toward the mine. As before, the haulage to No. 12 shaft and No. 3 incline were more or less direct through the side of the shed, but to reach Nos.10 and 14 shafts the ropes went by the fixed frames and pulleys. Even nature played its

No 12 mine looking west, in 1968. By then it had a dedicated winding house. In the background can be seen the drift mine No 6. To take this view the photographer was almost standing in the track leading to the disused No10 shaft.
MICHAEL MESSENGER

part! A convenient oak tree was used to support the pulley, which angled the haulage rope towards No. 14.

Underground lighting was improved in 1949 using carbide/acetylene gas lamps attached to helmets, instead of working by candlelight. Originally, the miners had to buy their own candles from local grocers, but by the 1940s the candles were supplied direct by Price's Patent Candle Co. Battersea, usually in 6 case lots. A case of candles cost 60s 9d in 1948. A hurricane lamp had been tried in an effort to improve lighting, but that consumed the oxygen too rapidly. Until that time the mines were thought to be free of gas, but a small amount of methane gas was generated by the decay of timbers from old mine workings. This could accumulate if mining was intermittent and resulted in one or two ignitions or explosions when company personel were burnt. A change to Oldham rechargeable electric light cap lamps was made and this type of light was used exclusively for the next 50 years. From then on smoking was banned underground and any combustibles such as matches or any other spark source was treated as contraband. On any shift a third of the men expected to be searched on a rotating basis, before going underground, and a £3 fine was imposed for smoking down a mine. This does not seem much today, but it was a week's wages then.

Hubert had helped to sink No. 14 mine in 1947, where he worked for some years, as well as other shafts such as No. 16. In 1962 Charlie Gover had made No. 14 shaft deeper, with clay being taken out at different levels during its life. Later a main lane was driven south, towards Norden Hill, looking for more PK clay, which was then in demand for wall-tile manufacture. In the old days there had been no demand for this clay; only the Best Blue was good enough. In 1965 Hubert transferred to the East Holme mine. About the same time, the Ridge Mine was sunk, a modern concrete shaft with a cage in which

Gordon Beazer with helmet light. AUTHOR

No 14 shaft in the evening sun on 15 February 1981. This mine was opened in 1947 and varied in depth from 85 to 102ft. It was made deeper by Charlie Gover in 1962 with clay being taken out at different levels during its life. The best Blue clay overlaid the PK or Excelsior, with Pink stained clay underneath. Behind the pile of pit props a wooden ladder led up to the stage. The large pit head supports were necessary to prevent the staging leaning over when the haulage took up the strain. In the days when it was connected to the winding house, together with 10 and 12, most visitors disappeared in a hurry when the winding began! AUTHOR

The cage and wagons at No. 14 shaft showing a full wagon just arrived at the stage. The cage was hauled up and down the shaft by a central wire rope attached to the spreader bar. This was heavily greased at each end to facilitate it sliding up and down two fixed timbers down the length of the shaft. A full wagon of clay was wound up the shaft, through a trapdoor and stopped several feet above floor level. The trapdoor was then closed down to cover the top of the shaft for safety and the wagon cage lowered on to it. The full wagon was then manhandled away for tipping and replaced by an empty. The cage was then raised again, so there was room for the trapdoor to be opened by pulling a lever, and the wagon lowered into the shaft. AUTHOR

men could ride, which also allowed a standard underground wagon to be transferred between the workings and the pithead. It was decided to change all the older shafts on the company to use cages, any movement of the wagon in the cage being prevented by a hinged steel bracket at either end. The idea of using timber guides in the shaft for the wagon lift was introduced by Ferdi Stanzel, the Mines Manager, and replaced the old system of fixed wire ropes as guides in Nos.10, 12, 14 and 16 shafts. By August 1979 a

new airshaft for No. 14 had been built and it also provided an emergency exit for the miners. At that time Charlie Fry was working as winch-winder and tipper at No. 14. The different clays were being tipped into storage bins to await collection and the wagons were prevented from overtipping by using a short chain, with one end attached to the floor of the stage and a hook at the other end holding the back of the wagon. Most early mines had used small turntables or curved track in the tranship shed leading to each bin, but this system gradually gave way to steel sheeting covering the timber floor over which the wagons could slide as they were man-handled for tipping.

The mines had a bell warning system between the miners and the winder, which was still used as well as the phone. The notice at each mine was in coal mining parlance, and indicated the following,

    1 ring = STOP
    2 rings = HAUL OUTBYE (out of the mine)
    3 rings = HAUL INBYE   (into the mine)
    4 rings = MAN IN SHAFT
    5 rings = MAN CLEAR

About five to ten times a day one or two sets of pit props would be sent down in an empty wagon and the miners would phone to say when they had enough. Charlie had first to lower the wagon cage to ground level and then leave the stage and go down the ladder to load the props into the empty wagon. He then returned to the stage to complete lowering the wagon to the bottom of the shaft.

Although mining production was not directly affected by weather conditions like open pits, it could be more wasteful as a thick clay roof about 15 to 20ft had to be left to protect the workings from the influx of water. The clay in the roof was either lost entirely or left until a later date when open cast work might recover it. In contrast to open work mining required expensive support. This came usually in the shape of round timber props. After 1946 steel arches were used for main roadways, either horseshoe or circular in shape, or in a few cases specially shaped concrete blocks were used to form a circular tunnel. However the advantage of mining was that where two or three commercial clays lay above each other, the lower one could be mined leaving the others for a future date. In an open pit there was no option but to remove the upper layer first. This created a storage problem if the top clay had no immediate sale. The support of the roof depended on the type of clay. Some being crumbly such as Creech Barrow required much more care and support close to the face. Softer but firm clays such as East Holme stood much better and were sometimes advanced for several hours before timbering up. The general rule in the 1950s was that the maximum distance between each set of timber should be three feet. The maximum distance between the last set and

Bottom of shaft 14, on 25 July 1980. Some of the metal pipes were still in place from the old system for taking compressed air to the working face. As the working face moved forward, a new length of pipe was added and a signal could be tapped on the metal if anything went wrong there, or in the lane. I had arrived down the vertical ladder on the right, which was for access by the miners to and from the surface. Riding up and down in the cage was not allowed, but it still happened. AUTHOR

the face was set at five feet. Of course the rules did not preclude supports being set at smaller intervals if deemed necessary. The final rule was 'No person shall withdraw support from the roof or sides of any place, otherwise than by a method or device by which he does so from a position of safety'. The custom of using local timber for support in the mines continued and was obtained from many sources. In 1948-9, 30 tons of timber came from the Digby estate, Sherborne, and 14 tons from Leonard Sturdy of Trigon. More timber came from D. C. Dudley Ryder then owner of Rempstone estate, and a substantial

On 21 July 1980, Arthur Hobbs was operating a pneumatic spade at a face of PK clay in No. 14 mine. This mine, built in the traditional manner, will be remembered as the last vertical shaft still working in the Purbeck ball clay area. The crushing pressure of the surrounding ground was forcing the shaft in and it was closed down when the expense of repair became too much. AUTHOR

Two of the miners who were working at No. 14 mine, on 25 July 1980 were Andy Ward on the left and Peter Welsh on the right. The clay face had yellow air stains, which would penetrate the face up to 5 or 6 feet. AUTHOR

Reclaimed rail at No. 14 mine. The bridge rail on the left would be re-used underground and the rail on the right was spare for use above ground. AUTHOR

No 16 shaft was 100ft deep, situated up a steep gradient and opened by January 1949. By the time of the photograph 1963 it was showing its age. In the 1950s, production was variable, anything from 40 or so tons a week to well over 100. In the first six months of 1961 the 100 ton average per week was reached only seven times, and the writing was on the wall! It was the only mine to let full wagons down a long gradient by winch before being picked up by the locomotive on the main tramway. It was also the last traditional timber shaft to be built in Purbeck, becoming just a flooded hole in the ground by 1969. The type disappeared completely when No 14 closed at the end of 1982. This rare photo was taken by Philip Hunt.

amount also came from the Hon. Sir Ernest Scott, cut at Arne. His timber was sold by the cu ft, a discount of 7.5% being allowed for bark. The Forestry Commission was by far the biggest source of timber, over 10,000 pitprops being supplied in the same period.

No. 14 had a long life by Norden standards, but by July 1981, the old wooden shaft was being forced inwards by the pressure of surrounding clay and was too expensive to replace. In the old days shaft righting was a regular overtime job, often carried out on Sundays so the clay getting shifts were not affected. Charlie (Mama) Welsh who was born in 1900, and transferred from Pike's to Fayle's in 1930 said he helped to re-sink

No. 12. He used to do shaft righting with his brother 'Curly' and they were paid £1 for working Sunday from 6am to 3pm. One of them would operate a windlass on the stage and tip clay when needed. In the shaft where the sides had become bad, they would build a temporary frame to stand on by nailing on supports and putting boards across. Two or three sets in the shaft wall would then be removed and the clay cut back, the sets then being renewed. Sometimes more than a day was needed, or even all night if the shaft was very bad. When the righting of the shaft was neglected, conditions would deteriorate until wagons became jammed. At No. 14 the cage had begun to foul the sides as it went up and down. At first the timbers were cut back to allow its passage, but this led to the shaft becoming more fragile, and with safety in mind the decision was taken in 1982 to close the mine down. Sadly this brought to an end the traditional all-timber working mine shaft in Dorset.

No. 15 mine was a shallow 30ft shaft sunk at the south end of Peaked Close. It was working in the summer of 1948. Yellow clay called Bristol Saggar or CY was being cut in an open pit, and the shaft was sunk in the bottom of the pit to reach some PK clay. As the open pit around the shaft went deeper, a double winch was installed on the stage at No. 15, one drum being used to haul wagons of PK up the shaft and the other to pull skips of yellow clay out of the open pit. The PK was tipped into other skips and both types of

The rail and siding for empties (on the left) at No 16 shaft. Hubert Coffen operated the winch here, which had two drums, one for winding the mine and the other for letting trains of four loaded skips down the hill to Eli, who would be waiting with the locomotive near No. 6 incline. PHILIP HUNT

clay were then hauled by another winch up to a second transfer point on the main surface tramway. George Andrews worked at this stage using an air winch to haul the wagons. The PK clay was then tipped into the 2ft gauge wagons to be taken for processing. The yellow/pink clay was railed to a third stage where it was loaded for Sharp Jones & Co, The Bourne Valley Pottery, at Branksome, who sent about six lorries a day to collect the clay. Such a shallow and labour intensive mine would not have been necessary in later years, as it became possible to remove large amounts of overburden and to have open pits 60 to 70ft deep. The yellow colour was due to the presence of iron oxide and one of its uses was as a base glaze on metal baths. This clay was also in favour with craft potters. If it had red streaks it was called 80, and this was later changed to AT. A section of the pit showed very clearly the concertina effect of clay layers being forced up over others by the enormous pressure generated by the folding of the chalk hills adjacent to the area.

No. 16 mine was 100ft deep and destined to be the last shaft sunk by Fayle's. It was situated in Middle Eight Acres, just on the lower slope of Norden Hill. It was sunk in the summer of 1948 and had its share of flooding problems, especially on 20 April 1951 when water and sand broke into the mine. Sometimes, several lanes in a mine could fill up overnight and if possible the sand

had to be dug out by hand until the clay face was regained. No. 6 incline suffered the same problem in 1983. The railway branch serving No. 16 mine came off the main line just west of No. 3 tunnel, and round a very sharp bend to the south, leading up the gradient to the stage. Hubert Coffen operated the winch at No. 16 mine for some time, which like No. 15 shaft had two drums for different purposes. One rope was used for winding the mine and the other to let loaded clay wagons down the steep incline, said to be 1 in 5, to the level area near No. 3 mine. There was a short siding for empty wagons beside the loading stage. The usual procedure was to have a train of four skips ready to load, held by the winch brake. The first three wagons could be alongside the stage at once, and when they were loaded, the brake was let off slightly to let the fourth move into position. When Hubert saw that Eli had arrived and was waiting near No. 3, the four loaded skips were let down the hill to be collected. Inevitably, on such a steep gradient, the wagons would sometimes run away. This usually happened when loading was going on at the mine; there would be a sudden bang and one or two or all four wagons would break away and accelerate down the hill, usually de-railing on the sharp curve near No. 6 mine, scattering clay everywhere. If the wagons stayed on the line, there was nothing to stop them continuing down through the works as far as the catch point near

Looking north down the gradient from No. 16 mine. Sometimes while loading the wagons, the rope broke, with the result that one or two wagons would run away and either derail on the sharp curve near No. 6 scattering clay everywhere, or continue on through the works as far as the catch point near the main road (A351). The Ruston 392117 can be seen shunting wagons near No. 6 tunnel. PHILIP HUNT

the Corfe road, where they would leave the track and go into the bank. A stop block had been installed near No. 3 mine to prevent runaway wagons going any further, but the impact of a loaded train easily demolished the block to matchwood. In earlier days, before the catch point was installed, wagons could and did rush unannounced across the main road! Fortunately, the traffic in those days was only intermittent. On one memorable occasion Eli was on *Russell* waiting near No. 3 mine. There was a shout of warning from Hubert, 'Look out, Eli, the rope has broken'. The next moment four loaded skips accelerated down the slope. There was a huge crash as the run away train ploughed into the empties and *Russell*. A cloud of clay and steel arose in what seemed like slow motion to Eli and the skip nearest the locomotive flew in the air and landed on top of Russell's chimney. After a few moments re-thinking the incident, Eli said, 'I never got out, and I had a mind to, but that's where the skip landed up'.

There were times when the wagon haulage was out of action and attempts were made to take the locomotive up the gradient. Eli once drove *Russell* at full steam ahead in an effort to reach

the mine. But splintering and cracking of the track near the points for the empties siding forced a hasty retreat, using large amounts of sand on the rails to prevent too great a speed back down the hill. On another occasion when the winch was not working, one of the Montania diesels which fortunately had a very low centre of gravity and good stability had a lucky escape. Bill Selby and Bert Reed hoping to get the fulls drove as hard as possible up the grade towards No. 16, but did not hear Eli shout out to leave a sprag or two in the wagon wheels to assist braking. Bill pulled out the sprags, but the sudden weight of loaded wagons threw the engine out of gear and the brakes were unable to hold the train on the steep slope. They were lucky not to be de-railed as the train accelerated down hill and ran away round the sharp curve. Eli gave a rare laugh and said, 'Never had engine in gear or nothing, they came down over there a-flying'. Production continued at No. 16 until 11 June 1963. By January of that year George Allingham had been made up to foreman and remembered the first job he had was to bring up the miners from underground to help clear the snow from the tracks so Eli could bring up empty wagons.

Most of the time in later years Eli drove the Ruston, which had a heating coil to assist its starting. When he arrived at the east siding bringing full trains from the mines, the siding gang led by Bert White, took over the wagons for weighing and shunting, the pegs on the wagons showing which mining gang to credit. The local shunting and tipping of any waste clay was carried out using the small diesel units. The siding locomotives used diesel stored in the mobile tank on a converted 'broad-gauge' wagon, and Eli had a fixed tank near the blacksmith's shop in which fuel was stored for the Ruston.

John Cooper reported that the post-war (1946) clay production of Fayles and Pikes was about 50,000 tons total. The efforts of Frank Longmire and John to re-develop the Norden Company, initially seeking a lease for mining at Arne from the Eldon (Encombe) estate, triggered a response from Pike Bros. at Furzebrook. The last member of the mining Pike family had died in 1939 and John Bond of the Grange estate had become the major shareholder in Pike Bros. Wareham. When Bond died in October 1948, followed soon after by Edgar White, their Managing Director, the idea of merging with Fayles seemed an attractive option. A valuation of the two companies was made, Fayle's being £28,000 of which the locomotives and rolling stock totalled £4,640. Pike's was valued at £82,431 and their locomotives and rolling stock came to £10,770. The certificate of incorporation of Messrs. Pike Bros., Fayle & Co. Limited was dated 29 April 1949 and from 1 May 1949 they claimed over 80% of clay production in Dorset. Gordon Beazer, the mines manager for Pikes since 1936, managed exploration and development for the new company, with the help of John Cooper and a mining consultant C. P. Bates, of Stoke-on-Trent. Gordon had joined Pikes from the Bristol coalfield and his experience of coal mining techniques helped in the development of the clay industry. A period of modernisation followed which brought considerable financial success. The use of compressed air lines was extended to all underground mines, and thereafter all workings, both surface and underground, were made using pneumatic spades.

For a period of six or seven years, Pike Bros. Fayle & Co. Ltd operated two surface railway systems, the 2ft 8in railway at Furzebrook and the 1ft 11½in tramway at Norden. The company inherited six steam locomotives, and for three or

Gordon Beazer, the Mines Manager was in the open pit at Norden, talking to foreman Bill Selby and Midge Welsh. Midge has a miner's lamp looped to his belt and the meeting took place soon after the 1949 merger with Pike's at Furzebrook to form the new company, Pike Bros. Fayle & Co. Ltd. AUTHOR

four years the weathering and transport of clay continued at peak levels. However, the processing of clay stocks was changing and a large increase in demand for powdered clay hastened the end of the traditional weathering beds. The run down of this system made much of the Furzebrook railway superfluous to the business and in 1954 John Cooper took the decision to replace the 2ft 8in railway with lorry transport. Two other reasons for the decision were the planned expansion of new mines at some distance from the original line and also the maintenance problems of the long Povington branch into the Lulworth army firing range. By 1957 the Furzebrook line had closed.

It was also decided after 1949, that any new mines were planned as inclines, and four were subsequently built at Norden before underground work ceased.

No. 4 opened by 20 March 1952, in East Eight Acres, the field south of Little Copse and worked 11 years, closing 1 June 1963. The mouth of the mine was situated close to Norden Hill and the main haulage was built using steel arches, following the direction of the hill west toward No. 16 shaft. Underground, the clay was trammed using the standard 22in gauge wagons. For seven years (1951-8) the winch man for No. 4 was Colin Varney. A new branch line was built to reach No. 4, which diverged off the clay main line near the compressor house in Dandy Hayes and curved south toward Long Close and the new incline. The building of the new branch resulted in the west works becoming situated in

No. 4 incline was in East Eight Acres and the main roadway of the tunnel was driven in a westerly direction, parallel to the chalk ridge. Fred White and Colin Varney worked as tippers here, and the picture in June 1952 shows the incline shortly after it was opened, before the stage was completed. AUTHOR

the fork of a railway junction. About half way to No. 4 mine, another branch line diverged to the west across Five Acres to No. 10 shaft, and this became a convenient place to leave empties while shunting at No. 4. Full wagons leaving No. 4 stage faced a sharp upward gradient and the usual procedure was to pull them up to level ground using a wire rope attached to *Russell*. As they went down the branch, Eli would leave the empties in No. 10 road. Then they would continue to No. 4 and see if there were any 'fulls' to pull out. The boy went down the grade to connect the rope and Eli hooked on to *Russell*. Then the pull out started with the locomotive going back up the branch about 100yds and the wire rope running on rollers between the rails. The boy followed the wagons up the slope to sprag them at the top and stop them rolling on. Eli would ease back to release the rope and then go forward so the wagons could be hitched direct to the locomotive. Then they set off down the slope to get the empties attached to the load, and the whole train was then shunted back up to No. 4, the empties being spragged before being let down to the stage at No. 4. Then they set off back to No. 10 mine to get their 'fulls'.

The working at incline 4 was Frank Longmire's idea, and it did involve a lot of shunting, but Eli said they pulled out hundreds of tons from there. After *Russell* broke down, the

No. 5 incline recorded on 31 May 1969, nearly two years after it had been abandoned. It was replaced by No. 6 incline. At the time, it was at the western end of the Norden works. The railway came in from the left and ran under the staging, where tipping of the clay took place under the sloping roof. The view is looking southwest and the incline went down underground behind the pit props and spoil heap to the right. When the change over to lorry haulage was made, only two mines remained to be converted. Of these, No. 14 continued until 1982 when it too closed leaving No. 6. GEORGE MOON

O&K diesels were used until the Ruston 392117 arrived in January 1961, and was pressed into service the very first day. While pulling out from No. 4 on one occasion the clutch handle came off. Eli managed to stop the loco, but being over the top the wagons ran on down on to the engine with the rope all tangled up. The working of open clay pits in the vicinity affected the stability of the branch to No. 10 and it was then abandoned. A replacement branch to service No. 10 was then built approaching the mine from the west. This was quite a short spur which came off the main line near No. 12 mine and it remained in position under newly growing trees long after the mine it served was closed. Eventually No. 4 closed down and the last train ran on 18 May 1963. The truncated remains of the original branch to No. 4 remained in use as a siding for redundant stock, until the final run-down of the system.

During 1951 a new tunnel was being planned to get clay further to the west. The incline was put down during 1952 and was designated No. 5 with production starting in August. It was a shallow mine situated at the western end of the main clay railway, beyond the old No. 3 tunnel and the turning to No. 16 shaft. Within a year the production from No. 5 mine resulted in the closure of No. 3 on 4 April 1953.

Eli said that one day, (it was actually 11 July 1955) he was working with Bert Richards in the engine shed. Frank Tubb had taken a small diesel locomotive and gone up to the British Railways siding with two of the flat wagons loaded with 26cwt bagged powder clay. Apparently, some of the load, or most of it had come off the wagon and Frank re-loaded the train himself and presumably unloaded it again at the siding. Shortly after, the engine was heard coming back

The stub point near the locomotive shed at Norden, looking west. The foreground line continued past the photographer to Goathorn in 3ft 9in days. By this time in 1969 the shed was little used but it was here that Eli pulled the O&K out and left it in the sun for me to photograph. This was the only stub point on the re-laid system and the place where the derailment occurred in 1955 when the train and Frank ran away. R. W. KIDNER.

quite quickly past the shed and Bert shouted, 'She's coming right off the line', which was a dead end since the line to Goathorn was lifted in 1939. They rushed out to the locomotive and found poor Frank dead, but still sitting upright in the cab, and concluded he must have expired somewhere between reversing his engine and two wagons on to the branch for the return journey and reaching the engine shed.

Pike Bros., Fayle & Co. Ltd issued a low key report saying Frank had been a foreman at the Norden Mines Works for most of the 42 years of his trusted service, but in fact it was 16 years at

In 1953 a short report said Pike Bros. Fayle & Co. Ltd was then producing more than 60,000 tons of clay each year, from 13 mines and 3 opencast sites. This was then 75% of ball clay produced in Dorset. The report stated that there were 5 small mines at Norden, on what was originally the Fayle working area. These would have been the shafts 10, 12, 14 and 16 and the incline 4. An open pit was being worked using a traditional incline. The best quality clays were located between strata of inferior clays, which gave protection from contamination by sand and water. The Fayle Company had despatched large tonnages of clay to Germany until the beginning of World War 1. By 1953, the largest opencast pit was at Kilwood, which contributed some 250 tons per week. The mine surveyor was R. L. King who worked closely with Gordon Beazer, the Mines Manager. He was responsible for accurate records of mine progress, the positions of test borings and all relevant data. About four fifths of the company production was obtained by underground mining.

No. 6 incline in 1969 basking in late evening sunshine. Time was running out for the surface railway, with a waiting line of empty skips. One of the wagons had steel eyes welded to one end, which may have been for lifting the wagon in a previous existence.
31 May 1969. GEORGE MOON

No. 6 incline, not long after building in 1960.
PHILIP HUNT

Norden following his early life at Newton Clay Works. As a foreman at the open pit he had extra responsibilities such as directing the extraction work and checking safety each day, but he was still part of the working force and would fill in where needed such as driving trains. He was said to have been driving on the tramways of the works yard, loaded with clay, when he collapsed and died over the controls, which was in a sense true, but without any of the drama related by Eli, with the train running away. However, the company produced a drawing of the end event, a normal procedure following an accident, which only recently came to light. The drawing bears out exactly the report given by Eli, showing the train de-railed just past the engine shed on a dipping gradient of 1 in 40. Frank was said to be foreman, Norden siding, Corfe Castle, and in error aged 59 years when he was actually aged 57.

On 11 June 1959, a second hand winch was obtained for No. 5 mine, a 30cwt Clarke-Chapman, No. 2582, driven by a 20hp electric motor, costing Fayle's £218. In October 1959, two un-used Holman type HY 5hp winches were purchased, each having a 1600lbs safe working load at 80p.s.i. They cost £105 each, both for use at Norden. As mentioned above, No. 5 tunnel was at the far end of the tramway, which ran into a conventional siding at the mine stage. It became a main production unit for the next 13 years, but stopped on 19 June 1965. The miners returned for a month in 1966, but no clay was taken in 1967. Eventually the mine closed down on 20 July 1968 and was superseded by No. 6 drift mine, which had been started in 1962, driven in a westerly direction to reach lower levels of clay than No. 5, but from a starting point closer to the old No. 3 mine.

The decision to shred and blend clay as the primary material in 1948 was followed by the merger between Pike's and Fayle's, the future processing of clay then coming under a unified management. John Cooper agreed to combine with Watts, Blake, Bearne & Co. (WBB) of Devon in the purchase of two American shredders, one of which was destined for Furzebrook. At first they were not entirely successful in use, so Brixey's of Parkstone carried out some modifications to the equipment. Clay in the shredded form was considered the most economic condition for large-scale bulk transport, or handling in a works, and is still the basic material today. Shredded clay consists of lump clay cut into pieces approximately ¼in to 2in in size by rotating hardened steel knives. Moisture content could not be guaranteed, but was usually between 14 and 19% on a wet basis. Clay prepared in this way underwent a homogenising, as well as a size reduction process, and was therefore very suitable for blunging, drying, milling or any other process. Blends of ball clay could now be despatched according to user's specification, for example, combining strength with light firing characteristics. By a special arrangement of the normal clay shredding plant, it was possible to prepare an extremely intimate mix of two, three or even four ball clays. Marketing of the clay types was done under the company name Pikefayle Ball Clays.

By 1956, Pike Bros. Fayle & Co. Ltd described in their catalogue of Dorset ball clays, how dried and granulated clay had been developed using the rotary louvre principle and had largely replaced dried lump clay. The heat control in this plant was fully automatic using a refined fuel. The operation at a low clay temperature gave a product free from contamination and with unaltered plasticity. The standard product had 5% moisture content. Some lump form was still sold at 18-23% moisture, but was artificially weathered giving a more homogenous product. The clay was sold by names which reflected either their traditional source, or from a particular mine. The two best qualities were Fayle's Blue and Pike's K, followed by No. 1 or Prima (Cotness and Creech mines) all used in the finest vitreous enamel ware. The next most important were refractory clays, PK (Povington and Norden 14 mine) and No. 71CW (Cotness and Creech) both used in electrical applications. Then came other types or blends such as TLD (Trigon light dark), No. 4 (Grange mine), SM (Sandy Mining), GR (Grange red), PNK (also known as 80 or AT), H (Squirrel opencast) and CY (Yellow due to iron content, from various mines). Graphs were included to show the characteristics of each clay from strength/firing temperature curves to irreversible thermal expansion so that each customer could chose the clay most suitable for their needs. For most uses the fired colour was important and this ranged from pale ivory for the Blue and K through light ivory and cream to very light pink and pink to a buff-red for CY

Powdered clay of medium fineness was then available at regular bulk density with a moisture content 4 to 6%. The fineness varied with different clays. By the late 1950s the company had a milling capacity of over 15,000 tons a year of powdered and air-floated clays, the standard product having 2-4% moisture content and a fineness of 90% passing 200 mesh B.S. Sieve. For special purposes a considerably finer and drier product could be obtained from the plant, 300 mesh or finer for refractories. The aim at Furzebrook was to provide the clay product in a form convenient for the customer.

Quality was further improved by setting up the works laboratory at Furzebrook. Soon after the merger, John Cooper heard that a friend of his, Harry Hall, was retiring. He had held the post of Technical Director at Carter's Tiles in Poole, so John asked him if he would help set up the laboratory. A modern looking building soon appeared at Furzebrook on the opposite side of the road to the processing plant. Les Berkin, a ceramics engineer from Stoke, joined the team whose work over the next ten years was not only to systematically check and control clay products prior to despatch, but also to produce both chemical and physical analysis of all borehole samples.

Openpits or surface mines had been increasing in size from the 1940s, and by 1960, depths up to 100ft were being considered. The 1940s increase had been due to the use of Priestman draglines, mostly by Pike Bros., which were obtained second hand from the water industry. They were first used in Purbeck, along with dumpers, to make the initial 'box-cut' in the removal of overburden. This material, removed from above the clay was then used for the construction of screening banks, or was stored for future infilling. When a sufficient area of clay had been exposed at the base of the box cut, pit roads constructed from railway sleepers were laid across the surface of the clay to provide access for lorries taking away the excavated clays. Fayle's continued to use the traditional inclined railway to haul clay out of open pits, and a similar track was used at Povington for sometime.

It was not long before the operators were using the draglines to cut clay as well. At first the getting of clay with a dragline was done behind the foreman's back, and on the usual piece rates for supposedly hand cut clay, the miners were earning big money! To disguise the fact, one of the miners Jim Courtney had a special blade made, which fitted over the bucket on the dragline. This disguised any markings that would have been on the clay from the bucket and the

This rare photograph, May 1967, shows small RH 179889 with a short train of loaded wagons taking refuge from inclement weather in the large storage shed near the weigh house, part of the east works and sidings. At the end of the track can be seen the converted 3ft 9in wagon with oval fuel tank standing in the doorway. MICHAEL MESSENGER.

blade was hidden away when not in use. Another favourite trick was to dragline the clay onto the lorry and then climb up in the back and cut up the lumps with spades. That was a lot easier than cutting the clay with spades in the pit. About 1962, Ferdi Stanzell was appointed Mines Manager and as an ex-miner known for his competitive edge and also an ex-foreman, he knew all the problems in mining and all the short cuts. After a while in charge and realising what was going on he announced a change in practice, which made the use of draglines to get clay official, but at new rates of pay. The men could still earn more money, but not so much as when claiming the clay had been cut with spades! In the 1960s, the draglines were superseded by hydraulic excavators of the Hymac type, known as backacters; the type of equipment still in use today. The selection of clay at the face had not been so good with draglines, but the new excavators were very accurate in control and as the men would say, 'you could get the clay down to a fag paper'. Starting from the far end of the access road, the clays were dug by the backacting machinery, standing on the top of the clay seams and reaching down to extract the clay. In extreme cases of selection, and at least until 1975, it was sometimes necessary to employ hand cutters using pneumatic spades, in which case the clays were cut and loaded into small hoppits which were then lifted to the surface by a dragline operating as a crane.

By the 1960s, Colonel Ashley Bond was Chairman and main shareholder in the Company and John Cooper was Managing Director. About this time Col Bond became

concerned about the future of the company if anything should happen to him. John had no ambitions to be Chairman and further discussions did not produce a likely successor to Colonel Bond. Reluctantly, the decision was taken for John to draw up a list of possible outcomes for the future of the company and for this to be presented to the board. After much soul searching the decision was taken to seek a buyer for the clay works, among those companies in similar extractive business. At that time various companies were interested in expanding by take-over. There had been a long history of acquisition and abrasive relationships within the companies making up the Cornish china-clay industry, both before and after the formation of English China Clays (ECC) in 1919. At that time, two of the other principal producers were Messrs. John Lovering & Co. and H. D. Pochin and Co. Ltd whose annual production was 260,000 tons together, compared to the 460,000 of ECC The same sort of rivalry existed between the Devon ball clay companies, whereas in Dorset there was less intensity, perhaps because Fayle's and Pike's had slightly different clays, and traditionally a quite different customer base. Discussions were entered into with English China Clays for the sale of the business to them. Eventually an offer was made in November 1967 of £478,864 in part exchange for the ordinary capital of Pike Bros., Fayle & Co. Ltd and the deal was concluded in 1968. Under ECC control, John Cooper and Sydney Swain became executive directors of Pike Bros., Fayle & Co. Ltd, but in 1970, John who was managing director of both Pike's and Hexter & Budge Ltd merged the two companies to form

ECC Ball Clays Ltd. It was the first company in the ball clay industry to have workings in each of the three sources of ball clay in Britain, namely South Devon, North Devon, and Dorset clay fields; its total production was close to 450,000 tons per year. All employees became members of a contributory company pension scheme, well ahead of most of the rest of the country. Things had come a long way from the days when you were not paid steam time, that is raising steam early in the mornings before winding could begin at the mines, and when there were no paid holidays. At Povington, which was to become the largest opencast operation, plans for extraction were based on a maximum depth of 65ft in 1973, which increased to 90ft in 1977 and 135ft in 1981.

The company offices had made a third move. Originally as Pike Bros., based at Creech, the 1949 merger with Fayle's led to new offices being opened in South Street, Wareham for Pike Bros., Fayle & Co. Ltd. These gave way in June 1967 to a newly built administrative block for ECC Ball Clays Ltd in North Street, where Benjamin Fayle's bust had a prominent position in the Boardroom window, overseeing a steadily growing business for the next 25 years. Sadly, this rather elegant building was demolished by January 1999 in a cost cutting exercise initiated at the St Austell Head Office, to make way for 17 dwellings and to save £140,000. This was seen as scandalous by some staff and local people.

At Furzebrook, the tramway had closed in favour of lorry transport (1957). However, the tramway at Norden was retained because the system was already geared up to bring clay from the mines direct to the mill, and while the Norden siding still operated, thousands of tons of

No. 6 showing wagons coming up the tunnel. AUTHOR

bagged clay were sent out by rail. When the Norden mill eventually closed in 1961 and was transferred to Furzebrook, the railway siding became redundant after 76 years. All clay was then taken by road to the central works for processing. The tramway was retained at Norden for another eleven years to link the mines with Cattle Creep, where the wagons were tipped directly over the side of the bridge into the lorry waiting below.

By 1969, the western end of the clay tramway terminated at No. 6 mine. Loaded wagons arriving from underground were manhandled across the stage to an Avery scale for weighing. Wagons were identified by the use of pegs with 1, 2, 3 or 4 grooves cut in them and stuck in the clay by the miners. A record was kept on a large blackboard

Frankie Foot weighs a wagon on No. 6 stage. Wooden pegs were used to identify wagonloads of clay. The pegs with 1, 2, 3 or 4 grooves cut in them were stuck in each wagon of clay when filled by the miners at the face. In this way a record was kept of the number of wagons sent by each gang. AUTHOR

No. 6 mine with full wagons arrived on the stage. AUTHOR

Above: On the stage at No. 6 George Fry was about to tip a wagon. The blackboard kept a record of wagons received, whether good or bad clay. AUTHOR

Top right: Some of the tunnels in No. 6 mine were made up using specially shaped concrete blocks. As the face was driven forward the blocks were made up into a circular shape on a former or template, with wood chocks placed between the concrete to prevent crumbling and breaking of the blocks. AUTHOR

The train was waiting for clay tipping to start at No. 6 mine. A vintage Muir Hill dumper had been placed in store. AUTHOR

The following pictures illustrate a journey down the line in the late 1960s. No. 6 incline was then the western extremity of the Norden workings and a run to the exchange sidings began there with a train of loaded wagons. The winding house for the mine can be seen above the O&K diesel. The overhead pipe and cylindrical chamber were part of the compressed air system, which drove the clay cutting spades and tuggers underground. The train is about to get under way on 12 September 1968. AUTHOR

When clay tipping was in progress the train was moved on slowly as wagons were filled. On the right was a pile of the shaped blocks for making concrete tunnels underground. 3 July 1969. GEORGE MOON

at the end of the stage, which showed the tonnage per mining gang. On the siding adjacent to the mine, rows of skips were waiting to be loaded and taken to the transfer sidings by Eli Kitcatt. For most of that year Eli used the Ruston DL, the first job being to shunt the wagons into position beside the loading stage. Tucked underneath the stage was an old wagon from underground, which was used to keep any broken spade blades

for the scrap man. When loading was complete, Eli checked the train and the journey down to the east sidings began. A series of photographs taken at different periods illustrate the run. After passing No. 12 mine, disused by 9 March 1968, a stop was made to collect full wagons at No. 14 shaft. Then they meandered on through the works area and down to the main road. With the road safely crossed it took a few minutes to traverse

Eli looks out from the cab of the O&K diesel No. 20777, which was brought into use when the Ruston was out of service. How it reached Dorset is a mystery; it was believed to be the spoils or war having worked on a V2 rocket site in France. The familiar diamond shaped O&K maker's plate can be seen on the side of the locomotive and all the dials and instructions in the cab were in German. Eli was born on 4 March 1905 and retired from ECC Ball Clays at Christmas 1987 after 70 years service. 4 July 1968. GEORGE MOON

A short way after leaving No. 6 mine the train passed the stage of No. 12 shaft and threaded its way past old wagon frames discarded by the line side. Wagon 34, loaded with bundles of heather was kept under cover at the old stage. The facing point, by then disused, previously fed a branch a short distance through some trees to No. 10 shaft. AUTHOR

About a hundred yards further down the line a short branch with a trailing junction, led up a sharp incline to No. 14 shaft. It was Eli's custom to leave the full train on the main line, which on that day included wagon 72, held by a block of wood across the rails. The Ruston then went up the branch to collect the 2 or 3 wagons at No. 14 and returned to couple up again to the main train. 3 July 1969. AUTHOR

A short time later the wagons, with No 80 at the front, were brought back to the main line to continue the journey. In the background can be seen part of the west works, power line and carpenter's shop. AUTHOR

the old Matchams area with glimpses of Corfe Castle through the undergrowth. Then more determined acceleration from the Ruston lifted the wagons over the Swanage branch up to the reversing point.

Standing near Cattle Creep with the grass grown high, it was strange to see the wagons being propelled toward you through a sea of green. A brief rattle over the bridge followed by a whiff of hot oil from the Ruston and the train began to slow for the sidings. On some days Eli stayed to push the wagons across the weighbridge, but generally one of the small Rustons took over. A line of empty wagons would be waiting in the loop and after a few minutes Eli hooked on and they clanked over the skew bridge on their way back to the mines. After the wagons were weighed the small loco propelled them the short distance to Cattle Creep where the tipping into the lorry began. Sometime later, Eli arrived with the last load of the day and preparations were made to close up for the night. At the time of course, the system seemed permanent, and closure within three years

O&K diesel 20777 picks up speed with a full train of clay past the works and also sister locomotive 21160 dumped in a siding.
12 September 1968.
GEORGE MOON

In a siding, just east of the works, four 1ft 11½in wagons of the early batch were sandwiched between O&K 21160 and the Simplex run-about. The main line continued on and crossed the chalk road leading to the main works entrance. The railway then curved to the right between low grassy banks and began the descent to the main Wareham road. The point consisted of a short lever, which operated a hooked rod connected to the point rod. The uneven nature of the line, which had suffered from heavy locomotives and poor maintenance, gave a rough but exhilarating ride.
19 May 1966.
GEORGE MOON

Just across the road. The pattern of the wagons varied a great deal, as this train showed. One frame had a piece of angle steel plate along the side. The sandbox and pipe spoiled the lines of the diesel locomotive but it was convenient to fill. GEORGE MOON

The Ruston with its train was passing over bridge 15 on a hot 4 July 1969. After bridge 15, the train crossed over the Swanage line. Through the gap in the hills a glimpse could be seen of the southern part of Purbeck, best known for stone and marble production. AUTHOR

At the weighbridge, the Ruston which had been propelling the train after crossing bridge 15 left the loaded wagons to be taken over by one of the smaller diesels and took the line of empties on the left back to the mines. AUTHOR

At the end of the day, the Ruston had taken the line running behind the weighbridge, curving east through the bracken and long grass towards the engine shed behind the trees. AUTHOR

This view was taken from about the same spot as the previous picture, but nearly 20 years earlier, with *Russell* taking the same line with a rake of wagons. The locomotive shed was the one on the left (above *Russell*), and the shed on the right had been used for the school wagon. AUTHOR

seemed unlikely. But by 1972 the surface railway was gone. Below ground it would be another 27 years before railway use finished. With the surface tramway closed, both mines were converted to road haulage, but because the mine stages had not been converted for lorry use on time, a system of PowerX skips hauled by a tractor was used to transfer the clay to Furzebrook. This unfortunately caused many delays to traffic on the A351 road, and it was a relief to all road users when the lorries were able to take over.

By 1974, total production had risen to 124,000 tonnes per year; by then sales were in metric units. In 1976, Alan Williamson, who was the Company's Production and Mining Engineer, had explained that an average good week's production was 3,000 tonnes. Most people, even local residents, are still surprised to hear that mining goes on in Purbeck. Because of its small

Lines of wagons assembled at the west works 31 August 1972 after the railway system had closed. The view was taken looking towards the main road. GEORGE MOON

Left: One of the 3ft 9in gauge wagons was converted using 2ft wheel sets and used for carrying a diesel fuel tank. It was seen standing on some jubilee or portable track with steel sleepers near the Norden works.
Above: This wagon had a flat top and was used for transporting pit props. The timber was cut in a shed with rail access situated between the A351 road and the Swanage branch. I found the wagon discarded after it had been run down the old No. 2 Matchams incline. AUTHOR

When the clay railway closed, Marcus Churchill drove a Fordson tractor hauling skip loads of clay from Norden to Furzebrook for about 2 years before the staging at the mines was altered to accommodate lorries. On 26 August 1979, the retired tractor with trailer was still at the works. AUTHOR

After the end of the railway, a lorry was being loaded with clay at No. 6 mine in place of the train. This mine was rebuilt in 1983, with greater height to improve access for larger lorries. AUTHOR

The carpenter shop is on the left, and the foreman's office on the right, looking west up the tramway towards the cluster of mines in and beyond Little Copse. A heap of pit props (sticks) has been dumped on the left. The large shed, which housed the Belliss compressors, was just out of the photo to the left. The metal piping can be seen passing under the track, and after a right angle turn following the tramway to distribute the air to spades, pumps and winches underground. J. W. MANN

Some of the miners were coming off duty. To the left were Peter and Keith Daynes, and Dave Day was leaning on the wagon. In the roof, extension pieces had been used in the arches to make a road wide enough for double track. This tended to be a weak point susceptible to ground pressure and in some mines a line of timber supports from floor to roof were used between the two tracks. AUTHOR

scale it is often overlooked. The 'box-cut' or overburden to be removed for Squirrel Cottage open mine in Holme Lane was 20,000 cu yds and being well screened with trees was not an obvious eyesore. In other cases, the overburden itself was often built into screening banks. The Company's output came from 16 production units, 8 mines and 8 openpits. As an indication of the scale of the operation, production from underground mines, including a minimal amount of waste clay, varied from 50 tonnes per week from the smallest, to 350 tonnes per week from the largest unit. In open pits, corresponding figures were 150 to 700 tonnes per week, the average being 250 tonnes. At that time the clay was carried in

conventional lorries, of 7 cu yd capacity to the central storage and processing area at Furzebrook.

The mining tradition, like so many other things, seemed a permanent feature of Purbeck to those who knew it well. Although the signs of its ultimate demise were there as the number of open pits began to outnumber the mines, new products and ideas were still being discussed and introduced. In August 1979, at Norden No. 6 mine, the main haulage was 600 yards long with an average gradient of 1 in 5 and was 160ft deep. On 25 July 1980, on a visit underground the round timber being used for support was de-barked. This had been in use since 1978 and was referred to as rind timber. A big advantage of the new props was the absence of clouds of midges in the works. These had previously hatched out from eggs in the bark of the sticks in those parts of the mine which were hot with moist conditions. At a productivity meeting in November that year, members agreed that the rind timber being supplied was not strong enough. It was recommended the suppliers be contacted to enquire if heavier timbers could be de-barked for underground use. A new airshaft was then built at the mine, which incorporated a powerful fan. The latter was used mostly at night, because the draught was too strong and cold during normal work. However, it had a considerable cooling effect on the hot spots of the mine. To assist the circulation of air around the mine, self-closing doors were installed at strategic positions, as in coal mining practice. The main tunnel at No. 6 had been repaired and upgraded during 1981, and in November the same year, the compressor house was being refurbished. Two Broom and Wade compressors were being installed. One of these came from the Ridge mine, which at that time was mothballed and ultimately never re-opened. The other came from the mine at South Creech, which had closed down. (Both these mines were previously Pike's.) The compressor shed was to be re-located, nearer to No. 6 mine, but the provision of a new power cable was considered too expensive. The shuttering for the new shed had been prepared on the south side of the line near No. 6, but before the concrete could be poured the decision was taken to retain the old house.

After 1983, with the closure of No. 14 shaft, No. 6 tunnel was the only mine left working at Norden with an expected life of seven or eight years. There was little blue clay left and mostly PK was being mined. Some lanes were driven further down and reached a depth of 220ft by 1983. The loading facilities for the mined clay were due for modernisation because the stage built for loading railway skips, was not high enough to service lorries efficiently. This was achieved without affecting production too much, by erecting the new stage beyond the old building with the mine still working. Road access to the new loading bays was planned for the north side of the mine, being the opposite side of the stage to the old rail and road system. The rails of the haulage were then cut off at the entrance to the mine tunnel, and the old stage demolished. An extension from the new stage was built out toward the mine, taking up part of the space where the old stage had been. A new slope down to the tunnel entrance was then constructed and the railway re-connected. Subsequently, the incline was covered with a timber and corrugated iron building and painted black. Clay coming to the surface could then be tipped and stored by grade in separate bins, being released through hydraulic doors when lorries arrived for loading. This system was already in use at other mines operated by the company.

By this time the average load of clay being taken from Poole to Spain for tile making had risen to 1,000 or 1,200 tonnes per ship. The volume carried from Furzebrook was achieved by hiring in lorries from Andrews of Wareham and other transport companies. One of the main recipients was Porcelanosa who shipped regular loads of 1,150 tonnes of shredded HSM clay to

On 20 June 1983, loaded wagons were again being wound out of the mine, in this case waste clay and spent props. AUTHOR

Castellon in 1984. For example, one load of 1,150 tonnes went in the *Puntasugar* on 16 April and was followed by another on 4 June, a third load being taken by the *Antxon Mari* on 15 October. In between, 1,115 tonnes were shipped in the *Alpacia* on 25 July. A further 480 tonnes of shredded Blue, plus 100 tonnes of KC clay went on the *Roy Clemo* to ECC Belgium on 4 December 1984. Other loads taken at random were 1,620 tonnes of shredded AT on the *Eider*, 12 September 1986, and 950 tonnes of shredded Prima clay on the *Warin* to Ifoverken, who were in business near Solvesborg, Sweden, 17 February 1987.

After 1980, there was a tendency to rely on old borehole information to predict suitable mining sites. Generally a 100 metre grid was adopted which was said to provide good information but was really too long a distance between holes for accurate work. In practice it was often found lacking and the actual yield, for example, 400,000 tonnes would fall short of the

The 1807 tunnel was flooded during the road improvement scheme. It was reported that originally the arch had barely enough height for a horse to pass and the harness was cut down to avoid catching on the top of the tunnel. AUTHOR

forecast 500,000 tonnes. The Production Manager, who at that time was Norman Vye, would call in a rig to put a hole down if there was some doubt about the volume of clay. At Dorey's opencast pit, just off Holme Lane, Norman began taking face samples every 10 metres using a pick, and whereas the drill might have said four metres of good clay, he often found just three. The week's take could then be plotted on a graph, and in many cases the actual clay mined fell short of estimates by the company. In another area of the same mine, compensation of £60,000 had been paid for farm buildings and to re-route the road for mining to take place, but when the ground was excavated there was no clay at all! The short fall had to be made up by blending with other clay, mostly from Arne.

During the 1980s, the Wytch oil field was being developed on the heath south of Poole Harbour and the main gathering station was built close to the former Norden to Goathorn clay railway. It became necessary to move some extremely large equipment and plant to the site by road, which involved the upgrading of some local roads and temporary movement of posts and signs along the carriageway. The second half of the Wareham by-pass road was completed

from the Worgret roundabout past Stoborough in order to accommodate the huge loads. In 1987 the A351 road at Norden was re-aligned and widened from the bridge over the old Swanage branch line to a new roundabout near Norden Farm. After 180 years the Middlebere Plateway tunnels were about to be changed forever. It was said the Dorset County Council Planning Dept. and its engineers had no idea of the tunnels original purpose and thought they were drainage culverts under the main road. The west ends of the tunnels were unaffected, but the building work affected the east facing portals. They disappeared under the new carriageway and the widened road also destroyed adjacent ponds and remains from the early 1800s clay working.

By the early 1990s, the company's extraction sites was down to seven, of which five were open cast workings and two deep mines. Mining had always been a dangerous occupation and the risk of injury or worse was accepted by the men, generally because they were better paid than taking other jobs available in the area. Over the years, lessons were learnt from collapsing shafts, lumps of clay falling from the roof or sides of lanes, unexpected water and bad air, and the results of methane ignition. Systems were introduced to raise awareness of danger in the underground environment and upgraded regulations came in 1985 known as RIDDOR, or the Reporting of Injuries, Diseases and Dangerous Occurrences. Incidents resulting in any injury were then recorded in the Accident Book, and many were the result of moving heavy items or the prevailing conditions in the mine. These included props or clay lumps falling on part of the body, lifting heavy items and slipping on wet boards or sleepers when walking down the incline. The tramming of loaded wagons by hand on the 22in roadway was also a risky business, especially when done at speed in the days when pay was piecework. More than one miner or runner suffered the accident of running into the water of a flooded lane, losing the candlelight, and having to crawl along the track in pitch black to another exit, and a very few accidents did have fatal consequences.

CHAPTER TEN

Locomotives and wagons, 'Narrow gauge' 1ft 11½in.
Called 'Narrow Gauge' by the mining community

Russell, working at Norden. Russell had been in Dorset two years when this photo of Eli Kitcatt driving was taken on 18 September 1950. The locomotive was often called *Jane*, after the glamorous film star of that era. However, the locomotive lost a little of its glamour when it proved rather too heavy for the track remaining around Norden and often derailed by dropping through the lines. Following a mechanical breakdown *Russell* was replaced with diesels in 1953.
GEORGE ALLIEZ

RUSSELL, STEAM LOCOMOTIVE 1FT 11½INS 1948-1953.

Russell was (and still is) a 2-6-2T (side tank) outside cylinder locomotive, originally built to a gauge of 1ft 11¼in. The engine carried a brass oval worksplate 'The Hunslet Engine Co. Ltd Leeds, No. 901, 1906', the order for the locomotive having been placed by the Portmadoc, Beddgelert and South Snowdon Railway Company on 13 February that year. However, after steam trials on 26 May 1906 *Russell* was despatched three days later to its associated company the North Wales Narrow Gauge Railway and named after James Cholmeley Russell, who had taken financial control in 1901. The service provided by this isolated railway had limited potential and gradually the business dwindled away in the face of road competition, leading to closure in 1916. A revival came after the war when, as the Welsh Highland Railway, a connection was built through to the Festiniog Railway, but eventually poor receipts again led to closure in 1936-7.

The derelict railway was dispersed in 1941 under the direction of the Ministry of Supply, to provide much needed metal. In May 1942 *Russell* was sold to the Brymbo Steel Company to work at their Hook Norton ironstone mines in Oxfordshire, but not very successfully as it turned out, with lots of derailments occurring, despite the experimental removal of some wheels. By June 1946, a decline in demand for ore led to the decision to cease operations at Hook Norton and *Russell* was again out of service until the Andover sale that brought the engine to Dorset in 1948. The engine's principal dimensions were cylinders 10¾in x 15in, working pressure 160lb per sq in, coupled wheels diameter 2ft 4in and coupled wheelbase 5ft 6in. *Russell* weighed in at 16 tons and in working order, 20 tons.

In July, *Russell* was sent to the Dorset Ironfoundry, in West Quay Road, Poole for overhaul and emerged from the paint shop in a dull maroon but this was changed in 1951 to green. A list of some of the work done 19 August 1948 included the following: 'Drilling out old stays in *Russell* boiler and supplying and fitting 2 new copper stays, Re-lagging boiler with own material, Re-fixing all sheeting

The original maker's plate from *Russell*, now at the National Railway Museum, York.

Another view of *Russell* showing how its profile had been cut-down. The work to lower the cab, chimney and dome was carried out at Dinas when *Russell* was working the Welsh Highland Railway, by then part of the Festiniog Railway. Staff from their Boston Lodge Works carried out the work and it was hoped the locomotive could be used on through workings between Blaenau Festiniog and its home base. Despite the cutting down in height, Russell's tanks proved too wide and were scraping rock outcrops in the narrow Moelwyn tunnel on the Festiniog section. In the event of a failure the engine-men would be unable to leave the footplate. For safety reasons *Russell* was then confined to the WHR, running only as far as Portmadoc Harbour. GEORGE ALLIEZ

with new steel band, removed for inspection. Taking out old and fitting new fusible plugs and fitting new bolts etc. cost £73 1s 6d'. Part of the work was allocated to Willkin & Willkins Ltd, Quayside, Hamworthy who carried out some fitting and engineering work for Fayle's. On 28 July 1948, their invoice simply said, 'Sorting out loco valve gear, etc £14 12s 6d'.

Most of *Russell*'s running problems in Purbeck were due to the locomotive's weight causing the fairly light track to spread, and the engine then becoming derailed by dropping down between the rails. Eli said the engine derailed about 7 or 8 times on the first day. However *Russell* was very suitable in other respects and worked for over 5 years in Purbeck. The leading axle gave trouble, and the bogie was again removed with no real improvement. But the engine was still held in some affection by the men at Norden who called her Jane, after Jane Russell the film star pin-up of the time. The railway men from Pike's, rather like the miners, took a poor view of what went on at Norden. Some of them had been sent over to do repairs

on *Russell*, when Gordon Hatherill happened to visit. The fitters said to Gordon, 'Come up to Furzebrook and we'll show you a real railway!'

On 14 September 1953, one of *Russell*'s coupled axles broke. A month after the axle fractured it was agreed the boiler was also in poor condition, and the clay company offered *Russell* to the Birmingham Locomotive Club at a scrap price of £70.

DIESEL LOCOMOTIVES 1FT 11½ IN GAUGE 1948-72. During most of the five years 1948-53, when *Russell* was first choice for the heavy haulage, the first reserve was a German machine. Just how this diesel locomotive manufacturered by Orenstein and Koppel AG (O&K) arrived in England remains a mystery. It was said to have been working at a V2 rocket site on the French coast during the Second World War. When overrun by the Allied Forces, it became part of the spoils of war.

Prior to the 1920s, Montania was a separate company manufacturing small locomotives and when taken over by O&K it was decided to use

The O&K diesel loco 0-4-0DM 20777 1936. Eli had arranged to pull the O&K diesel outside the shed and leave it for me to photograph during one afternoon in September 1969. AUTHOR

the name as a trademark for all their small engines so locally the German locomotive was referred to as 'The Montania'. Unfortunately O&K's pre-war records have all been lost, but the company told the author that 0-4-0DM locomotive No. 20777, which carried its number on the back of the cab, was a class RL3 probably constructed in 1936 and originally supplied to Marine Sperrzeugant, Kiel, Germany, before active service in France. The Germans had built two huge bunkers and rocket assembly plants at Watten and Wizernes in Pas de Calais, the former being attacked by 185 B17 Flying Fortresses in August 1943 with a view to destroying it, but they were unable to penetrate the extremely thick concrete. By the beginning of September 1944 the Nazis were ready for the rocket offensive against London. However by then, all of northern France and most of Belgium had been liberated by the Allies. The Germans were forced to withdraw and the V2 batteries arrived at The Hague for the attack on Britain. It would seem that the O&K diesels, when captured in France had been used only in the construction of the bunkers.

The side panels of 20777 were typical of the make, displaying the O&K legend painted green and removable to give easy access to the engine. The locomotive wheels were painted red and the weight was 6½ tons complete with covered cab.

John Cooper paid £350 or £400 for the Montania at a Ministry of Supply sale, which was

probably organised by Bungey of Hayes. George Bungey had advertised seven O&K 2ft gauge diesels for sale on 11 February 1949 and No. 21160 was noted in his yard in October that year. John was unable to recall exactly, but thought No. 20777 had remained unsold along with the sister Montania, No. 21160 built 1938, and he was able to negotiate the above price for both locomotives, with the latter in a partly dismantled state. It was originally intended to use No. 21160 solely as a source of spares. It was later sent to a small engineering company in Hamworthy to be rebuilt and emerged with a new cab and a

The second O&K diesel 21160 was rarely used. By 17 April 1954, when Martin Galley took the photograph, the locomotive had been rebuilt with a Leyland radiator.

Ruston diesel No. 175413 passes with a well-loaded wagon 69. Driver George Fry looks out from the cab as Tom Burden greets the photographer. George switched from Pike's to Fayle's in 1941, mainly for the advantage of using compressed air spades instead of hand picks, and began mining Best Blue at No. 10 mine. AUTHOR

George and Tom Burden tip a wagon of waste clay one day in September 1968. Knowle Hill in the background dominates the view. AUTHOR

Leyland radiator, at a cost of £600, but did not see much use due to clutch problems. Montania spare parts were available through Wm. Jones at Charlton.

The O&K 20777 proved to be a powerful machine, used quite regularly when *Russell* was under repair. One day, coming up over the Swanage branch the clutch jammed and if Eli had not acted quickly to shut off the diesel they would have gone right over the end of the reversing siding and down the waste tip. Eli was not so lucky another time when the loco jumped out of gear on the way down to the main road and the train was derailed at the catch points. The engine was half-buried in the bank and to help the re-railing process the tractor from Norden farm was summoned. The German engines had a large starting handle, needing the strength of at least

two men to turn. The action was made even more awkward because the single buffer got in the way. This buffer had one edge cut off so in its original position it jammed under the buffers of the skips and would throw them off the line. This problem was cured, by inverting the buffer of the locomotive, so the flat edge was underneath. This was probably done by Willkins of Hamworthy, who among other items, invoiced 'Turn screw & drill loco buffer rods' for £2 10s 8d on 21 March 1949.

Two small diesel locomotives were located at the weighbridge sidings for most of the time. They were used to take over any trains arriving from the mines for shunting and weight recording, and also to deal with any wagons of waste clay to be tipped in that area. In 1969 waste was being tipped in the old Matchams incline area. The two locos were painted grey and of similar appearance and at first sight the only clue to their separate identities were their brass number plates carrying the maker's name Ruston and the numbers 175413 and 179889. However, each locomotive had a cab of slightly different design, which was the easiest way to distinguish between them.

No. 175413 had a locally made cab-roof constructed of two flat plates, slightly raised where they met in the centre line giving a pitched roof appearance. It was built in January 1936, designated by the makers as 18/21hp and previously worked at the Gillingham pits of Hine Bros (Ringwood) Ltd, cost to Fayle's 6 July 1948, £300.

Small Ruston diesel No. 175413 waiting for its next job, coupled to a flat wagon. In the background to the left, was the small cottage like office where the foreman was based, and where most expeditions into the mines started. Beyond the rather scrappy hedgerow is Five Acres field with Little Coppice behind the office. The Ruston had a home made cab but the toolbox at the rear was original. AUTHOR

Small Ruston No. 175413 photographed with wagon 18 at the wieghbridge. AUTHOR

Ruston 175413 parked in a siding at the workshops, 18 September 1950. B. M. BARBER.

Some jobs are lined up outside the blacksmith's shop. Motor Rail 4wPM was un-numbered and said to have been purchased from the Standard Steel Co Ltd, Croydon. It needs some refurbishment and wagon 60 is receiving attention. AUTHOR

Small Ruston, No. 179889 with curved roof cab and flat wagon. AUTHOR

No. 179889 was a 20hp machine and had an original Ruston cab, with its top plate. curved over the roof from one side to the other, which marked it out from No. 175413. It was also constructed during 1936 in September and went to work for the Severn River Catchment Board before coming to Dorset. Both locomotives were fitted with Lister 18/2 engines. In fact RH 175413 and 179889 were identical machines when supplied, but Ruston changed the class designation from '18/21 HP' to '20 HP' during 1936.

Other small jobs, (1953) could be done using a Simplex petrol-engined loco. This small machine had boat-shaped frames, generally referred to as bent frames by the men at the Motor Rail & Tramcar Company's works, Bedford, where it was made. in large numbers, many for use on light railways by the War Department. (In 1928, after many more had been constructed for various customers, the design was changed to a straight channel frame being cheaper to build, and in 1931 the company name changed to Motor Rail Limited).

Running without any cab, it was rated at 20hp had four chain driven wheels and was identified by a small plate with the wording, 'Standard Steel Co. (1929) Ltd, Croydon Ref. 422.' Having acquired the Simplex by 1945, it was despatched from their works at 72 Purley

Way on 25 May 1948, the Simplex was invoiced to Fayles at £80. It seems likely the MR works plate was removed and replaced by the Standard Steel type during overhaul to ensure any spares required in the future would be ordered from them and not the original maker. Some photographs show it with an original type radiator. Some time later, the radiator was replaced with one from a Karrier bus. It did not get used a great deal, and was scrapped in 1961.

A similar Motor Rail locomotive, with cab, had been transferred from the Furzebrook works in October 1959. This was a four-wheeled petrol

Ruston 179889 was outside the large shed with the 48DL on the right. AUTHOR

Back in service, the Simplex had acquired a Karrier radiator. AUTHOR

The 4wd Simplex 5242 was seen on 28 July 1956 while working at Furzebrook on the 2ft 8in gauge before conversion to 1ft 11½in and its transfer to the Norden system. MARTIN GALLEY

years, it lay derelict alongside O&K 21160 before being scrapped late in 1967

The main workhorse towards the end of the working railway at Norden was another Ruston and Hornsby 4-wheeled diesel loco painted green, with an impressive manifold and brass pipe exhaust added after manufacture, which was clearly seen on hot days when the engine casing was left open. This was the engine most used through the 1960s until the line closed. The locomotive, No. 392117 left the Lincoln factory in 1956, being a 48DL class; that is a 48hp diesel mechanical loco with a four cylinder Ruston engine driving both axles by a chain drive via a three-speed gearbox. It has been reported that 392117 was one of 28 such locos built new in 1956 for contractor Charles Brand for the building of the new tunnels at Hadley Wood, when the main line was being quadrupled north of Potters Bar. At the end of the contract it came to Fayle's on 20 January 1961. Delivery of the locomotive was from the Merton depot of Charles Brand and Son in Surrey, where it had been standing surplus since the tunnel contract was completed in September 1958. However, Fayle's purchase records show it was supplied by G. W. Bungey Ltd, the cost being £900 delivered. The truth was that George Bungey was only acting as agent for the sale, because his original company had gone into liquidation in 1958. The engine, which weighed 7 tons, was a slow speed model with a top speed of 8.46 mph in third gear.

loco, 20/35hp No. 5242 built in 1930, and previously working at Folkestone Quarries Ltd, West Hythe Ballast Pit and Crushing Works, West Hythe, before coming to Pike's in October 1951. The supplier was Bungey of Hayes, where the engine was seen in the yard during March 1951. It is said that 5242 was originally a two-foot gauge petrol loco that was rebuilt with a diesel engine and converted to 2ft 8in gauge by Bungey's for supply to Pike's. The Furzebrook works then carried out reverse conversion from 2ft 8in to 1ft 11½in before sending the loco to Norden in a livery of unlined mid-green. After some rather intermittent use over a period of 8

The diesel that was most used in later days was the green four wheeled Ruston model DL48. It was No. 392117 built in 1956 and came to Fayles in 1961. AUTHOR

It was designed to start a load of 171 tons on the level, in first gear. This reduced to 82 tons on a gradient of 1:100. A supply of spares came from Bungey's on 12 June 1961, invoiced £75. The arrival of RH 392117, now painted green, coincided with the closure of the mill at Norden and its transfer to Furzebrook. The exhaust pipes, which gave the engine its distinctive appearance, replaced the four original pipes, which passed through the side of the engine compartment. For some reason the exhaust pipes had been modified using some brass boiler tubes left in stock from one of the old steam locomotives. The pipes extended vertically through the top of the engine compartment and may have been more efficient in dispersing the exhaust gases.

ROLLING STOCK 1FT 11½IN 1947-1972.
A number of second-hand steel V-shaped side-tipping wagons were bought for the new system, each with a capacity of 1½ cu yd. The wagons were a mixture of Hudson Victory wagons (built 1920 onwards) and Rugga wagons, and also some from W. Jones Ltd. Records from 1950 show that some of the wagons needed attention, such as replacement roller bearings supplied by Robert Hudson Ltd.

Continued scanning of the large dealers' catalogues resulted in more wagon purchases and it was Cohens of Hammersmith, who invoiced Fayle's for 25 more wagons on 18 June 1948. They were listed as 36 cu ft, 24in gauge, Hudson side-tipping wagons at £26 each, duly paid on 10 July.

Three flat wagons were reported supplied by R. A. Lister of Dursley, Gloucs, in 1948, but may have been bought second hand. They were used to transport bagged clay in powdered form, each wagon loaded to 6 tons, and one or two more

One of the Lister flat wagons. R. A. Lister & Co Ltd of Dursley constructed two or three of these flat wagons in 1948. At Norden, they were used for the carriage of bagged clay from the mill, round to the weighbridge and then to the sidings, the maximum load being six tons. They became redundant after 13 years when the mill was moved to Furzebrook. John Cooper told me he thought he had bought them second-hand. 29 May 1969.
GEORGE MOON

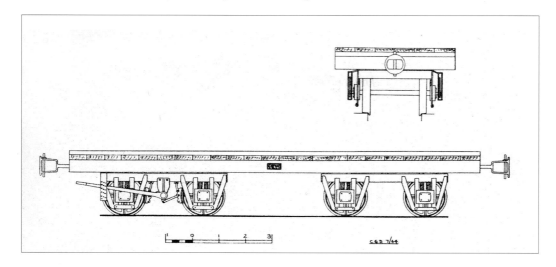

Drawing of Lister flat wagon.
CHRIS DOWN

Home made flat wagon, built by the carpenter to supplement the Lister built wagons, standing in a siding near the old mill with a heap of waste clay behind, probably tipped from the tramway embankment at the top. There may have been a couple of these wagons, fairly lightly built in contrast to the Lister product. Did it work with no buffers? With two bogies of unknown origin, it looks higher off the track and was probably easier when loading sacks by hand. 29 May 1969. GEORGE MOON

Top left: Wagon 6, appropriately at No. 6 mine, one evening in 1969.
Top right: Wagon 113 on the weighbridge at Norden.
Bottom left: Wagon 17 on the weighbridge showing the different style frames of the wagons.
Bottom right: Wagon 118 on the weighbridge, with a rivetted plate joining the frame member. ALL AUTHOR

similar wagons were constructed locally by the clay company. The Lister wagons had steel frames, with decking consisting of 23 transverse planks and 6 longitudinal ones on top. Their length overall was 17ft 9in, the height 2ft 5½in and wheel diameter 18in. The wagon bodies had a length of 15ft 6in and width 4ft 6in and were carried on two bogies, 8ft 4in apart at their centres. Each of the bogies had a wheelbase of 3ft and on each wagon one bogie had brake gear fitted using fibre-lined brake blocks. Another company who proved valuable in the search for railway stock was the Standard Steel Co (1929) Ltd, This was followed up with several batches of wagons, a total of 50 from that source, costing £24 10s each.

Considerable expansion of the mines and their output occurred during the next few years, and the company was again on the lookout for second-hand wagons, preferably with larger capacity and more rugged construction. Fayle's purchase records, from 1958 to 1963 show that over two dozen side-tip wagons were bought from such companies as Cohens, Bungey and M.E. Engineering at prices ranging from £29 to £45. Most were of 2 cu yd capacity but some were 2⅓ cu yd. Some rail was acquired as well. The railway was very busy during this period so 136 wagons were needed to service 6 to 7 mines. Four shafts were open, Nos.10, 12, 14 and 16, as well

as the open pit. At least 2 inclines were working, Nos. 4, 5, or 6, so three or more trips daily, about 36 full skips, were necessary to transfer clay to the weighbridge.

Much later, in 1969, a list of wagon tare weights was kept at the weighbridge to record the exact weight of mined clay. The operational wagons were then numbered from 1 to 119, and 140, a total of 120. Because of the various sources, there was quite a mix of weights. For example wagons in the 11cwt range were 28, 29, 30, 50 to 53, 57, 59, and 63 to 66. Most of the later wagons weighed in between 17 and 18cwt,

Wagon 21 had a very angular design and looked like a German or Continental type. The wagon behind it, No. 22 looked similar. Could these have been spoils of war, like the O&K diesels? AUTHOR

On 6 December 1965, wagon No. 21 was in use next to the Ruston 175413 at the Norden east siding. A similar wagon was at the end of the train, probably No. 22. AUTHOR

This wagon with a cylindrical diesel tank was converted from one of the old 3ft 9in wagons, recorded on 29 May 1969. AUTHOR

examples being 91 to 95, 97, 98 and 101 to 107. The rest weighed anything from 10 to 27cwt.

The steel chassis of a homemade 4-wheel 'flat' wagon was on site in 1969. It had been run away down a slope southeast of the skew bridge, and it was apparently used for moving pit prop timbers. WAGONS CONVERTED FROM 3FT 9IN TO 1FT 11½IN.

Two wagons were in use regularly for the transport of diesel fuel. They had been converted to 1ft 11½in from 'broad gauge' wagons using just the 'chassis' adapted to support the fuel tanks. One tank was circular in section, and the other oval.

Another converted wagon, with an oval fuel tank. AUTHOR

Norden No. 7 last underground clay mine in Dorset, 1992

An event, which surprised everyone connected with the clay industry, was a new drift mine being built about 30 years after No. 6. When work commenced in 1992-93 the main intention was for No. 7 to replace mine No. 6 to reach deeper deposits of clay, but no one realised this would be the last underground railway operating in Dorset. Before then, no clay mine had been purposely driven to meet with other existing workings underground, but a connection with No. 6 mine would provide an alternative safety exit for the miners as well as ventilation. The main tunnel and haulage railway would be over 400 metres long the longest in Dorset, and the miners would be about 280 ft. below the surface.

The plan was to excavate all of the saturated sand and gravel down to the clay, put in the first 200 feet of tunnel to that point and backfill the excavation. The upper part of the tunnel was made of pre-cast concrete 'rings' having an oblong section, of which 34, each 2 metres wide, would be used giving a length of 68 metres or 221ft from the entrance gate. Each block weighed about 10 tons. Excavators provided an initial slope of 1 in 4 down to the clay area and a concrete 'road' was laid to the width of the tunnel sections. The sections were designed to withstand different stresses with depth and therefore numbered in the order to be installed and would be moved down the slope to their final position in the tunnel. This was achieved using two small winches and small diesel engines. Each block was sealed to the next using a bitumastic strip where the overlapping lip of two sections met, thus forming a continuous watertight tunnel.

By May 1993 the stage was being built using the hydraulic bins and girders from Greenspecks mine, which had just closed. A Clarke Chapman winch was installed and a Joy compressor brought from the Devon ball clay operation was being installed in the compressor shed to partner the Broom & Wade. The slope down to the entrance of the tunnel was roofed over and the sides were slat timbered in order to let warm air being ventilated from the mine escape to the atmosphere. This avoided any condensation

Building the incline to No. 7 mine. By 14 October 1992, eleven blocks were in position, ready to receive the next segment of the tunnel. AUTHOR

The half built steel structure of No 7 incline. The hydraulic bins have been installed for clay storage before loading into lorries. Level with the top of the bins going right is the tipping stage and a further extension to the embankment built up on the right. Both of these would have the mine shed structures built on them housing the winch, a re-charger unit for cap(helmet) lights and other mining equipment. AUTHOR

The slope down to the mine entrance being timbered in. AUTHOR

inside the colder stage housing. The rails forming the mine haulage had also been installed up to the stage level and most of the metal sheeting had been fixed to the floor of the stage to minimise wear from the wagon wheels.

At the end of January 1994 a two-man mining team, Robert (Bob) White and Chris Creech, started cutting the clay in the tunnel driving forward at three to five feet a day. There was only room for one gang to work in the tunnel, so progress would get slower the deeper they went. While the wagon was being wound out they had to take refuge, so there was up to 15 minutes down time before an empty wagon arrived back at the face. At 150 metres (early 1995) the mine started to pay with the face consisting of the top ¾ PK clay and the bottom ¼ red clay. The gradient of the tunnel was slackened from 1 in 4 to 1 in 6 and then to 1 in

13 and eventually to 1 in 18 during June 1995 to avoid old clay workings and accumulated water. The roof for the new tunnel needed to be 7 or 8 metres thick to support the old ground and as there was water about 4ft below the new drive, getting the slope right was quite critical. By the following spring 1996, the tunnel was about 300 metres long and the miners were about 180ft below the surface. They would soon reach the point where the gradient eased to 1 in 100 at the sidings area, which would be double track for about 80ft. For the twin track area the clay face was widened to 12ft allowing for wider girders than usual to give a siding for empty wagons. Andy Ward was making the first set of points at the Furzebrook shops, which would be normal blade action going into the haulage and a fixed crossing to go out at the other end.

During the night of Wednesday 28 August 1996 water broke into No. 6 mine and because the new mine was then open to those workings, and lower in depth, the whole area became flooded reaching about 200yds up the tunnel of No. 7. A round the clock clean up operation began but the new mine was so badly affected the drive would not be back to normal until February 1997. Whereas the forecast had been for 30 years work at the mine, this was now put at 10 years only. The additional cost to the clay extraction would also affect the viability of the mine; Norden mined clay went up from £32 to £51 per tonne after the flooding costs had been added. Material cost had been £90,000. Digging the initial hole had cost £15,000 and the concrete tunnel sections had swallowed up £40,000. The other main expenditure had been moving the stage and making the concrete base.

By 1998, there was less urgency for Norden production because the amount of PK clay required to make the Excelsior blend, had been cut from 5,000 tonnes per annum to 3,500. More open pit clay from Povington was being used instead and the future of underground mining was hanging by a thread. During 1999 there was talk of a take-over bid for ECC. On 27 August the decision was taken to stop pumping at the mines, so both underground operations ceased. Switching off the life support to the mines saw the end of a special breed of men as most of the miners took severance pay and left the industry. It also meant the end for rail-operated transport

A quick visit to the Furzebrook blacksmith shop found a set of points being fabricated for the main haulage at No. 7 incline. This double track section would be widened to 12 feet to give a siding for empty wagons, about 80ft long and 190ft below the surface with a 1,400ft haul out. At the entrance would be the normal blade action point, the straight track was for pulling out loaded wagons, while the loop going off to the right was for empties entering the mine. The double track would merge again at a fixed crossing before going deeper into the mine. Haul out time about 4 minutes. AUTHOR

and underground clay mining at the former Fayle pits after 194 years. Subsequently, Imerys Minerals Ltd, the new owners, donated the mine structure to the Purbeck Mineral and Mining Museum. It was dismantled, removed across the A351 road and rebuilt as the centrepiece of the museum opened in 2013 near Norden Station on the Swanage Railway.

21st Century, still a healthy demand for Purbeck clay, but...

On average four production clays 'as dug' from the mine are mixed to give a saleable blend of consistent quality to suit different manufacturers. The blends depend on the higher quality clays being mixed with lower quality and without the quality base it becomes impossible to meet the specification. In 2002, some 26 clays were being mixed in various proportions to make 24 saleable blends. Another way to provide the specification might have been to refine lower quality clay by the removal of impurities, but because the clay is so fine grained it is impracticable and energy consuming to alter the fundamental mineral. This might become possible with further research. Underground mining, and loads of higher quality clays hand trammed by rail, might become feasible again, but only if lower ball clay production overall led to a greatly increased price on world markets. This would be preferred to disturbance of the ground by open work so long as any new mine buildings were the same size as the traditional loading stage. However, because the old mines have been dismantled any renewed underground working would require re-development of shafts and underground roadways. The general feeling of the remaining workforce in the clay industry is that the days of clay extraction in Purbeck are numbered.

So although the local planning policy is to shift ball clay extraction into the area north of the River Frome, the loss of quality clays would seriously affect blending and the company's viability. An added cost is the increased demand for the restoration of disturbed ground. Whereas, at one time, old clay workings were left to return to nature over a number of years and provided valuable habitat for wild life, the policy now is to regenerate the area much more quickly, and even re-create new types of heath-land, through to valley mires. Even so, a time factor of 20 years is built into the development of such areas and more if deciduous woodland is part of the plan. Green issues tend to dominate and take precedence over mining requirements. New people now living in the area do not understand the value of a local employer and traditional industry.

Following the take over of ECC Ball Clays by Imerys Minerals Ltd in 1999, clay production still continues from open pits located away from the Norden mines and hopefully the future of the industry will be perpetuated there. Trigon, Povington, Arne, Dorey's and Furzeyground are the remaining clay extraction sites. These are located on what was the former Pike's mining territory around Creech and Furzebrook and in 2005 planning was being sought for an extension to the Trigon workings. Despite this being a preferred area it was over a year before permission was granted.

By March 2006, John Bowring, the company's Finance Controller, reported other costs rising dramatically, such as energy, which had virtually doubled in one year. For the same reasons, manufacturers were moving to the Far East, North Africa or Brazil to save labour costs, and because clay is expensive to move around the world, they were looking for cheaper sources nearer to consumption. For example, by the year 2000, using modern shallow draught ships, individual cargoes of clay for export had risen from 3,000 to 5,000 tonnes, although there were still some ships taking orders of 1,500 to 2,000 tonnes. With new working practice, 5,000 tonnes of clay could be loaded comfortably in two days, a job which previously took three days. In 2002 the Poole Harbour cargo 'dues' for clay was £0.45 per tonne and the loading cost £2.07 per tonne. On 17 April the *Celtic Commander* sailed for Castellon with 5,300 tonnes for which the dues came to £2,385 and the loading cost was £10,971. Most of the clay in 2002 went to Castellon and Tarragona in Spain, but a few loads went elsewhere to Villagarcia, also in Spain south of Corunna, Antwerp, Genoa Italy, Solvesborg Sweden, Leixoes Portugal, Rotterdam and Dordrecht, Nederlands.

John's parting remark was, 'Here in Purbeck we are sticking to shredding and milling which we do best, and hopefully the Company will be around to celebrate 250 years'. The longevity of the clay mining industry speaks volumes for the generations of clay getters who have toiled away to send millions of tons of Dorset clay around the

During the year 2000, 58 ships called at Poole to load clay. A record had been set the previous year, the total being just under 150,000 tonnes, but that had already been exceeded by the end of October 2000, with 156,234 tonnes. The author was visiting the Harbour Office soon after and was escorted down to see one of those ships in the final stages of loading for Spain and the tile making industry. The *Pedernales* had arrived in Poole Harbour from Bilbao on 13 November 2000. In two days with poor weather, 1,690 tonnes of clay were loaded at the Ballast Quay followed by preparations for getting the ship under way. Quietly, at 12.30 on 15 November the ship moved imperceptibly away from the quayside and slid down the channel bound for Castellon. AUTHOR

world. Two years later in January 2008 the works were still busy with clay arriving by lorry from different directions, but Arne was being worked out with no further permissions and Furzeyground with its shallow clay and the cheapest to extract was also running low. The market for refractory clays had virtually disappeared and future business would rely on Dorey's, Povington and Trigon with possible new extraction at Hawkpost. Some new orders came in for bagged clay, which was being shipped in containers to India and China via Southampton. By 2013 the orders amounted to about 5,000 tonnes per annum used to produce electro-porcelain. Extraction at Arne was then finished and the area back-filled to the harbour. Dorey's pit was due to be closed and replaced by a new opencast site near the Grange Road and Trigon was forecast to go on producing TLD (Trigon Light Dark) and SM (Sandy Mining) clay until 2018. An extension eastwards was planned for Povington.

It seems like only yesterday that on those journeys to school back in the 1950s, whistles were being exchanged between our passing Swanage branch train and the polished steam locomotives preparing for work on Pike's 2ft 8in system. The scene is etched on the mind after a thousand journeys. At that time I was unaware that the Furzebrook railway system also had a history spanning well over 100 years. But that is another story.

The back plate to *Tiny*'s cab was retained at Norden and used as part fencing to retain sand, gravel and other materials. It was purchased by Alan Keef and is still used for a similar purpose at Ross on Wye. One side was apparently longer than the other to accommodate the hand brake.

Thames was sold for scrap in September 1948, but someone rescued the nameplate and the worksplate. These two items were sold in a Great Central Railway auction in October 2011 for £1,250. The nameplate made of cast brass, measured 22½ x 5¾ inches and had its front re-painted. In Manning Wardle's records it said of the nameplate *Thames*, the first letter was 3½in, remainder 2½ in. The worksplate also cast brass, measured 11 x 6 inches with the front re-painted.

After *Russell* failed in 1953, the management of Fayle's, by then Pike Bros. Fayle & Co Ltd, was approached by the Birmingham Locomotive Club with a view to purchasing the locomotive for preservation. A sale was eventually agreed for £70 and the locomotive was transported to the Talyllyn Railway, Narrow Gauge Museum, Towyn, in August 1955. After ten years, stored out of use at Towyn in mid Wales, *Russell* was moved to Porthmadog and eventually restored and put back to work again on the Welsh Highland Heritage Railway, Porthmadog (WHHR). *Russell* was successfully steamed in 1986 and back on Welsh Highland metals after an absence of almost 50 years.

One of the original nameplates fixed to *Russell* 1906-1942 is at the National Railway Museum (NRM) in York, but the whereabouts of the other nameplate is unknown. The original worksplate from *Russell* can be seen in the 'Warehouse' open store at the NRM.

When *Russell* was refurbished in 1942 by the steelworks in Brymbo near Wrexham, two new brass nameplates were made and carried by *Russell* for the next ten years, until the locomotive was withdrawn in 1953. One of those is owned by the WHHR. The other was thought to be lost. However it was saved by an enthusiast and passed to the Industrial Railway Society (IRS) on his death. The IRS has now placed it on loan with the WHHR.

In August 2007, *Russell*'s frames were observed receiving attention at the WHHR workshops. They were hoping this rebuild would be completed for the proposed 2009 reinstatement of the entire line from Carnarfon to join the Festiniog at Porthmadog, but progress was slow and *Russell* was then expected to be in traffic again by 2011. In April 2012 the Board of the WHHR decided to send *Russell*'s rolling chassis, boiler and fabricated components to Alan Keef Engineering Ltd at Ross on Wye to complete the overhaul/restoration of the locomotive. In June 2012 an appeal for £125,000 was made to complete the work. There was a flood of contributions. In February 2013, a donation of £25,000 was received from a longstanding donor, who offered to match other donations received to the end of May, up to another £25,000. By May 2014 Patrick Keef reported that *Russell* was almost completed but unpainted. There had been a delay in the delivery of side tanks. It was hoped the locomotive would be steamed in May/June 2014 and shortly after that to be working again on the WHHR.

When the Norden clay line closed the two O&K locomotives were bought by Barry Curl of Durley and the chassis of 21160 was subsequently sold in 1992 to Jim Haylock of the Moors Valley Railway (MVR) at Ashley Heath near Ringwood to be rebuilt, Mr Curl retaining the engine. The chassis consisted of the wheel sets and suspension, some brake rodding and other gear and Jim thought O&K had probably derived the diesel design from a former steam locomotive. He subsequently rebuilt it, with the help of Tim Woron, to a 0-4-0T steam locomotive, with 6in x 10in cylinders driving 18in diameter wheels. At the reopening of the Lynton and Barnstaple Railway in May 2003, at Woody Bay Station, the locomotive was named *Emmet* after the pet cat on the MVR, the livery being maroon, edged black and lined out in yellow. In 2013, *Emmet* visited the Swanage Railway Gala weekend 6 to 8

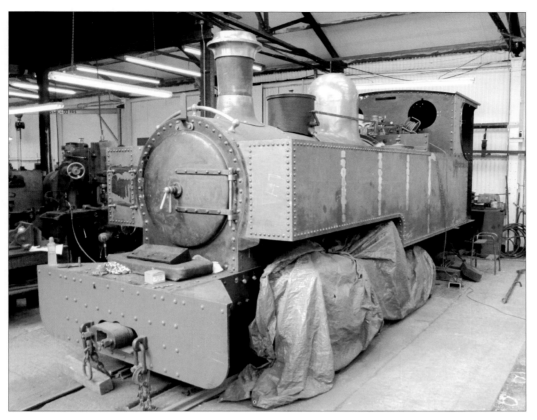

The restoration/rebuild of *Russell* is coming to a climax in the Alan Keef engineering works at Ross on Wye. By June 2014, new tanks had been fitted to the locomotive, shortly to be removed again to allow final painting. It was hard to find a moment without tools, equipment, forklifts and workers around the engine. A sheet protects the motion while the loco is worked on. Russell has since returned to Wales and is steaming on selected dates at the WHHR, Porthmadog. PATRICK KEEF

September and was in steam at the Purbeck Mineral and Mining Museum. *Emmet* was the first steam locomotive at Norden since *Russell* failed in 1953.

When Barry Curl died, his wife decided to sell the O&K 20777, which came on the market at an Auction on 6 October 2012. Although there were hopes the O&K might return to Norden it was bought for the Statfold Barn Railway for £26,000. The best hope for the future would be a guest appearance on the Norden museum line.

RH 392117 has survived, initially purchased by a syndicate at Four Winds, Durley, Southampton, where the engine was running at week-ends until the Hampshire Narrow Gauge Railway Society moved from that location. The locomotive was then sold to Dave Knott, then to Richard Bentley, and has since been refurbished at the Old Kiln Light Railway. The engine will return to its home at Norden in 2016 and after some mechanical attention will run again at the mining museum.

The two small Ruston locomotives, 175413 and 179889 were bought by A. M. Keef, then of Bampton, Oxon in August 1972 and sold for further use to a logging company in Singapore.

Alan also bought the remaining rail at Fayle's and the converted 3ft 9in wagon chassis on which the oval fuel tank was carried. By then the tank was missing, perhaps returned to Furzebrook works for further use. Alan laid the rail to form a metre gauge track at the Cotswold Water Park, South Cerney, which was used for a few years to run some Belgium tramcars.

Hudson skips, Nos. 9, 13, 17, 38 72 74 and 101 went to Seaton Tramway by 1973. Some were widened to 2ft 9in gauge for use on the tramway.

The Purbeck Mineral and Mining Museum is now fully open with its rebuilt stage from Incline No. 7, and a section of underground mine tunnel. Part of the former mineral tramway is running again and together the museum gives a fine interpretation of the history and technology of the ball clay industry. A future aim is to relay the tramway over the skew bridge just south of Norden Station to re-create scenes last experienced in 1971. For full details visit www.pmmmg.org or email curator@swanage-railway.co.uk. In 2013/14 the Museum received a National award from the Heritage Railway Association.

APPENDIX TWO
BALL CLAY MINING AT ROLLINGTON

The record shows that Rollington Farm, which was part of the Rempstone Estate, had been leased by John Calcraft to John Symonds of Bushey from 13 December 1761. The term was for 14 years at a rent of £141 10s per annum, and the land included the Heath called Thresher's Heath adjoining the farm. The rights were reserved to Calcraft, the whole area being honeycombed with old workings.

During the time that Fayles were mining at Arfleet, another company started prospecting and extracting clay at Rollington, on what was now Ryder's land under East Hill, situated on the opposite side of the Studland road to the Arfleet workings. Ryder was a descendant of the Calcrafts. The new clay company originated through the working of ball clay in south Devon, when in 1919, F. W. Marshall, formed the Mainbow Clay Co. Ltd., to work ball clay at Mainbow. In 1920, the company was taken over by H. D. Pochin and Co. Ltd., and in 1923, when they acquired the ball clay deposits at Rollington, a new company was formed, Pochin Ball Clay Co., to work both Mainbow and Rempstone.

The mining at Rollington was largely open cast, but as the pit became deeper, a series of lanes were driven off in an eastward direction toward Rollington Farm, and also toward East Hill. The clay itself was good quality, but was interpersed with unwanted mineral, and was deposited more in layers with pinny or flinty clay above, rather than in a deep lens. Ultimately, it was the geological problems that shortened the life of the mine; the same problem that plagued the clay from Thresher's pit in Wedgwood's day.

By the late 1930s, foreman Taylor was in charge, who had come up from Devon, along with Rayleigh Keam, who operated the main winch, and Ernie Kerswell, a miner from lvybridge. Some of the clay cutters were, Bill Diffey and Harold Tatchell who later worked for Fayle's, and Bill Collins who came to work here from Pike's Creech Common mine. William Collins was bom about 1890, and his father Benjamin born 1851 was also a clay worker, above ground.

Another of the miners who worked at Rollington was Colin Vamey. He was born in 1923, the grandson of Charlie Jeffries, the most experienced Fayle's miner. Living in Essex at the outbreak of war, Colin's family evacuated to Corfe Castle and he started work at Pochin's in 1940. The tunnels into the clay were supported by 5ft. 3in. timbers, with one gang working in each tunnel. The clay was loaded into wooden wagons at the face, each holding about 8 cwt, and winched out of the tunnel where it was tipped into larger metal skips, holding about 2 tons. Two of these skips were then hauled up to level ground using a gantry, said to be out of sight of the winder, whose winch shed was, up under the hill ! The clay was despatched in three ways, most of it going via Corfe Castle station. Some was weighed into hessian bags with a 2 cwt capacity. The necks of the bags were stitched up by a few of the older men in the village and much of this clay was carted to Corfe station for despatch to India and South America. Bulk loose clay was also sent from the station and, for export, loose clay went by lorry to Poole, to be loaded into ships from the quay side.

Waste clay from the workings was hand trammed through a short tunnel under the Studland road and dumped in the old Fayle workings at Arfleet. There has been some speculation that the tunnel under the Studland road was somehow connected with the Arfleet branch of the Norden to Goathorn line, and allowed Tiny to access the works at Rollington. This never happened. The two workings were quite separate and operated by the two different companies. The Arfleet mining by Fayle's was almost finished, before Pochin's began work at Rollington.

Colin Varney joined the Army from 1942 to 1946, and returned to Rollington after his service under Class B release. When Pochin's closed down in 1951, he transferred to Fayle's where one of his main jobs was winchman at the No. 4 incline, from the time it opened, to the time he left in 1958, when the mine was still working. Colin returned in 1969 to Furzebrook works, where he worked in the mill for 14 years.

SOURCES AND ACKNOWLEDGEMENTS

I have derived great pleasure from the research involved and the writing of this book. Following that 1969 visit described in the introduction, one of the first people who pointed me in the right direction was Patrick Henshaw, who gave me a copy of an essay he had written on the *First Railway in Dorset, Fayle's Tramway*. George Moon shared research notes from 1969 onwards to the present day and I am greatly indebted to George for all his input and photographs. We were linked to another mutual friend Gordon Hatherill with all his knowledge and contacts on the engineering side. More helpful information came during the 1970s and 1980s in correspondence with C. N. Sykes, who had written newspaper articles on the Goathorn tramway; gleaned when he lived at Studland. A visit to Westbury added copies to the photo collection from S. W. Baker, who lent his negatives for printing and agreed their use in any subsequent history. Michael Blackmore helped to bring to life the early days of the Middlebere plateway through his drawings.

Roger Kidner exchanged letters about his visits to the tramway. Our discussions always produced more information and he also was quick to lend negatives for printing and write the latest news. At the same time all this was happening, I found a welcome at the mines office at Furzebrook, largely due to family friend Ferdi Stanzell, Mines Manager. Over many visits there, I had complete access to all the mining maps for study and photography. This privilege, more than any other thing, gave me a clear insight into how the industry had developed over the years. Ferdi also took me on a visit to the Povington open clay pit. Brenda Chappell local researcher gifted me the set of B. Fayle & Co, photos taken on the opening of the 1907 tramway. John Rowley has kept me in touch with developments at the Purbeck Mineral & Mining Museum (PMMM) and supplied valuable information from his own research such as the 1870 account of a passenger train on the Middlebere plateway. Jimmy Samways, ex engineer-fitter above and below ground, has a virtual museum of clay mining artefacts in his garden and many a story

to tell. A few of us had some good evenings sharing memories around his fire.

I have received so much help in writing up the history that someone is sure to be missed, and I hope they will forgive me if they have been overlooked. If they were contacts who worked for Pike's, rather than Fayle's, they will appear in a later history. Some of them were old friends of the family, who directed me on to others who became friends in turn. On other occasions there were memorable evening meals with John and Sheilah Cooper. John had been Managing Director of Fayle's before the merger with Pike's and subsequently of ECC Ball Clays Ltd., Wareham, and his family included Frank Longmire and Richard Pinney, former managers of Benjamin Fayle and Co Ltd. John arranged various visits to mines for the author. Cecil Ellis also supplied details of his employment and directorship of the company. Over afternoon tea in Swanage, W. J. (Tom) Stiff kindly supplied family information, photographs (from his sister Nancy) and copy documents from when their father (Sydney James) ran the business from 1903 to 1945. The other bonus for me, when making visits near Wareham, was having time to sneak up to Grange and enjoy the wonderful views and scenery of Purbeck, taking time to visit a mine or knock on an old friend's door. Elsie Tomes answered my questions about life at Newton and Goathorn and her forebears, the Tubb family who were so involved with the running of the Goathorn end of the clay works for several generations. Ian Makinson also shared knowledge of his family connections to the Tubb family, and I explored the churchyards at Studland and Corfe Castle. When John Cooper moved to ECC head office at St Austell, local promotions followed, and Alister Currie was made Operation Manager UK. Andy Hill, who I had also known since he joined the company as a surveyor, became Development Manager, ECC International, by then a member of Imerys Minerals Ltd.

After endless more visits to Purbeck it would not be surprising if my welcome had worn thin. I am glad to report quite the opposite. A series of early morning visits and photo shoots during the building of No.7 incline were encouraged by Norman Vye, then Production Manager, who became a good friend. John Bowring, Finance Director, whose office had been re-located above the Furzebrook Laboratory allowed me access to several cupboards full of old ledgers moved when the Wareham office closed. A number of visits and hours were spent searching these for information. John often welcomed me by saying, 'Thought you might like to see this' and out would come some old production, shipping or correspondence ledger. My most recent foray in searching for more records included a visit to Stuart Knott of Imerys Minerals at Furzebrook. Stuart has taken on the running of the local mining operation and somehow accepted me as part of the furniture, finding time to help my enquiries in the most positive way. The loan of working maps for copying has been a case of going the extra mile. Brian Jones wrote in detail on the geology and origins of ball clay.

Help and encouragement was always available from the more formal places of enquiry. The Dorset County Record Office, now renamed the Dorset History Centre were very efficient at producing documents such as Tithe maps showing the tramway, leases for clay extraction and estate records such as the Scott's of Encombe, the Calcrafts of Rempstone and the Bankes of Kingston Lacy. At that time, hours could be spent perusing and copying any clay reports in filmed copies of the Dorset County Chronicle located at the Reference Library. Richard de Peyer, Curator of the Dorset County Museum, kept me informed of any clay photographs added to their collection and I was privileged to visit the storage cellars and read some of the original Dorset newspapers. Mike O'Hara and Ben Buxton of the Wareham Museum provided copies of other photographs.

Further afield, I was aided by Gaye Blake Roberts, Curator of the Wedgwood Museum, Barlaston, Stoke-on-Trent. Martin Phillips of Keele University, where the Wedgwood Archive was then stored gave valuable advice. Special thanks to Helen Burton, the Archivist for the Wedgwood collection, who beyond the call of duty, always had papers ready for me to read after a long drive to Stoke. The City of Birmingham Reference Library provided material from the Railway and Canal Historical Society Collection. Lloyd's Register of Shipping, London gave information on ships collecting clay, as did Frank Turland of Poole Maritime Trust. The Central Library, Sheffield holds records on British patents. The Greater London Council Record Office, as it was in 1980, provided information on *Thames* and the work carried out on the Northern Outfall Sewer enlargement 1902-08. The Harbour Office at Poole, not only allowed me space and time to copy ship movements and the loading of clay, but also provided copies of the relevant costs of shipping, and mugs of coffee as the days wore on. Thirty years of records and more besides! Early charts of Poole Harbour were examined at the British Museum Map Room and information on the ship *Gustafsberg* was supplied by Marianne Landquist, of Aktiebolaget Gustavsbergs Fabriker, Gustavsberg, Sweden. Mike Wilmott sent details of his research into the Middlebere plateway, particularly on the position of existing blocks and gauge. Clive Dowding spent some time with me excavating and photographing blocks near the mouth of the 1807 tunnel. Paul Webb, another researcher has conducted walks taking in the routes and remains of the various clay lines, and another stimulus in recording the history of ball clay mining in Purbeck has been the work of the Ball Clay Heritage Society based in Newton Abbot. Roy Link did some early work on the publication.

I am indebted to the following people for information on Fayle's clay mining activity.

George Allingham, foreman at Norden 1980s who arranged visits underground.

Allan C. Baker gave technical information on the tramway.

Gordon Beazer, mines manager.

D. Bennett of Thor Tools, suppliers of pneumatic spades.

Michael Boquet on shipping.

Leonard (Bob) Bugler, clay mill operator at Norden.

J. O. (Jim) Bugler, clay miner, and pit winder.

John Burgess was fitter & engineer at Norden.

Brenda Chappell, photos showing the opening of the Norden to Goathorn Railway.

Harry Clark, Steward of the Rempstone estate.

Hubert Coffen, was winch-man at various mines for 35 years.

Alister Currie, was Imerys Operation Manager UK.

Dr Chris Down, drawings of Lister wagons.

Graham Feldwick for sharing his experience of narrow gauge.

Frankie Foot, a pit winder at No.6 incline.

Charlie Fry was pit winder at No.14 shaft.

George Fry, miner and later driver of small Norden diesel locomotives.

Arthur Gaskell, geographer.

Fred Green, clay miner at Arfleet and Rollington.

William (Ernie) Gover from the weathering beds.

Dennis Guy, miner.

John Hartill of Minton china works.

Andrew Hawkes of Poole gave details of the tugs and early lifeboat activity.

Eli Kitcatt, who first drove horses, and then steam and diesel locomotives.

Dr M. J. T. Lewis, for his expert knowledge of early railways.

Derek Parham, Company Engineer.

Douglas Ryder, then owner of Rempstone.

Frank Selby, miner and foreman.

Ferdi Stanzel, mines manager.

Bert Stockley, son of Thomas James (Tommy) Stockley who drove Tiny.

Wilf Stockley, miner.

S. W. (Bill) Swain, Company Secretary.

Colin Varney was first a miner and then mill worker.

Norman Vye, first a miner, foreman and then production manager.

Charley (Mama) Welsh, miner.

Ernest (Midge) Welsh, miner and foreman.

Alan Williamson, mining engineer.

The response from photographers has been both generous and almost overwhelming. Sometimes, one person has provided almost a collection in itself, while from another just one or two shots have been equally valued in building up the jigsaw.

James Aston, S. W. Baker, Gordon Bartlet, Andrew Bibby, J. I. C. Boyd, Dennis Cullum, Peter Deegan, Martin Galley, Ken Hartley, Humphrey G. W. Household, Frank Jones, Roger W. Kidner, Dr Michael J. T. Lewis, John Loakes, Michael Messenger, S. C. Nash, Andrew Pilborough, D. Pinniger, R. G. Pratt, John Scrace, John B. Snell, Tom Stiff, Colin Sykes, R. Tunstall, Russell Wear, H. Wheeller and George Woodcock. Dick Riley sold his black & white photo collection of Purbeck mineral railways jointly to George Moon and the author. Gordon Lillington lent a rare photo showing some miners at work in the 1930s. Dr M. R. Galley sent photographs from Canada and Philip Hunt sent a batch of colour slides from New Zealand, taken at Norden in 1963.

You have all been amazingly helpful, and I hope the satisfaction of recording the working life of the ball clay industry for future generations to enjoy will be sufficient reward for all our efforts.

BIBLIOGRAPHY

PRINTED SOURCES, BOOKS.

Arkell, W. J. *The Geology of the country around Weymouth, Swanage and Corfe Castle*, HMSO,1947.

Ball Clay Heritage Society, *Ball Clays of Devon & Dorset*, Cornish Hillside Publications, 2003.

Ball Clay Mineral resources Consultative Committee, HMSO 1973.

Baxter, B. *Stone Blocks and Iron Railways*, 1966.

Beamish/Dockerill/Hillier, *The Pride of Poole 1688-1851*, Borough of Poole 1974.

Beaton, David *Dorset Maps*, Dovecote Press 2001.

Baynton-Williams, Ashley *Moule's County maps of the West of England*, Bracken Books, 1994.

Bristow, C. R. et al. *Mineral resources of East Dorset*, British Geological Survey, 2002

Clammer Richard *Cosens of Weymouth 1848-1918*, Black Dwarf Publications 2005.

Cochrane, C. *Poole Bay & Purbeck 300BC-AD1660*, Friary Press, 1970.

Cooper, Ilay, *Purbeck Revealed*, James Pembroke, 2004.

Cox, Peter & Hearne, C. M. *Redeemed from the Heath, archaeology 1987-90*, Dorset Natural History & Archaeological Society, 1991.

Curr, J. *The Coal Viewer and Engine Builders Practical Companion*, 1797 (rep. 1970)

Deegan, Peter *Introducing Russell*, Russell restoration Fund 1969.

Dendy Marshall, C. F. *A History of British Railways down to the year 1830*, Oxford University Press 1938, 1971.

Dorset County Council, *Ball clay in Dorset*, County Planning Department, Dorchester, May 1982.

Dorset County Council, *Ball Clay in Dorset, Technical Memorandum*, 1982

Dorset County Council, *Dorset Minerals and Waste Local Plan (Draft)*, 1991-94.

Dorset County Council, et al. *Dorset Minerals and Waste Local Plan*, April 1999.

Fairclough, T & Shepherd, E. *Mineral Railways of the West Country*, Bradford Barton, 1975.

Farey, J. A. *General View of the Agriculture and Minerals of Derbyshire*, 1813.

Griffin A. R. *Coalmining*, Longman 1971.

Hadfield, C. & Skempton A.W. *William Jessop, Engineer*, David & Charles, 1979.

Hateley, Roger *Industrial Railways of South-west England*, Industrial Railway Society, 1977.

Highley, D. A. et al. *Sustainable development issues for Mineral Extraction; The Wareham Basin of East Dorset*, British Geological Survey 2002.

Hillier, John *Ebb-tide at Poole*, Poole Historical Trust 1985.

Hutchins John *History of the County of Dorset*, 3rd edition, 1861.

Hughes, Stephen *The Brecon Forest Tramroads*, Royal Commission on Ancient and Historical Monuments in Wales, 1990.

Ingham, Paul *Two foot Gauge Rails to the Ironstone*, RCL Publications 2000.

Jackson, B. L. *Swanage 125 years of Railways*, Oakwood Press 2010.

Kelly, Alison *Mrs Coade's Stone*, Self publishing 1990.

Kelly's Directory of Dorsetshire, various dates.

Kerr, Barbara, *Bound to the soil*, John Baker Publishers, 1968.

Kidner, R. W. *The Railways of Purbeck*, Oakwood Press, 1973.

Kidner, R. W. *Mineral Railways*, Oakwood Press, 1967.

Lead, Peter *The Trent & Mersey Canal*, Moorland Publishing 1980.

Legg, Rodney *Purbeck Island*, Dorset Publishing Company, 1972 & 1989.

Legg, Rodney *Purbeck's Heath, Claypits,nature & the oilfield*, Dorset Publishing Company 1987.

Lewis, M. J. T. *Early Wooden Railways*, 1970.

Lucking J. H. *Railways of Dorset*, RCTS 1968

Meates, Joyce *Goathorn, a forgotten Clayworking Community*, Purbeck View Publishing 2013.

Messenger, Michael *Industrial Railways of the South West,* Twelveheads Press 2005.

Messenger, Michael, *North Devon Clay,* Twelveheads Press 2007.

Meteyard Eliza, *The Life of Josiah Wedgwood,* Hurst & Blackett, 1866.

Mitchell, V. & Smith, K. *Branch lines to Swanage,* Middleton Press, 1986

Neale, A. *Russell,* The Welsh Highland Railway (1964) Ltd.,1996.

Outram, B. *Minutes to be observed in the Construction of Rail-ways,*1801.

Page, W. *The Victoria History of the County of Dorset,* vol. 2 Archibald Constable, 1908.

Payne, Donald *Dorset Harbours,* Christopher Johnson, 1953.

Pigot's Directory, various dates.

Rattenbury, G. & Cook, R. *The Hay and Kington Railways,* Railway Canal Historical Society, 1996.

Ripley, David *The Little Eaton Gangway and the Derbyshire Canal,* Oakwood Press, 1973/93.

Robinson, C. E. *A Royal Warren or Picturesque Rambles in the Isle of Purbeck,* The Typographic Etching Co. 1882.

Ryder, Richard D. *The Calcrafts of Rempstone Hall,* Halsgrove 2005.

Schofield, R. B. *Benjamin Outram,* Merton Priory Press, 2000.

Stevenson, William *A General View of the Agriculture of Dorset,* 1812.

Stone, Colin *Rails to Poole Harbour* Oakwood Press, 1999.

Stretton, John *The Welsh Highland Railway Vol.1 A Phoenix Rising,* Past and Present Publishing 1999.

Thomas, John *The Rise of the Staffordshire Potteries,* Adams & Dart 1971.

Turner, Alun R*ussell, the story of a Locomotive,* The Welsh Highland Railway (1964) Ltd., 1990.

Van Lemmen, Hans *Coade Stone,* Shire Publications 2006.

Wear, R. & Lees, E. *Stephen Lewin and the Poole Foundry,* Industrial Railway Society, 1978.

Weinstock, M. B. *Old Dorset,* David & Charles 1967.

Woodward, Ida *In and around the Isle of Purbeck,* The Bodley Head 1908.

PRINTED SOURCES, BOOKLETS AND PERIODICALS.

Baker, S. W. 'Narrow-gauge Lines in the Isle of Purbeck', *Railway World* July 1953.

Dorset County Chronicle, 1824-1957.

E.C.C. Review 'Ball Clay Country', *E.C.C. Journal* 1970.

Fayle Mines visit. *Proceedings of the Dorset Natural History and Archaeological Society,* 1930.

Hamilton Ellis, C. 'Locomotives built by Stephen Lewin', *Railway Magazine,* April 1934

Holdridge, D. A. *Clay Variability and its Consequences,* Stockholm 1966.

Holdridge, D. A. 'Composition Variation in Ball Clays', *Transactions of the British Ceramic Society,* Vol. 58, November 1959.

Holdridge, D. A. *Isomorphous replacements in Kaolinite,* undated.

Latham, J. P. M. *Dorset Clay to Staffordshire Pot,* Paper read at V&A Museum 1976.

Legg, Chris 'Digging out the clay', *Dorset County Magazine* No.24 1972.

Legg, Chris 'Middlebere Plateway', *Swanage Railway Magazine,* Autumn 2000.

Legg Rodney, 'Down the Mine', *Dorset County Magazine,* 31 1975.

Lloyd's Register of Shipping, various dates.

Locomotive The, November 1934.

O'Sullivan, N. *The clay boats and Clay Trade,* Poole Maritime Trust 1987

Penderill-Church, John *The Dorset Ball Clay Industry,* E.C.C. T I B 771103, St Austell.

Pike Bros, Fayle & Co Ltd. *Catalogue of Dorset Ball Clays,* 1957.

Pinniger, David, 'Norden Clay', *Narrow Gauge & Industrial Review,* 2001.

Popplewell, L. 'Purbeck Narrow Gauge', *Railway World,* June 1978.

Pottery Gazette and Glass Trade Review, 'Ball Clay from Dorset', August 1953.

Riden, Philip 'The Butterley Company and Railway Construction 1790-1830'. *Transport History,* Vol.6, 1973.

'The Corfe-Goathorn Mineral Railway', *Railway Magazine,* September 1940.

Tolson, J. M. 'The Swanage Branch', *Railway World,* January 1969,

INDEX